3

# THE DOOLITTLE RAID

# THE
# DOOLITTLE
# RAID

## DUANE SCHULTZ

**ST. MARTIN'S PRESS**
**New York**

C1
11/88

Design by Claudia Carlson

Maps by Bruce S. Houghton

Library of Congress Cataloging-in-Publication Data

Schultz, Duane P.
   The Doolittle Raid / Duane Schultz.
      p.   cm.
   "A Thomas Dunne book."
   ISBN 0-312-02195-X
   1. Tokyo (Japan)—History—Bombardment, 1942. 2. Doolittle, James Harold, 1896–    . 3. World War, 1939–1945—Aerial operations, American. I. Title.
D762.25.T6S35 1988                                      88-11564
940.54′21—dc19

First Edition
10 9 8 7 6 5 4 3 2 1

The selection of Doolittle to lead this nearly suicidal mission was a natural one. . . . He was fearless, technically brilliant, a leader who not only could be counted upon to do a task himself if it were humanly possible, but could impart his spirit to others.

—GEN. HENRY H. ARNOLD

They were picked crews. They were the crews that had the most experience with the airplane, and, right from the start, they were absolutely top-flight.

—GEN. JAMES H. DOOLITTLE

My cap is off to Jimmy and his brave squadron . . . their flight was one of the most courageous deeds in all military history.

—ADM. WILLIAM F. HALSEY

# CONTENTS

1. A Shiver over Japan, 1
2. That Might Be a Good Idea, 5
3. I Have Never Felt Fear, 19
4. The B-25B Special Project, 43
5. Tell Jimmy to Get on His Horse, 59
6. I'll Be Seeing You, 76
7. This Is a Breeze, 91
8. This Force Is Bound for Tokyo, 109
9. Army Pilots, Man Your Planes, 124
10. They Were Shooting at *Us*, 139
11. If My Wife Could See Me Now, 159
12. Thanks for a Swell Ride, 177
13. We Lost Some of the Boys, 203
14. Days of Stark Horror, 226
15. I've Been Away, 243
16. I Request that the Penalty Be Death, 260
17. You Can Go Home Now, 274
   Appendix 1: Tokyo Raiders, Order of Take-off, April 18, 1942, 292
   Appendix 2: Japanese Regulations for Punishment of Enemy Air Crews, 296
   Acknowledgments and Sources, 298
   Chapter Notes, 302
   Bibliography, 312
   Index, 317

*Photo Section follows page 158.*

MAPS

1. The Pacific Theater and the route of Task Force 16, ix
2. Japan, 138
3. Eastern China, 176

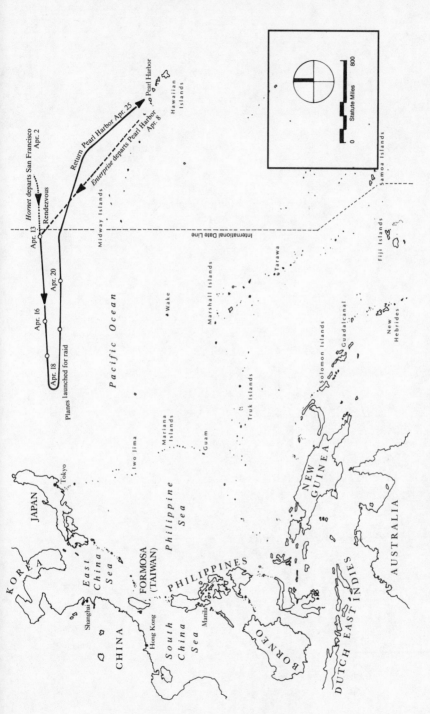

Pacific Theater showing route of task force

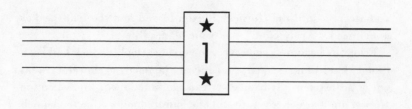

# A Shiver over Japan

Jimmy Doolittle stood on a cold, barren hillside in eastern China, staring at the shattered remains of his plane.

"Damn it, Paul," he said to his crew chief, Sgt. Paul Leonard, "they'll never give me another plane. They'll ground me from now on, and I'll be lucky if they don't break me."

It was Monday, April 20, 1942. Two days earlier, Doolittle had taken off in his twin-engine North American B-25 bomber from the flight deck of the aircraft carrier USS *Hornet*, some six hundred miles from the coast of Japan. Fifteen more B-25s were ready to take off and follow him on the United States's first attempt to strike back at Japan since the disaster at Pearl Harbor four months before.

The mission was a daring gamble, a calculated risk, the kind Jimmy Doolittle was used to taking, the kind that had made him a world-famous flier long before the start of World War II. But this time the prize was not another trophy or a speed or altitude record. It was survival, for himself and his crew and all the other B-25 crews, eighty men in all. He was responsible for them, accountable for them. He had trained them and led them from the day they

1

volunteered until the *Hornet*'s klaxon blared and the loudspeaker announced, "Army pilots, man your planes."

From the beginning, however, the famous Doolittle luck had been tested. Fuel tanks leaked, gun turrets jammed, carburetors went out of adjustment, hydraulic systems malfunctioned. And when the *Hornet* and her convoy were still one hundred miles from the launch point, a Japanese picket boat spotted them, and the fliers were forced to take off hours earlier than planned. They had enough gas to reach their targets, but they were no longer sure they could fly on to a safe landing field in China, twelve hundred miles from Japan.

Doolittle hadn't made it. Luck turned against him, against them all. His flight across China at night instead of in daytime, over poorly mapped terrain with eight-thousand-foot mountains, was not what he had anticipated. The weather unexpectedly closed in, and visibility dropped to zero, encasing his airplane in clouds, rain, and fog. The radio homing signal that was supposed to guide the planes to a secure airfield was not being transmitted.

Flying blind and low on fuel, Doolittle ordered the other four men in his crew to bail out, and he followed them into the dark, cold night. It was not until the following afternoon that he saw them again. All were uninjured, and for that he was grateful, but he knew nothing of the fate of the other fifteen planes and crews.

Had they taken off from the carrier? No one had ever done so before in a heavily loaded B-25. Because of limited fuel, Doolittle had not been able to circle the ship to watch his men take off. And if they had reached Japan, had they been able to hit their targets, or had Japanese defenses been alerted by his own attack? Had enemy fighters swarmed over the bombers that were supposed to follow him, one at a time, for the next hour?

What of those who might have made it to China? The weather and the darkness, the unseen mountain peaks, were the same threats for them as for him, the radio homing signal just as silent. So far as Doolittle knew, he and his crew might be the only survivors of this, his first combat mission. The raid on Tokyo, once a vision of such promise, seemed to be turning into another shattering, humiliating defeat of the kind that had dogged American forces in the Pacific ever since the words "Pearl Harbor" and "infamy" had become linked in the national consciousness. Only this time the disaster would be associated, forever, with Doolittle's name.

Doolittle sat down heavily on the ground in front of one wing of his plane. A portion of the other wing rested a quarter-mile away. The fuselage was a heap of twisted metal, and one engine had rolled down the hill and smashed on some rocks. Chinese peasants had ransacked the wreckage, taking everything they could cart away. Doolittle found only the blouse of his air corps uniform. It was soaked with oil, and its shiny brass buttons had been ripped away.

"It's been a complete failure," he told Sergeant Leonard.

★ ★ ★ ★

In Tokyo, some twelve hundred miles northeast, another man also believed he had failed in his mission. Adm. Isoroku Yamamoto, supreme commander of the combined fleet and planner of the surprise attack on the U.S. Navy at Pearl Harbor, was so mortified, so stricken with shame when American bombs fell on Tokyo on April 18, that he fled to his quarters aboard his flagship and refused to come out. His steward reported that he had never seen the admiral so depressed.

"In Admiral Yamamoto's mind," said Comdr. Mitsuo Fuchida, leader of the attack on Pearl Harbor, "the idea that Tokyo, the seat of the emperor, must be kept absolutely safe from an air attack, amounted almost to an obsession." Yamamoto's chief of staff, Rear Adm. Matome Ugaki, wrote in his diary the night of the Doolittle raid that "today the victory belonged to the enemy."

The bombs caused relatively little physical destruction—there were, after all, only sixteen planes—but the psychological damage was severe and long-lasting to Yamamoto and other military leaders. Yamamoto's biographer wrote that the admiral's "normally clear judgment was warped by the Doolittle raid." The military had failed to protect Japan's sacred soil. The emperor's life had been endangered, and the solemn promise to the Japanese people that they would never be bombed had been broken. Worse, the attacking planes had all gotten away unscathed.

If the Americans could do it once, they could do it again, perhaps with larger planes and more of them. That realization, said Capt.

Kameto Kuroshima, a staff officer, as well as the shock of the bombing itself, "passed like a shiver over Japan."

Yamamoto knew there was only one way to safeguard the homeland against further air attacks. He would have to extend Japan's wall of defense in the Pacific.

He emerged from his self-imposed isolation on April 20 to attend a joint army-navy conference. On the same day Doolittle was contemplating his wrecked plane and brooding over the fate of his men and his mission, Yamamoto was pressing for the most momentous decision of Japan's war. For some months he had been urging a further eastward expansion, but had found it difficult to persuade army officers, and even some of his fellow navy officers, of its necessity.

His plan had been balked in favor of expansion to the south, to cut off the shipping lanes between the United States and Australia by capturing Samoa, Fiji, and New Caledonia. Now Yamamoto's arguments for a thrust to the east carried more weight. Pacific waters had to be cleared of any base the Americans might use to launch more attacks on Japan. One island in particular, tiny though it was, appeared, to Yamamoto, too dangerous to leave in American hands. The homeland would not be safe until it was occupied by Japan.

In addition, the invasion of that island base could bring Yamamoto what he desired most, a major sea battle with the U.S. Pacific Fleet. This time he would destroy the carriers, a job left undone at Pearl Harbor.

Japan's military leaders agreed to Yamamoto's plan—the Doolittle raid had persuaded them—and set the date for the invasion of the American island base for the first week of June. The destination was Midway.

Yamamoto had his great sea battle and was beaten decisively. The Battle of Midway was a pivotal event, altering forever the course of the war in the Pacific and marking the beginning of the end of Japan's conquests. It would not have occurred, at that time or that place, had it not been for sixteen planes and eighty men and a mission Jimmy Doolittle considered a failure one cold Monday in April of 1942.

# That Might Be a Good Idea

The Doolittle raid began with a line painted across a runway in Norfolk, Virginia. There was nothing unusual about the line. Most naval air stations had one to mark off the length of the deck of an aircraft carrier, to help pilots practice short-run takeoffs and landings. It was a lot safer to practice on land than on a carrier deck. Navy fliers saw such lines every day and thought nothing of them.

On Saturday, January 10, 1942, Capt. Francis Low, a submariner, took a look at the line across the runway at Norfolk and saw in it a way to strike back at Japan, a way to avenge what the Japanese had done to the U.S. fleet at Pearl Harbor. As operations officer for Adm. Ernest J. King, Commander in Chief of the United States Fleet, Low had been in Norfolk to inspect the navy's newest carrier, the USS *Hornet*. As Low's plane took off for the return flight to Washington, he glanced at the line painted on the adjacent runway.

At that instant, a pair of twin-engine army bombers swooped down on the simulated carrier deck in a practice bombing run. As the shadows of the two planes raced across the concrete, an idea flashed through Low's mind. If army bombers could take off from an aircraft carrier, and if the carrier could bring them near enough without being detected, then they could bomb Japan!

The idea of bombing Japan was on the minds of most military leaders in Washington during the first agonizing weeks of the war. Japan's surprise attack on the Pacific Fleet the month before had humiliated the United States militarily for the first time in history. Since then, a string of defeats and disasters had filled the newspaper headlines: Clark Field, Manila, Guam, Wake Island. And now American troops were trapped on the Bataan peninsula, in the Philippine Islands, with no hope of rescue or relief. That would turn out to be the largest surrender in the U.S. Army's history.

The British had already surrendered Hong Kong and were rapidly losing Malaya. At sea, two magnificent ships, pride of the Royal Navy—the battleship HMS *Prince of Wales* and the battle cruiser HMS *Repulse*—had been sent to the bottom by Japanese airplanes. Japan was on a rampage, apparently invincible. American morale, both civilian and military, was as shattered as the ghostly remains of the fleet at Pearl Harbor.

President Franklin D. Roosevelt was obsessed with the idea of striking back at Japan as quickly as possible, of dealing a blow to her fierce sense of national pride. The president had, as news correspondent Quentin Reynolds noted, "a fierce, consuming hatred for the Japanese."

Roosevelt had wanted to attack the Japanese Empire even before Pearl Harbor. On July 23, 1941, three days before he announced an embargo on the sale of oil to Japan, the president had approved the shipment of sixty-six twin-engine bombers to China. The planes, bearing Chinese insignia, were to be flown by American crews secretly released from the U.S. Army and Navy and paid by a private but government-financed company. Their mission was to bomb Tokyo and other Japanese cities before the end of 1941.

The scheme had been devised by Claire Chennault, a former Army Air Corps pilot and adviser to China's leader, Generalissimo Chiang Kai-shek. Chennault was then in Burma training the 250-man air group that would become known as the Flying Tigers. That outfit, flying P-40 fighter planes to defend the Burma Road, had been designated the First American Volunteer Group.

The Second American Volunteer Group was to fly Lockheed Hudson and Douglas DB-7 bombers in offensive raids against Japan's home islands.* Production and shipping bottlenecks delayed the arrival of these planes in China, and it took longer than expected to recruit the crews. The initial group of forty-nine ground crewmen did not leave the United States until November 21, 1941, and the men were still at sea when Japanese forces attacked Pearl Harbor. Only eighteen bombers were ready for shipment, and they were still sitting on the ground at Lockheed's Burbank, California, airfield when the war began.

Japan won the race for executing a surprise attack, and this fact may have increased Roosevelt's antipathy. At every meeting with his military leaders in the weeks following the Pearl Harbor disaster, the president stressed how much he wanted a bombing raid on Japan. He told them they must "find ways and means of carrying home to Japan proper, in the form of a bombing raid, the real meaning of war." His service chiefs—Gen. George C. Marshall of the U.S. Army, Gen. Henry H. "Hap" Arnold of the U.S. Army Air Corps, and Adm. Ernest J. King of the U.S. Navy—passed on that sense of urgency to their staffs. Captain Low certainly knew about it, and this made him see the line painted across the Norfolk runway in a way no one else had.

Every staff officer in Washington had the notion of a raid on Japan uppermost in his mind, and so did much of the American public. Many corporate executives and wealthy industrialists contacted the White House, offering large sums of money to be awarded to the first person to bomb Tokyo. Roosevelt even suggested that if our military was not yet able to bomb Japan, then perhaps we could persuade our allies, the Russians, to do it for us. However, the Russian dictator, Joseph Stalin, hard-pressed by the German army, was unwilling to antagonize Japan. He feared that the Japanese, as

---

* The Douglas DB-7 was the export version of the A-20.

treaty partners with Nazi Germany's Adolf Hitler, would force him into a two-front war.

Roosevelt asked the Russian leader if American planes could use the seaport of Vladivostok, located on the Sea of Japan about six hundred miles from Tokyo, as a base for an American attack on Japan. Stalin turned down that request, too. If the mission was to be launched, it would have to be done by American forces on their own, weak and ill prepared though they were.

It seemed an impossible demand, but Roosevelt kept the pressure on his military chiefs. Perhaps no service felt that pressure more keenly than the navy. In the public mind, and in the awareness of many navy officers as well, including Admiral King, it was the navy that had suffered the greatest blow to its prestige in those opening weeks of the war. And the navy, far more than the army or the air corps, felt driven to redeem itself, to erase the shame that had dogged its wake since December 7.

The navy had been strongly criticized by journalists and news commentators, and by the other services, for allowing the fleet to be caught unawares in Hawaii. In addition, Secretary of War Henry L. Stimson, Army Chief of Staff George Marshall, and Gen. Douglas MacArthur were all blaming the navy for its failure to even attempt to break through the Japanese blockade of the Philippines and bring reinforcements to the beleaguered troops on Bataan. "Where is the navy?" General MacArthur asked, and newspapers and magazines from coast to coast echoed his query.

The army was holding on at Bataan. The Marine Corps had kept Wake Island for sixteen days, beating off the first invasion attempt. The air corps was producing its share of popular heroes with Capt. Colin Kelly and other valiant fliers in the Philippines. But the navy appeared to be doing nothing, so far as the American public knew.

When the navy first tried to strike back at Japan, the results were so embarrassing that the incident was kept secret until after the end of the war. On the evening of December 15, 1941, a small task force consisting of the aircraft carrier USS *Saratoga*, three cruisers, nine destroyers, an oiler, and a seaplane tender converted to a troop transport, sailed from Pearl Harbor for Wake Island.

The ships carried reinforcements for the garrison whose gallant stand had galvanized the home front. The reinforcements were meager—only two hundred marines and eighteen obsolete Brewster Buffalo fighter planes—but they were all the navy could muster.

Seven days later the fleet's commanding officer, Rear Adm. Frank Jack Fletcher, learned that Japanese troops had landed on the tiny island. Wake's senior navy officer, Comdr. Winfield Scott Cunningham, had cabled:

ENEMY ON ISLAND, ISSUE IN DOUBT.

The cable prompted the navy to recall the task force, although it was within twenty hours' sailing time of Wake. Despite the country's desperate need for a show of force against Japan, the risk of a second naval disaster so soon after Pearl Harbor was too great for the navy to consider. A number of officers aboard the flagship urged Fletcher to ignore the recall order, make a fast run for Wake, and attack whatever enemy force they found, but the admiral had no choice. The little fleet turned around and sailed out of harm's way.

When word of the recall spread through the barracks and the officers' clubs in Honolulu, and the bridges and wardrooms of ships at sea, the sailors and the marines were angry and ashamed. One Marine Corps general called it "the blackest day in the history of the U.S. Navy," and a retired admiral regarded it as a disgrace. Navy fliers of Fighter Squadron Six, aboard the carrier USS *Enterprise*, wrote in their unofficial log that "everyone seems to feel that it's the war between the two yellow races. Wake was attacked this morning and probably surrendered with the *Saratoga* but 200 miles away and us steaming around in circles." When Secretary of the Navy Frank Knox told President Roosevelt about the task force's recall, the president considered it "a worse blow than Pearl Harbor."

A few days later Americans stationed throughout the Pacific heard the taunting voice of Tokyo Rose on the radio.

"Where, oh, where, is the United States Navy?"

All this was on Captain Low's mind as his plane landed in Washington. He hurried to the Navy Yard, hoping he might have the answer to that question. If his idea could be implemented, it would show the world where his navy was—off the coast of Japan, launching planes.

★ ★ ★ ★

The U.S. Navy was not alone in its obsession with the bombing of Japan. Japanese navy leaders were equally concerned. Admiral Yamamoto, architect of the attack on Pearl Harbor, worried constantly, in the weeks following his triumph, about American retaliation. His foremost duty, and that of all Japanese military leaders, was to protect the Emperor. Failure to do so would be the gravest dereliction of duty and a source of overwhelming shame.

The Japanese people had no such worry, for they were repeatedly assured, by radio broadcasts and newspapers, that their sacred homeland was safe from attack. No hostile foreign force had touched Japan's soil since 1281, when a Mongolian fleet had been defeated, thanks, in part, to a violent storm the Japanese called the "divine wind" or *kamikaze*.

But Yamamoto knew better than to believe the propaganda, and just as Admiral King transmitted his concern to his staff, so did the Japanese admiral. Yamamoto's chief of staff, Rear Admiral Ugaki, reflected Yamamoto's anxiety in a diary entry written less than three weeks after Pearl Harbor.

"It is almost certain that the U.S., after reorganizing their forces, will come against us in retaliation. . . . Tokyo should be protected from air raids; this is the most important thing to be borne in mind."

No matter where he was, on land or at sea, Admiral Yamamoto demanded the weather report for Tokyo. His staff thought it was just one of his eccentricities, and they never understood why he was always more cheerful when the weather over Tokyo was bad. He knew enemy bombers were unlikely to come over in bad weather. He fretted when the skies over the capital were clear.

Although the means for protecting Japan from air attacks rested with the army's planes and antiaircraft guns, the responsibility for safeguarding the homeland rested with Yamamoto, because the only way the Americans could attack was by sea. It was the navy's job to ensure that no carrier force got close enough to Japan to launch planes.

Yamamoto knew Americans well, so well that he had opposed going to war with them, convinced that Japan could not win a protracted confrontation with an industrial giant. From his years in the United States, first as a student at Harvard University and later as Japan's naval attaché in Washington, he was aware of the bold, aggressive spirit that characterized the American people. And he believed that spirit would impel America's military leaders to take revenge on Japan for the Pearl Harbor attack.

Yamamoto himself had provided America with an example of how best to accomplish that—through a surprise carrier attack—and he was concerned about how the Japanese people would react when the inevitable attack came. In 1904, during the Russo-Japanese war, the Japanese people had panicked when Russian ships appeared outside Tokyo Bay. The city's residents had fled to the mountains, and when they returned, they stoned the house of the admiral whose fleet had failed to protect them. A young officer at the time, Yamamoto had been appalled by the public reaction and had seen it as a sign of instability in the Japanese character. He feared it would erupt again if American bombers appeared over Tokyo. Then it would be *his* home the people would stone.

To keep enemy carriers beyond air striking distance of Tokyo, Yamamoto established an early-warning line consisting of a fleet of small boats to patrol one thousand miles north and south, and six hundred to seven hundred miles east. The boats on picket duty to the east would cruise directly in the path of an American carrier force, one that did not yet exist even on paper, the one that would carry the Doolittle raiders.

★ ★ ★ ★

Captain Low reached the Washington Navy Yard and was taken immediately to Admiral King's stateroom aboard the USS *Dauntless*, a 257-foot yacht, formerly the property of the Dodge family, which was moored in the Anacostia River. King, Low, and several other senior staff officers had quarters on the *Dauntless*, so that King, after a day of meetings at his office, could continue his work in the evenings. King was reserved, austere, arrogant, and totally dedicated to his job, to which he had been appointed only three weeks before. A strict disciplinarian, it was said he "inspired respect in many but affection in few."

Low knew Admiral King was always receptive to new ideas and strategies, no matter how unorthodox they might appear, but he also knew the admiral did not look kindly upon the air corps. Indeed, the competition between the navy and the army air services was keen. Yet Low was about to suggest to the admiral an attack on the enemy that depended on the use of army planes.

Low believed there was no other way to do the job. Navy dive bombers had such a short range that a carrier would have to bring them suicidally close to Japan's shores. Because army bombers could fly greater distances, the navy could launch them some four hundred to five hundred miles from Japan's coast. A risk to the carrier remained, of course, but at that distance the ship would be beyond the range of Japan's land-based fighters. So far as the navy knew then, the Japanese did not have picket boats patrolling that distance offshore.

King looked up as his operations officer knocked and entered the room.

"What is it, Low?" he asked.

It had not been a good day for Admiral King. Since December 24, only four days after his appointment to his post, King had been involved in the Arcadia Conference, meeting almost daily with representatives of Britain's Royal Navy and with more than eighty military and civilian members of Prime Minister Winston Churchill's staff, to chart the course of the war. The sessions had often been acrimonious and frustrating, and always long and tiring.

Also, the war news had been bad again. There had been no major American losses during the previous 24 hours, but the troops on Bataan remained besieged. The British had abandoned Kuala Lumpur, allowing the Japanese another step closer to Singapore. The enemy continued to advance in Borneo, and the Dutch East Indies appeared ever more vulnerable.

Low spoke quickly.

"I've been to the Norfolk yard, as you know, sir, to see the progress made on the *Hornet*. At the airfield they had marked out a strip about the size of a carrier deck, and they practice takeoffs constantly."

"Well," King said, puzzled at why Low was pointing out the obvious, "that's a routine operation for training carrier-based pilots."

"If the army has some plane that could take off in that short distance," Low said, "I mean a plane capable of carrying a bomb load, why couldn't we put a few of them on a carrier and bomb the mainland of Japan?"

Admiral King leaned back in his chair. Low paused, expecting that his idea was about to get a curt rejection.

"Low," King said, "that might be a good idea. Discuss it with Duncan and tell him to report to me."

Low quickly put in a call to Capt. Donald Duncan, King's air officer, an experienced pilot with an M.S. degree from Harvard. Duncan agreed to meet Low the next morning at headquarters, on the third floor of the Navy Department building on Constitution Avenue.

"How would you like to plan a carrier-based strike against Tokyo?" Low asked him when they met. He went on to explain his idea for using army bombers.

Duncan's initial reaction was that even if army bombers could take off from a carrier deck, they could never land on one. They were not equipped with arrester hooks to grab the steel cables stretched across the deck to bring a landing plane to a quick halt. In addition, army planes had higher landing speeds. And because their wings did not fold up, they could not be stored below decks.

Still, Duncan thought, that might not rule out Low's idea. The important thing was to transport the planes to the target, and Duncan was certain the navy could do that. As for what the planes and crews would do after they were launched, well, that would have to be worked out. If nothing else, they could ditch alongside the carrier and the crews be brought aboard.

Overall, Duncan was receptive to the idea of a carrier-based strike against Japan. He, too, knew how much the navy, and the nation, needed a victory. The opportunity to achieve something as spectacular as a raid on Japan's capital city was clearly worth the risk.

"I started in right away," Duncan recalled, "and made a preliminary survey of the situation, considering such factors as the availability of a carrier, the practicability of some takeoff trials, the performance data of the various army aircraft which might be used, the weather, things the pilots might strike in Japan with the force that could be provided."

He spent five days developing his plan, working in absolute secrecy. He wrote a thirty-page report in longhand, not even permitting his trusted clerks to type it for him.

The first problem he dealt with was the choice of aircraft. There were several possibilities: the B-23 Dragon, the B-26 Marauder, and the B-25 Mitchell. All three planes had the necessary range and bomb-carrying capacity.

The B-23, an improved version of the B-18, was ruled out because its extra-long, ninety-two-foot wingspan made it too wide for a carrier takeoff.* The B-26 was eliminated because it needed a longer takeoff run than a carrier deck would allow. That left the B-25, which, theoretically at least, should be able to take off from a carrier. It had a wingspan of only sixty-seven feet and required a shorter takeoff run.

Duncan proposed that the army fliers be trained in takeoff procedures by navy carrier pilots. He suggested reducing the weight of the B-25s as much as possible by discarding all nonessential equipment. Extra fuel tanks would be installed to increase the planes' range.

Two carriers should be used for the mission, Duncan wrote, one to carry the bombers and the other, with navy fighter planes aboard, to provide air cover for the carriers and their escort of cruisers, destroyers, and oilers. The navy fighter planes of the carrier carrying the B-25s would have to remain below decks until the

---

* The B-23 never flew in combat. Only thirty-eight were built, beginning in 1938, and they were eventually used as transports (UC-67s) and for towing gliders in training.

bombers were launched; the bombers themselves would take up the entire flight deck. Duncan designated the USS *Hornet* as the primary aircraft carrier. According to his calculations, she had room for sixteen B-25s on her deck.

The *Hornet*, due to end a shakedown cruise within weeks, was scheduled to proceed through the Panama Canal to Pearl Harbor, with a stop at San Francisco. Thus her movement to the Pacific theater would occasion no undue comment, and the B-25s and their crews could be taken aboard secretly in California.

The plan called for the task force to proceed at high speed to within five hundred miles of the Japanese coast, launch the bombers, and depart the area as quickly as possible. The planes would strike military targets in the Tokyo-Yokohama, Osaka-Kobe, and Nagoya areas. Duncan recommended a low-altitude mission. This would allow the bombers to escape detection as they neared the coast and avoid antiaircraft fire over land, and it would also increase bombing accuracy.

After the raid, the planes could return to the carrier and ditch alongside, or continue to unoccupied territory in China, to the air bases that had been prepared by Chennault for his earlier planned bombing of Tokyo. Duncan preferred to leave the choice to the air corps. If they chose the latter option, the planes could then be used by Chennault's forces.

A careful study of weather patterns persuaded Duncan that the raid would have to take place before the end of April to ensure the most favorable conditions. This timetable meant that the aircraft would have to be modified, the crews selected and trained, the task force assembled, and the seven thousand miles of ocean crossed, all within twelve to fourteen weeks. It might have sounded impossible to some, but Duncan thought it could be done.

A perfectionist who later became vice-chief of naval operations, Captain Duncan reviewed his plans, checking and rechecking his calculations, making sure he had overlooked nothing. Finally he was satisfied. It looked like an "almost foolproof . . . although hazardous, undertaking." It was time to take the plan to Admiral King.

The next day, Friday, January 16, Duncan briefed King, in company with Captain Low. When he had finished, King, unsmiling as usual, leafed through Duncan's handwritten report. He sat in silence for a moment before making any comment.

"Go see General Arnold about it," King said, "and if he agrees with you, ask him to get in touch with me. But don't mention this to another soul."

★ ★ ★ ★

Hap Arnold, so called because he was almost always grinning, had already been thinking about army planes taking off from aircraft carriers before Low and Duncan came to see him. Like King, Arnold, as air corps chief of staff, had been trying to devise a plan to bomb Japan, but he was no closer to success than the navy.

The Army Air Corps had few long-range bombers left. The Japanese attack on Clark Field in the Philippines on December 8, 1941, had caught the B-17 force of thirty-five planes on the ground. Only seventeen of those planes were still flyable, and most of them were now in Mindanao, far to the south of Manila. There were few big bombers available in the United States, and even if any of them could have been spared, they could not be flown across the Pacific against Japan because the refueling stops at Wake Island and Guam were now in enemy hands.

The air bases nearest to Japan were in China, and the bombers there, operated by the Chinese Air Force, were obsolete and incapable of carrying a sufficient bomb load. To send the available short-range, twin-engine bombers to China by ship from the United States would take months. The air corps, therefore, had been forced to conclude that the bombing of Japan in the foreseeable future did not seem feasible.

That impression had been reinforced for General Arnold on December 24, in a meeting with Britain's Air Chief Marshal Sir Charles Portal. Portal asked what Arnold was planning to do about bombing Japan. At the time, Roosevelt was awaiting a reply from Stalin about the use of Vladivostok as a base for American bombers, and Arnold told Portal about that possibility. Arnold also alluded to the use of air bases in eastern China, once the American aircraft industry had produced enough four-engine bombers and flown them there.

Portal said that, in his view, an attack on Japan was a job for the navy. Carriers could launch a surprise attack on Tokyo, just as the Japanese had done at Pearl Harbor and the British had done at Taranto, Italy, in 1940. There, carrier-launched torpedo planes had sunk three Italian battleships in a strongly defended harbor. In both cases the attacking naval forces had gotten away unscathed.

"Your carriers are fast," Portal said. "The ocean is big. I believe such an attack would cause the Japanese fleet to return to home waters."

Arnold was suspicious of Portal's motives in arguing that the navy and not the air corps should bomb Japan. Britain was in desperate need of all types of American aircraft, and was pressuring Roosevelt to send every plane that could be spared, including B-17 bombers and crews, for the planned bombardment of Germany. Arnold wrote after the war that he thought Portal was "afraid [that] if our Air Force planned to use heavy bombers against Japan . . . it would cut down the number he would receive." Also, Arnold believed it would be too great a risk to bring carriers within the three hundred miles of the enemy coast necessary to launch navy planes. The ships would be too vulnerable to attack by Japan's land-based air force.

On January 4, 1942, the subject of aircraft carriers arose again, this time in a White House meeting of the combined American and British chiefs of staff. One topic under discussion was an invasion of French North Africa.

Admiral King suggested that three carriers be used, one to transport navy planes to defend the task force, and two to carry army fighters and bombers to be off-loaded by crane or flown off if possible. Arnold said nothing about King's idea at the meeting, but that night in his office he wrote: "By transporting these army bombers on a carrier it will be necessary for us to take off from the carriers, which brings up the question of what kind of planes—B-18 and DC-3 for cargo?

"We will have to try bomber takeoff from carrier. It has never been done before but we must try out and check out how long it takes."

Arnold turned the problem over to his war plans division, but had not received an answer about the feasibility of a carrier takeoff by January 17, the day navy captains Duncan and Low arrived with their plan to bomb Japan. What they presented Arnold with was a neat combination of Portal's idea of a carrier strike and King's suggestion to transport air corps bombers on a carrier.

Arnold did not tell Duncan and Low that his staff was already working on the problem of carrier takeoffs. He listened quietly while Duncan outlined the navy's proposal, and he responded with immediate and wholehearted enthusiasm. He agreed that Duncan should continue to plan the navy's part in the mission and to coordinate the overall operation. He would find someone to handle the air corps' role. Not to lead the raid—the man he had in mind was too valuable for that—but to assume the demanding tasks of modifying the planes, training the crews, and overseeing the technical details vital to the mission's success.

The job required more than an experienced pilot. He would have to be an aeronautical engineer, a brilliant planner and manager, a natural leader who would inspire confidence in his men, and a fighter who could cut his way through bureaucratic red tape. Someone who cared less about securing a promotion than about getting the job done.

Arnold knew there was only one man who had all these qualifications. His name was Jimmy Doolittle, and his office was just down the hall.

# I Have Never
# Felt Fear

James Harold Doolittle was famous long before the raid on Tokyo became linked with his name. He was a legend, a hero, a celebrity in the 1920s and 1930s, the golden age of aviation, a time when daredevil pilots were idolized by the American public. Of all the pilots whose exploits thrilled spectators on the ground, only Charles Lindbergh received as much adulation as Jimmy Doolittle.

It was the time of the air races in which small, fast, single-engine planes zoomed at dizzying speeds at treetop level and careened sharply on one wing around pylons. Doolittle won almost every speed trophy offered, some of them twice. He won awards for his stunt flying, for aerobatic maneuvers such as the outside loop, never before attempted. He also won fame and prizes for his cross-country flights, being the first to fly coast-to-coast in under twenty-four hours. Later he became the first to make the trip in less than twelve hours. His short, athletic figure and his quick, engaging smile became familiar sights in magazines, newspapers, and newsreels throughout the nation.

But Doolittle was more than a daring flier risking his life in what appeared to be crazy stunts and death-defying maneuvers. He was also a scientist, a holder of one of the first doctoral degrees in aeronautical engineering from MIT, who was intent on pushing back the frontiers of aviation. His stunts were dangerous, to be sure, but they were calculated risks, carefully planned, with every variable examined before he tried them in the air. "I have never felt fear," he told a television interviewer at the age of ninety. "I am single-minded. I think of only one thing at a time, and if I'm in a very hot spot indeed, I'm thinking about how to get out of that hot spot."

Doolittle developed the techniques and flight instruments needed for flying blind, and became the first person in the history of aviation to take off and land on instruments alone. Thanks to his work, planes no longer had to be grounded because of poor weather conditions or darkness. This was a great advance for both commercial and military flight. Doolittle was also responsible for the development of high-octane aviation fuel, without which bigger, more powerful engines—and the resulting increase in speed and payloads—would not have been possible. Jimmy Doolittle changed the nature of aviation.

He had come a long way from an undersized street brawler in the rough, lawless town of Nome, Alaska, at the turn of the century. Born in California in 1896, he was taken by his mother to Nome when he was three to join his restless, adventurous father who was seeking his fortune in the Gold Rush. His father never found gold, but he managed to make a living at his trade as a carpenter.

His son, the smallest boy in school, whose hair was kept in long curls like a girl's, learned to fight in order to survive. He was fearless even then, and lashed back at every bigger boy who challenged him to a fight, until he proved his courage. He grew up tough, wiry, aggressive, and highly competitive. He loved to fight—and, of course, to win—and to excel at everything he tried.

He also became adventuresome, like his father. When Doolittle was seven, he accompanied his father on a brief visit to Seattle. He had never been in a city before, or seen an automobile, a train, a trolley car, or colorful buildings. "My values changed," he recalled. "I saw everything in a new perspective and I wanted very much to be a part of the exciting life I saw so briefly on that memorable trip." When he returned to the drab mud and ice and tundra of Nome, he read every book and newspaper he could get his hands on, and resolved that one day he would leave Alaska and see the world.

His mother helped. In 1908 she insisted that the family move to Los Angeles. His father stayed only a short time, and the boy once again had to prove himself with his fists at his new school. His skill at fighting was noticed by his high school English teacher, who was also the boxing coach. The man taught him how to fight properly, and Doolittle became, at age fifteen, the West Coast's amateur bantamweight champion, weighing in at 105 pounds. Now he could fight with approval and even win prizes for it. He won some twenty official bouts, but his temper also led him into a number of street brawls.

His mother tried to dissuade him from fighting, in the streets and in the ring. She believed there was no future in boxing, and worried that he might get hurt. One Friday night she had the chance to teach him a lesson. Doolittle got into a fight at a dance hall and was arrested. When the police telephoned Doolittle's mother, she told them to keep him in jail over the weekend. When Doolittle was released, he was shaken by the loss of his freedom and vowed never again to break the law or to let himself be ruled by his emotions.

Deciding to do something else with his hands, he built a glider from plans published in the magazine *Popular Mechanics*. Two years earlier he had attended a ten-day flying meet in Los Angeles, the largest ever held in the United States, and had seen his first airplane. Every sort of plane and dirigible available had participated in the races and flying stunts before a huge, awestruck crowd. Fascinated by it all, he was determined to fly himself, in a homemade biplane glider with an eighteen-foot wingspan. It was a flimsy affair (but all aircraft were flimsy in those days), not unlike modern hang gliders, with the pilot strapped below the wings in a harness.

It didn't work. Doolittle took a running leap off a thirty-foot cliff and plummeted to the ground, damaging his pride and his glider, but leaving him with only scratches and bruises. He tried twice more, once being towed by a car and another time powered by a small motorcycle engine he bought with money earned by boxing under an assumed name. His plane was pulled aloft by the car but crashed, and his powered craft was destroyed by a thunderstorm the night before he was to fly it. That turned out to be a stroke of luck, for he later learned that he had violated several basic aerodynamic principles. Had the contraption gotten off the ground, he might have been killed.

Doolittle gave up all thoughts of flying and turned to new pursuits, a motorcycle and a pretty girl. His mother bought him the motorcycle in return for his agreeing to quit boxing and flying. He souped up the engine and enjoyed zooming around the city at top speed. Even an accident that put him in the hospital for six weeks and on crutches for three more didn't slow him down. Jimmy Doolittle liked to travel at high speed.

He also liked Josephine Daniels, nicknamed "Joe," a serious student with a Southern accent who seemed unimpressed by his speed on a motorcycle or his skill at boxing. No matter how hard he tried, she would not change her mind. He was the one to change, instead. He took more of an interest in his appearance and in his studies. He even talked about attending college to study mining engineering.

In his last year at high school, he asked Joe to marry him but she refused, whereupon he announced that he would go to Alaska after graduation. When he had made enough money, he would send for her.

He was no more successful earning his fortune in Alaska than his father had been, years before. There were no jobs, and Doolittle's small savings ran out quickly. He was reduced to fishing in order to eat, and it would be twenty years before he voluntarily ate salmon again. Beaten, he took a job as a cabin boy on a boat to Seattle and stowed away on another bound for Los Angeles. He told Joe they would have to wait a while before getting married.

She reminded him that she had not yet agreed to marry him. She thought that he should go to college and get a job first. He took her advice and for two years studied mining engineering at Los Angeles Junior College, and he became a gymnast. He proved to be an agile tumbler, expert on the horizontal bar and the parallel bars.

He later said that his athletic prowess made him a better pilot. "I feel that two things were very helpful to me in my flying career. One was tumbling, where you get a sense of balance. And the other was boxing, where unless you [want to] get pretty badly mauled, your reactions have to be extremely quick. So the balance and the quick reactions that came from boxing and tumbling, I think, were definitely helpful to me in my career."

In 1916 he continued his studies at the University of California at Berkeley, where he also resumed his boxing career. This time he fought in the 165-pound class because the team had no vacancy in the lighter categories, where someone five feet six inches tall, weighing 130 pounds, belonged. He beat three taller, heavier contenders in two days to become university middleweight champion.

He continued boxing as a way of making money, and even considered turning professional. He earned up to thirty dollars a bout, but he used the name Jimmy Pierce to keep it secret from his mother and Joe. He did well until he was beaten by an old pro. After that humiliating defeat, Doolittle decided to stick to mining engineering.

In April 1917, world events altered his plans. The United States and Germany were at war. Young men, caught up in a patriotic frenzy, flocked to recruiting offices to fight for their country—and for the promise of adventure. That summer, Doolittle decided he was going to become a hotshot fighter pilot.

This new career did not have an auspicious beginning. Once he had enlisted in the Army Air Corps, he was told to go home and wait for a call. He had already left school and had no money, so he took a night-shift job at a tin-can factory and also worked in a quicksilver mine. In the fall, he was ordered to preflight ground school on the Berkeley campus. He was back where he had started, taking classes in subjects ranging from aerodynamics and navigation to military justice and close-order drill. He was sure the war would pass him by while he did nothing more exciting than study for exams.

But he was determined that Joe Daniels would not pass him by any longer. On his Christmas leave, he hurried to Los Angeles to propose again. Both his mother and Joe's counseled her against it, but she married Doolittle on Christmas Eve, 1917, at the Los Angeles City Hall. She had to pay for the license with money her mother had given her, and the newlyweds went to San Diego for a honeymoon on her remaining twenty dollars.

The following month, January 1918, Jimmy Doolittle learned to fly. As he and his instructor taxied out in a Curtiss JN-4 Jenny at San Diego's Rockwell Field for his first flight, two other Jennies collided and crashed nearby. Doolittle and the instructor ran to the wreckage and found one man dead and two others badly injured. Minutes later, with Doolittle making an effort to conceal how shaken he was by the accident, he and the instructor took off.

After seven hours of training, he felt confident enough to solo, but the instructor had one more lesson to teach him. "I want you to fly across the airfield at exactly three feet," he said. "I don't want you to hit the ground and I don't want you to get over three feet."

"I tried that for a while," Doolittle recalled, "and found it very difficult indeed. I bumped the ground, and I sailed up to twenty feet, and for the first time got a slight realization on my inadequacy.

"Just after I had completely lost my confidence, he stepped out of the airplane and said, 'Now you fly it around.'"

He managed to fly the Jenny around and discovered that he loved flying and was good at it. He couldn't wait to get into action against the Germans. But when he received his wings and his commission as a second lieutenant on March 11, 1918, he learned that he was not going to France to fly fighters. Indeed, where he was headed, he would not fly at all. Camp Dick, Texas, had no airplanes.

Doolittle and the other pilots stationed there passed their days training ground troops and plotting wild schemes that might get them into combat. None of the plans worked. In June, Doolittle was transferred to McCook Field (later renamed Wright Field), outside Dayton, Ohio, where he studied aircraft and engine maintenance. From there he was shunted off to Camp Dix, New Jersey, the major port of embarkation for France. He left there in August, but in the wrong direction, southwest to Gerstner Field, near Lake Charles, Louisiana, for training in combat tactics and gunnery, skills that it seemed increasingly unlikely he would ever use.

A few weeks after Doolittle arrived, a hurricane roared through the area, leaving five dead and many injured. Three hundred planes and all the buildings on the base were destroyed. The military personnel were dispersed, and Doolittle was sent back to Rockwell Field in San Diego, where he had first learned to fly. He was glad to be reunited with Joe, who had taken a job in a shipyard, but he was even farther from France and the war.

Detailed as a flight instructor, he seized every opportunity to fly, perfecting maneuvers and stunts, such as wing-walking. He acquired a reputation as a daredevil pilot and a maverick. He admitted to "a certain amount of mischief, and I did on occasion utilize an airplane for the purpose of having a little good clean fun."

Because he persisted in breaking the rules, he was occasionally confined to the post. He was not grounded, however. He was too good an instructor for the brass to do that. In one incident, he swooped low over two soldiers who were walking along the road. He felt the plane lurch as a wheel hit something solid, and when he looked back he was horrified to see one of the soldiers lying on the ground. Doolittle was so shocked that he failed to pull up in time to avoid a barbed-wire fence. He wasn't hurt, and neither was the soldier, to his immense relief.

Most of Doolittle's antics occurred at Ream Field, a small auxiliary field south of San Diego. But before long his reputation reached the colonel commanding Rockwell Field. One of the commanding officer's aides, Lt. Ira Eaker, came to his office to complain.

"Colonel," Eaker said, "there's a man down at Ream Field whose conduct is so bad it requires your personal attention."

Eaker explained that Doolittle had bet another pilot five dollars that he could sit on the bar connecting the main landing gear while the pilot came in for a landing. Doolittle won the bet, but the colonel grounded him for a month. The commanding officer's name was Hap Arnold, and he would not forget Jimmy Doolittle.

On November 11, 1918, a few months after Doolittle's transfer to Rockwell, the war ended and with it the dreams of glory in air combat. Doolittle decided that he liked the military life—and liked flying even more—and that the only way to earn a living as a pilot, except for barnstorming, was to stay in the service. Also, with all the veterans returning from France and flooding the job market, finding a civilian job would not be easy. The pay wasn't much—$140 a month—but it was steady. And the flying was more fun than any other job could possibly be.

But there was little for the military to do, with the war over. The army was reducing the size of all its branches. Doolittle was ambitious, both for himself and for aviation, and he thought the one way to enhance public interest in flying was to demonstrate the great potential of airplanes. Five of his fellow instructors at Rockwell had made a historic flight from California to Florida, but Doolittle proposed a cross-country flight that would attract more attention, from San Diego to Washington, D.C. Linking a military base on the West Coast with the nation's capital would show that aircraft could provide a fast courier service.

The flight was a disaster. Doolittle and two other pilots, flying Jennies, got no farther than Needles, California, only 120 miles from Rockwell Field. The two other planes crashed, and Doolittle was ordered home.

Still hoping to publicize and promote aviation, he turned to stunt flying, organizing a team called the Five Daring Acrobats. They performed at a post–Armistice Day air show in San Diego, and again in Los Angeles, and were an immense success. Doolittle loved aerobatics and spent hours in the cockpit practicing, but he also spent hours at his desk analyzing the maneuvers and determining how best to perform them within the limitations of the aircraft of the day. For the first time he began to apply the scientific method to flight, and he saw, in his own continually improving performance, how beneficial the methodical approach could be. He was making the transition from a seat-of-the-pants flier to a pilot-scientist.

In July 1919 he was transferred to Eagle Pass, Texas, where his job was to fly patrols over the desolate Mexican border, looking for smugglers, illegal aliens, and bandits crossing into the United States. Conditions were primitive. The men lived in tents in the desert heat and flew the notorious De Havilland 4 (DH-4), known as the "flaming coffin," over miles of empty space, with orders not to fire on any Mexicans crossing the border, even if they fired first.

Most of the time the pilots flew along the Rio Grande and saw no signs of life. Doolittle got so bored he grew a beard, which disappeared only hours after Joe arrived to join him. The only excitement was occasionally being shot at by Mexicans, usually from clumps of bushes. The pilots would swoop away to search for a herd of cattle. They would round up the cattle by buzzing low around them, and drive them toward the bushes. "The brush would erupt sombreros," one of Doolittle's friends wrote, "and into the river they would pile, shaking their fists at us and screaming all manner of Spanish nasties. It made us feel ever so much better."

Doolittle endured Eagle Pass for a year before being transferred to the Air Service Mechanical School at Kelly Field in San Antonio, Texas. He was promoted to first lieutenant and commissioned in the regular army, which meant greater security (reserve officers could be discharged at any time). The extra money that came with the promotion was especially welcome because the Doolittles' first child—James Junior—was born in October 1920.

At Kelly Field, Doolittle involved himself even more with the scientific and engineering aspects of flight. He had the opportunity to experiment with a variety of aircraft, including captured German fighter planes, as well as different engines, propellers, and lubricants. He was learning how such factors affected flight performance, and the subject increasingly fascinated him.

In May 1921, he was temporarily detached from Kelly and sent to Langley Field, near Norfolk, Virginia, where he was assigned as an engineering and flight officer for the newly designated First Provisional Air Brigade. The outfit had been assembled by Gen. Billy Mitchell, deputy chief of the air service, for the purpose of testing his claim that airplanes could sink battleships. The navy thought the idea was ridiculous. Josephus Daniels, former Secretary of the Navy, stated that he would gladly stand bareheaded on the deck of any battleship Mitchell tried to bomb. Daniels's assistant said it was highly unlikely that airplanes could ever attack a fleet successfully under battle conditions. The assistant's name was Franklin Roosevelt.

That summer, off the Virginia capes, Mitchell's bombers demonstrated their effectiveness by sinking several captured German warships, including a destroyer, a light cruiser, and one of the world's largest battleships—the *Ostfriesland*—which was said to be unsinkable.

The navy claimed the tests proved nothing, but Doolittle and many others believed they demonstrated conclusively the almost limitless potential of military aircraft for determining the outcome of future wars.

Doolittle also envisioned the peacetime use of aircraft for passenger and cargo services. If planes could carry a ton of bombs, as Mitchell had demonstrated, then they could carry a ton of anything. But for commercial aviation to develop, it would have to be proven that airplanes could carry passengers over greater distances and in a shorter time than trains.

He decided to try for a new cross-country speed record, to span the continent in under twenty-four hours. To accomplish this, he would have to make no more than one refueling stop, a feat never before attempted over such a distance. He crammed as many extra gas tanks as possible into a DH-4, and in July of 1922 he flew, in stages, to a beach near Jacksonville, Florida. The news of his intended flight back to the West Coast had leaked, and newspaper reporters and sightseers flocked to the beach for the takeoff. Doolittle warmed to the attention. On August 6, waving jauntily to the admiring crowd of nearly a thousand, he gunned the engine and headed down the hard-packed sand.

Suddenly the plane's wingtip caught in the surf and the DH-4 flipped upside down. Doolittle found himself underwater. His helmet covered his eyes, and his goggles had been pushed over his nose. He could not see or breathe, and was sure he was going to drown. He thrashed and sputtered and finally broke the surface, gasping for breath. When he stood up and took off his helmet, he found that the water was only two feet deep. His audience broke into laughter. It was all very embarrassing.

It took a month to repair the plane. On September 6 he took off successfully, this time with no crowds in attendance and no advance publicity. Only ten hours and five minutes later he landed at his scheduled refueling point in San Antonio. He reached San Diego in a total of twenty-two hours and thirty minutes, including an hour and fifteen minutes on the ground in San Antonio. It was an astounding performance. Previous transcontinental trips had taken days, with many refueling stops and almost as many crashes along the way. Doolittle's flight was a major step forward for the airplane, and influential people began to think that perhaps those contraptions were not toys after all.

In September 1922, Jimmy and Joe and their two sons went to Dayton, Ohio, where Doolittle was assigned to the Army Air Service's research and development center at McCook Field. He served as a test pilot while attending the service's engineering school. It was not easy being a student again, adapting to the rigor and discipline of classroom instruction, but he gradually came to enjoy the challenge it offered.

In that same year he received his B.A. degree from the University of California, which awarded degrees to all who had been seniors when they enlisted to serve in the war. The degree prepared him for the next step in his education, a doctorate in aeronautical engineering from the Massachusetts Institute of Technology.

The army decided to send six of its most promising pilots, who had demonstrated talent and interest in engineering, to MIT for advanced study. Doolittle was among those chosen, and he moved his family to Boston in July 1923. The competition from his fellow students was tougher than it had been at McCook and other army flying fields. He later liked to say that he was not a brilliant student and would not have succeeded without Joe's assistance in typing his notes and term papers, helping him to express his thoughts clearly, and worrying with him about his exams.

In the spring of 1924 he was recalled to McCook for several weeks to serve as test pilot for a plane on which the wings had fallen off a previous model, killing the pilot. Doolittle's task was to put the plane through high-speed dives and other maneuvers to see if the wings held. In his final dive, in which he pulled almost eight Gs, eight times the pull of gravity, the wings weakened dangerously, but they held. Doolittle took advantage of the strong G-forces to study, personally, the problem of pilot's blackout, the loss of consciousness during exposure to high Gs. He learned that, contrary to what pilots believed, vision was not the only faculty to be impaired during a blackout, and it was, in fact, the last faculty to deteriorate.

Doolittle received his Doctor of Science degree in July 1925 and returned to McCook Field. After two months the army set him a different kind of challenge, racing seaplanes. He was posted to the Anacostia Naval Air Station, in Washington, D.C., to learn to fly seaplanes as preparation for the Schneider international speed trophy competition. He was also selected as one of the army's pilots to enter the Pulitzer speed trophy race for landplanes.

The Pulitzer race was held at Mitchel Field on Long Island, New York, in October 1925. To generate publicity for the event and for aviation in general, Doolittle and his racing partner, Lt. Cyrus Bettis, were dispatched to entertain New Yorkers at lunchtime. After performing aerobatics over the city, the two pilots "played tag with their Curtiss racers among Manhattan's peaks. Winging among the skyscrapers they flew past the Woolworth Building, waving to gapers at the windows; they swooped down upon Central Park skimming the treetops; and for a finale . . . they thrilled the crowd gathered at the Battery in lower Manhattan by diving at them." That night a formation of army planes trimmed in red, green, and white lights flew over the city and released a huge fireworks display at eight thousand feet.

Doolittle did not fly in the Pulitzer race—Bettis won the coin toss—but he did entertain the crowd gathered at the field with a half-hour demonstration of aerobatics, culminating in a long dive. He leveled off near the ground, turned over, and flew across the field upside down. He pulled up in an inverted climb and, just as he reached stalling speed, righted the airplane and dove at the crowd again. As he did, balloons were released from the ground, and he raced after them, popping them one by one with his propeller. The army then won the race.

The Schneider seaplane race was held a month later in Baltimore, Maryland. Doolittle flew in this one, and he put his scientific training to work to gain an edge over the competition. He had observed during the Pulitzer race that the pilots lost speed at the pylon by approaching the sharp turn in level flight. He calculated that if he approached the pylon in a slight dive, he would not lose the speed he had built up over the straight portion of the course. He also altered the pitch of his propeller, well before variable-pitch propellers were developed.

Doolittle won the Schneider trophy and established a new world speed record for seaplanes, averaging a speed in excess of 232 miles per hour, thirty-three miles per hour faster than the British pilot who came in second. The following day, Doolittle asked the race officials to let him fly a straight three-kilometer course to try to establish a faster record. In three passes he maintained an average speed of 245 miles per hour.

American aviation enthusiasts were wildly excited that the United States had won the prestigious Schneider cup, but navy pilots were not thrilled to have been beaten by an army pilot who had only just learned to fly seaplanes. Doolittle became even more famous. *The New York Times* praised his accomplishments in an editorial. When he returned to Dayton, his army friends celebrated his victory by giving him a full-dress navy uniform and chauffeuring him around town in a car with signs on the doors announcing the occupant as "Admiral James H. Doolittle."

In 1926, after serving a year as chief of the test flight section at Wright Field (formerly McCook Field), Doolittle embarked on a tour of South America. Taking a leave of absence from the army, he was paid by the Curtiss-Wright Company to demonstrate their P-1 Hawk pursuit plane to South American governments to try to drum up sales.

At his first stop—Santiago, Chile—he was invited to a party at which he drank a particularly strong native cocktail. The guests were talking admiringly about the American actor Douglas Fairbanks, Jr., praising the acrobatic leaps and tumbles he routinely performed as a swashbuckler in the movies. Doolittle, perhaps emboldened by drink, said that any red-blooded American boy could do those tricks, whereupon the former college gymnast executed a couple of flips and crossed the room in a handstand.

Then, as Fairbanks inevitably did in his films, Doolittle went to the window. Warmed by the applause and cries of admiration, he maneuvered himself onto a narrow ledge overhanging the courtyard one story below. He grasped the ledge with one hand and extended his body parallel to the ground. It was at this dramatic point, the peak of the demonstration of his athletic skill, that the sill crumbled and he fell twenty feet, breaking his ankles.

With both legs in casts for two months, flying seemed out of the question, and so did a bright future. How would Doolittle ever explain his stunt to the army and the Curtiss-Wright Company? When they heard that his own foolish actions had ruined the tour, he might never be given another position of responsibility. In Doolittle's view, there was only one thing to do—continue with the tour.

At Doolittle's request, his Curtiss-Wright mechanic attached metal clips to the bottoms of Doolittle's flying boots to fasten his feet to the rudder bars. Brought to the field every day by ambulance and helped into the cockpit, he completed the demonstrations, performing all the maneuvers of which the plane was capable. He even engaged a German war ace—who was trying to sell South American governments a much more powerful plane—in a dogfight. Doolittle won, but the strain of the escapade cracked his casts, and each time he stepped on the rudder pedal, he almost fainted from the pain. The local doctors refused to treat him again because he had ignored their prohibition against flying.

He found a maker of prosthetic devices who fabricated heavier casts, reinforced with steel corset stays, and was able to finish the tour on schedule. He had to use crutches to walk, but in the air nothing stopped him, not even crossing the Andes at almost twenty thousand feet in a single-engine plane. He didn't bother with a parachute. With both legs in casts and his feet fastened to the rudder bars, he would not have been able to free his feet by himself in an emergency. Doolittle became quite a hero in South America.

He sailed home in late September 1926 to face six months of confinement in Walter Reed Army Hospital in Washington. Joe and the boys joined him during this difficult period of recovery. For the first month he was not even allowed out of bed, but if he couldn't be active physically, he kept his mind absorbed by trying to figure out how to perform an outside loop. It had never been done before.

Inside loops were routine. The centrifugal force pinned the pilot to the seat, forcing the blood to his feet. In an outside loop, the pressure would force blood to the head and tend to push the body out of the seat. No one knew what the effect of that force would be. Could the human brain withstand the pressure without bursting its blood vessels? How would the internal organs be affected? Would the force break the seatbelt and shoulder harness and push the pilot out of the cockpit? And would the plane itself hold together?

These were intriguing questions for the temporarily earthbound pilot-scientist. In the spring of 1927, when Doolittle returned to Wright Field, he was determined to find the answers. Little by little, in measured steps, he flew his Curtiss Hawk fighter to simulate the pressures to which he and the plane would be exposed in an outside loop. After each flight he meticulously examined the ship and analyzed his own reactions.

On May 25, 1927, four days after Lindbergh's historic flight from New York to Paris, Doolittle performed the first outside loop in the history of aviation. Again, he was the subject of newspaper headlines. When asked by reporters what had made him attempt the feat, he said he really didn't know why he had done it—it was just something he thought of on the spur of the moment.

That kind of flippant answer, so characteristic of him, reinforced the image of Doolittle as an impulsive, daring pilot who would try anything once. The careful scientist, who assessed every contingency in advance, was known only to his friends. To the public, he was more the colorful adventurer than the scientist, and along with Charles Lindbergh, Jimmy Doolittle became an international celebrity. But in the army he was still a first lieutenant, after more than ten years of service.

In 1928 the army granted Doolittle another leave for a second sales-demonstration tour of South America. He did not break any bones this time, but he was bitten by a dog and lost one of his planes. When a British navy officer, an adviser to Chile's navy, told Doolittle he had experience flying the Curtiss seaplane that Doolittle was trying to sell, Doolittle believed him. He let the fellow take the controls and settled into the rear seat. They never got off the water. The Englishman was a poor pilot, and Doolittle, helpless in the rear with no controls, could only watch for the crash he knew was inevitable. He saved the man from drowning but was furious with himself for his poor judgment in endangering their lives and destroying the plane.

The tour was a success, nonetheless. Doolittle proved to be an excellent goodwill ambassador, charming all the dignitaries he met and collecting many honors, medals, and awards. He sold some planes and became the first person to fly over Brazil's uncharted Mato Grosso jungle, a flight of more than seven hours. But when he came home and saw no prospect of promotion, he began to question the wisdom of remaining in the air corps.

He postponed the decision for a year because of a unique civilian research venture in which the army allowed him to participate, the opportunity to head the Full Flight Laboratory at Mitchel Field. The project was financed by the Daniel Guggenheim Fund for the Promotion of Aeronautics, an organization operated by two former navy pilots. Yet, when they sought a director for the new laboratory, which would be devoted to research on flight under adverse weather conditions, they chose an army man.

In September 1928 the family moved to Long Island, and Doolittle set to work, ably assisted by an aeronautics professor from MIT, an army pilot, and a crew chief for the two airplanes the lab had purchased. For the next year the team worked on the problems of flying in fog, rain, snow, and other low-visibility conditions. If aviation was to progress, the problem of all-weather flight would have to be solved. Working with engineers in private industry, Doolittle also directed the development of new flight instruments, such as an altimeter accurate to within five feet (the old ones were accurate only to the nearest fifty to one hundred feet), an artificial horizon indicator, and a directional gyroscope, all essential to blind flying.

During this period, Doolittle was asked by the army to mount an aerobatics display at the National Air Races in Cleveland, Ohio. He had been flying slow planes for the research projects, so he decided he needed some practice in his favorite pursuit ship, the Curtiss P-1 Hawk, before performing in public. He took off early on the morning of the scheduled performance and was rehearsing his aerial stunt routine when the wings cracked and folded back. The plane cartwheeled toward the ground. Doolittle instantly released his safety harness, was tossed out of the cockpit, and parachuted to safety.

He landed out of sight of the airport, and when he showed up at the field carrying his parachute, army officials were greatly surprised. "Gentlemen," he said, "I guess I'll have to borrow another plane." A half hour later, as though nothing unusual had happened, he performed one of the most sensational aerobatic routines ever witnessed.

In September 1929, Doolittle made the world's first all-instrument flight. With a hood covering the cockpit, sealed to keep out all light, he took the plane to one thousand feet, made a 180-degree left turn, flew that course for several miles, made another 180-degree left turn, a gradual descent, and a good landing. The flight lasted only fifteen minutes, but it changed the nature of aviation. *The New York Times* wrote that Doolittle's research had led to the greatest single advance ever recorded in flight safety. Once again, Jimmy Doolittle had made history.

In December he left the army and went to work for the Shell Oil Company's aviation department in St. Louis, Missouri. He was reluctant to leave the service, but his army pay—less than two hundred dollars a month—was inadequate for his family and for the mounting medical expenses of his mother and mother-in-law. "The reason for leaving the service was a purely monetary one," he said. His work for the Full Flight Laboratory, during which he had received more than three times his army pay, had ended, promotion to captain was unforeseen, and Shell was offering a substantial salary plus a $25,000 Lockheed Vega for his personal use. His job would be to compete in air races and shows to publicize Shell's aviation fuels and related products. It was too good an opportunity to turn down. He remained in the air corps reserves, however, and to his surprise was given the rank of major, bypassing the grade of captain.

On the night of February 16, 1930, at Long Island's Mitchel Field, he loaded Joe and the boys and their luggage into the sleek white Vega for the flight to St. Louis, where he would begin work the following day. The weather was bad, with blustery winds and snow blowing across the ice-rutted ground. Waving good-bye to friends who had braved the cold to see them off, Doolittle gunned the 425-horsepower engine and taxied down the field. Although the engine was running at full power, the plane seemed sluggish.

The wheels struck a mound of frozen earth, and the door behind the pilot's seat flew open. Doolittle was thrown back into the passenger compartment. A forward bulkhead cracked, the landing gear collapsed, and the plane skidded across the ice and plowed into a snowbank, trapping the family inside the aircraft until a crash crew arrived.

It was an ignominious beginning. Doolittle was embarrassed to report to his new employer that he had caused ten thousand dollars worth of damage to the company's plane. Worse, one of the world's best pilots had to travel to St. Louis by train.

The Shell Oil executives did not mind the expense. They knew that the favorable publicity Doolittle would generate for them over the coming years would more than compensate for the loss of the plane. They were right. Doolittle stayed with Shell for ten years, and it was a time of excitement, glamour, and growing prestige for him. He continued to win air races and awards and to make significant contributions to aviation.

Shortly after joining Shell, Doolittle embarked on a ten-week tour of Europe, from Greece to Scandinavia, to demonstrate Curtiss-Wright airplanes that used Shell products. As usual for Doolittle, the tour was an immense success. He impressed the leaders of every country he visited, and learned much about European advances in aviation. He became concerned, however, about Germany's emphasis on higher airspeed, which he interpreted—correctly, as it turned out—as presaging the development of military planes. Military aircraft were forbidden to Germany under the terms of the Versailles Treaty. Doolittle's observations were made three years before Hitler came to power.

In 1933, Jimmy and Joe made a five-month business trip through the Orient and Europe. This time he was even more alarmed about advances in military aviation in Germany and in Japan. He worried that the United States was falling behind, not only in military flight but also in commercial aviation. When he returned to the United States, he used every opportunity his fame afforded to voice his worries in speeches and press conferences and to lobby government and military leaders for greater financial support for American aviation. Few people, other than fellow pilots, heeded the warning, but Doolittle continued to press his case.

His distress about America's lag in military aviation became all the more intense during European trips in 1937 and 1939, the latter shortly after Germany's occupation of Czechoslovakia and annexation of Austria. In 1937 he visited with Ernst Udet, head of the Luftwaffe's technical department. Udet enabled Doolittle to have almost unlimited access to information about Germany's air force. "He did me the courtesy of turning his airplane and pilot over to me," Doolittle said, "and giving me an entrée into all the things that I wanted to see in Germany, including the aircraft factories."

On Doolittle's 1939 visit, Udet was no longer so friendly, and he permitted Doolittle only a limited glimpse of Luftwaffe facilities. What Doolittle did get to see confirmed his fears about America's sorry state of military aviation. He shared his views with the American air attaché in London, but the man seemed unconcerned. At home, Doolittle tried to prod government officials to attempt to catch up with German progress, but there were few listeners. Doolittle believed a major war would soon erupt in Europe. If the United States was caught up in it, she would not be ready.

During the first few years of his decade with Shell, Doolittle participated in the increasingly popular air races. He knew these contests were beneficial to aviation because the ever-greater speed needed to win led to improvements in airplane engines and aircraft design.

In 1931 he won the Bendix Trophy, given to the winner of the annual race from Burbank, California, to Cleveland, Ohio. Not content with his record-breaking flight between those cities, he quickly refueled and set off for Newark, New Jersey, arriving eleven hours and sixteen minutes after leaving California. This bettered the transcontinental record set the year before. Nine years earlier, Doolittle had been the first pilot to cross the country in less than twenty-four hours. Now he was the first to do so in under twelve.

In Newark, Doolittle posed for photographers while his plane was being refueled, then he flew to Cleveland to greet his wife and on to St. Louis for a party Shell threw in his honor. In one day he had won a major speed trophy, set a transcontinental speed record, and flown more than 3,500 miles.

Shell sought to capitalize on Doolittle's celebrity, and sent him on a series of record-breaking flights between St. Louis and other U.S. cities. Following that tour, he flew from Ottawa, Canada, via Washington, D.C., to Mexico City, in less than twelve hours, linking the capitals of the nations on the North American continent. On the last leg of his flight to Mexico City, the small container of tetraethyl lead he had on board to boost his fuel octane rating leaked into the cockpit. The fumes caused several brief lapses of consciousness and left him nauseated. He taxied up to the reviewing stand and promptly vomited.

The next year he took Joe and two other passengers on a trip that broke no speed records but nevertheless generated considerable favorable publicity. They took off from St. Louis in the morning, stopped for breakfast in Jacksonville, Florida, lunch in Havana, Cuba, and dinner in Miami. The flight made the idea of air travel seem easy, normal, safe, and glamorous. Soon hundreds, perhaps thousands, of people would fly every day, for business or for pleasure, and do so as routinely as Doolittle. This was part of his vision for American aviation.

Another publicity gimmick dreamed up by Shell executives in 1932 was in celebration of the bicentennial of George Washington's birth and the one hundred fifty-seventh anniversary of the Post Office. The idea was to retrace by air the routes Washington had traveled and drop mail at the historic sites along the way. Taking a descendant of Washington's as a passenger, and a Shell Oil Company employee to drop the mail, Doolittle crisscrossed the eastern half of the country from Maine to North Carolina, Ohio to Pennsylvania, to Washington, D.C., keeping to a precise timetable. He covered more than 2,600 miles in one day, demonstrating that airplanes could fly to any number of towns, carrying mail and passengers, and adhere to a schedule.

In September 1932, Doolittle entered the Thompson Trophy race at Cleveland, Ohio, flying one of the most dangerous aircraft ever designed, the Gee Bee. Highly unstable in flight, with unusually short wings and a barrellike body, the powerful plane was difficult to handle in turns. One pilot had been killed in it and another hospitalized, but the plane had one advantage—it was the fastest ship in the air. If a pilot could control it, he would probably win the trophy. A month before, Doolittle had cracked up the plane he had planned to fly in the race, so he accepted the designer's offer of the use of a Gee Bee.*

In the qualifying runs, Doolittle's average speed set a record of 296 miles per hour, his best time being 306 miles per hour. The engine caught fire when he started it, but he won the race and vowed never to fly the plane again.

A few weeks later, Doolittle announced his retirement from air racing, for both personal and professional reasons. He felt he had more than used up his share of luck. He admitted to being disturbed when he had learned that press photographers had crowded Joe and the children in the stands during the Thompson race, waiting to record the horror on their faces if he crashed. He had already won every race and broken nearly every speed record. It was time for other challenges.

Also, Doolittle had come to think air racing had outlived its usefulness and was no longer worth the high price in pilots' lives. The races brought public attention to aviation as a sport, but it was

---

* Over the next three years, three more pilots died in crashes of Gee Bees. Two others crashed and survived.

time for flying to move beyond that, to the serious development of military and commercial aviation and to improvements in safety and reliability. The spectacular crashes at the air races, caught dramatically on newsreel film, did little to promote flying as a means of transportation. They brought crowds to the shows, but Doolittle wanted to see those crowds as passengers on airliners.

If commercial aviation was to prosper, airplanes would have to be larger in order to carry enough passengers to be cost-effective. In the military sphere, the army was already proposing bigger bombers, capable of carrying heavier bomb loads. These developments required more powerful engines, which, Doolittle knew, would require higher-octane fuel for better performance. He urged Shell Oil to develop 100-octane fuel to replace the 91-octane product then in use.

The company's managers were initially reluctant to invest in a product no one yet wanted to buy, but Doolittle persuaded them that the market for high-octane fuel would surely develop. Shell built a plant and waited for customers. No one came.

Doolittle continued to insist that the air corps and the airlines would soon be swamping them with orders, and on his recommendation Shell constructed three more plants to refine the fuel. Some executives referred to the project as Doolittle's "million-dollar blunder," but in 1938 the army decreed that 100-octane fuel would become standard for all Army Air Corps planes except trainers. It was a victory for Doolittle and another advance for aviation.*

In August 1939, when Doolittle returned from Europe convinced that war was imminent, he went to see Hap Arnold, chief of the air corps. Doolittle offered his services in any capacity, military or civilian. Arnold wanted Doolittle back in uniform, but under present law, reserve officers above the rank of captain could not be recalled to active duty. "I want you back on active duty," Arnold said. "However, it will take an act of Congress to get you back." It was almost a year before Congress revised the law, and when they did, in

---

*Unfortunately, the army's first contract for the new fuel went to a rival oil company, but soon Shell was selling all it could produce.

July 1940, Jimmy Doolittle was the first man the air corps recalled to duty.

He met with some jealousy from men who had stayed in the service during the ten years he had been living the more exciting life in private industry. Some resented his skipping the grade of captain, and others envied his high salary. Doolittle had no time for such concerns. He was busy with his assignment at the Central Air Corps Procurement District in Indianapolis, Indiana. The Allison Engine Division of the General Motors Corporation was having difficulties with the production of the large, liquid-cooled engines that powered the P-38, P-39, and P-40 planes, at the time America's best fighter aircraft. Doolittle reorganized the division and soon had the production lines flowing smoothly.

Given a P-40 for his own use, he installed additional instruments in the cockpit to enable him to fly in all kinds of weather. This was contrary to air corps policy, which prohibited pursuit planes from flying in bad weather. Doolittle thought the policy was unwise, particularly for wartime, so he concentrated on developing training techniques and modifying his instruments to enable air corps fighters to fly in all weather.

In November 1940, Doolittle was transferred to Detroit, Michigan, to expedite the conversion of the automobile industry from manufacturing cars and trucks to building airplanes. The project was encountering snags. The car makers wanted to keep making cars, and the aircraft industry did not want to release its design secrets. "I was to act as midwife at a wedding that nobody wanted to take place," Doolittle said. Displaying tact, persistence, goodwill, and his excellent organizational and leadership skills, he got the job done in the face of the determined resistance of both parties.

Despite these successes, he was bored with the paperwork and the lack of action, particularly after a visit to England to inspect British methods of maintaining and repairing aircraft. He wanted to fight, but there were no combat jobs in a nation not yet at war. The situation changed on December 7, 1941, and on December 8, Doolittle requested a transfer to a combat unit. He was turned down. As in 1917, he was faced with the prospect of missing the war.

On December 12 he received a telephone call from Hap Arnold.

"How quickly can you be here?" Arnold asked. "I want you on my immediate staff."

"Will tomorrow be all right?"

"So that's when I went to General Arnold's staff as trouble-shooter," Doolittle recalled. "It had been found that the bombs wouldn't drop, that the machine guns wouldn't fire, and that a lot of things just wouldn't work, and my job was to make sure that all our equipment was battleworthy."

He was promoted to lieutenant colonel and given the job of saving the Martin B-26 Marauder, a fast twin-engine bomber, from being canceled. The plane had a reputation as a killer. "Our new pilots were afraid of the B-26," Arnold wrote, "and we had one accident after another. Seemingly, all that was necessary was for one engine to go sour on a B-26 while in flight and it would crash."

Doolittle test-flew the plane and decided there was nothing wrong that proper pilot training would not remedy. He flew the aircraft to the B-26 training field and landed smoothly with only one engine working. He taxied up to a group of student pilots who had watched the landing in amazement. He got out and said, "Now what is it you don't like about this airplane?" Within a few days, he had them all making landings and takeoffs on only one engine, and the B-26 became a vital weapon in the air corps' arsenal.

On January 17, 1942, Doolittle was called into the air corps chief's office, shortly after Arnold had met with navy captains Duncan and Low. Arnold handed him the assignment that would change his life.

"Jim," Arnold said, "what airplane have we got that will get off in five hundred feet with a two-thousand-pound bomb load and fly two thousand miles?"

"General, I'll need a little time to give you an answer," Doolittle said.

"OK, Jim, but keep this quiet and let me know as soon as you can."

# The B-25B
# Special Project

Doolittle reported back to Arnold the next morning with his answer to the general's question. He had considered the same planes Captain Duncan had—the B-23, the B-25, and the B-26. He ruled out the B-26 because it could not take off in five hundred feet with a full bomb load. The other planes could do so if their weight was reduced.

"It narrows down to either the B-23 or the B-25," he told Arnold, "but either one will take some modifying."

"One more fact you should know that I didn't tell you," Arnold said, "is that the plane must take off from a narrow area not over seventy-five feet wide."

"Well, then, the only answer is the B-25. It has a sixty-seven-foot wingspan. The B-23 would never make it off safely. Now, what's behind all this?"

Arnold described Duncan's plan to have army bombers brought by aircraft carriers to within striking distance of Japan. Doolittle was immediately enthusiastic, particularly when Arnold said he was to supervise the air corps' part of the project. Doolittle's job would be to prepare the planes and train the crews, but from the moment he heard about the raid, he was determined to lead it. Here was his chance to get into combat. He knew it would be difficult to get permission. Arnold would say he was too valuable to risk losing. Doolittle decided first to prove himself indispensable to the success of the mission, then he would ask about leading it.

Arnold ordered him to work closely with Duncan on the modifications of the planes and the training of the B-25 crews. Duncan would coordinate the operation and organize the task force.

Finding a sufficient number of B-25 bombers presented no problem. There was only one operational unit of the planes, the Seventeenth Bombardment Group, about to be transferred from Pendleton, Oregon, to Columbia, South Carolina, to conduct submarine patrols over the Atlantic. Once the planes were ready for the mission, Doolittle would ask the Seventeenth for volunteers. He hoped enough men would volunteer. There wouldn't be time to train new crews to fly the planes.

On January 22, Doolittle began the process of modifying the planes for the mission. Based on his analysis of the requirements of the raid, he knew that extra fuel tanks would have to be installed to increase range, and new shackles designed to carry and release the bombs. In addition, the B-25B, the only model in operation, was poorly armed. He had to find a way to make it more readily defensible against Japanese fighters. All the work would have to be completed in a matter of weeks. Even with the top-priority orders Arnold had given him to expedite the job, it would be close. Doolittle would need to push everyone hard, himself included.

Some of the modifications would be undertaken by Mid-Continent Airlines in Minneapolis, Minnesota. Others would have to be done later at Eglin Field in Florida, while the crews were in training. Doolittle requested that a B-25 be sent to Mid-Continent the following day, with seventeen more planes to follow as soon as possible. He later increased the number to twenty-four. He flew to Wright Field to consult with air corps engineers on how best to make the necessary changes, but he told no one there or at Mid-Continent the reason for the work.

The most extensive changes involved the addition of three fuel tanks, which almost doubled the amount of gas that could be carried from the normal complement of 646 gallons to 1,141 gallons. Initially, a large steel tank to hold 265 gallons was installed in the bomb bay. It turned out to leak excessively and was replaced by a 225-gallon bulletproof rubber tank. It, too, would cause problems throughout the training period and, on one plane, even up to the day before the raid.

A tank holding 160 gallons of fuel was placed in the crawl space above the bomb bay. It was essentially a collapsible rubber bag. Once it was empty, it could be flattened and shoved aside so that crew members could once again move forward and aft through the passageway. This tank also developed leaks.

Another auxiliary fuel tank for sixty gallons was installed where the belly turret was located. That turret had never worked well, and Doolittle was said to have remarked that it would be easier to learn to play the violin than to operate that recalcitrant piece of machinery. A metal plate was riveted over the opening where the lower turret protruded, and the new tank, a two-foot cube, replaced the turret mechanism within the fuselage.

Finally, ten five-gallon gas cans were stored in the radio operator's compartment at the rear of the aircraft. The plan called for the rear gunner to empty those cans into the turret tank as its level went down. He was then supposed to punch holes in the cans so they would sink when he threw them overboard and not leave a floating trail that might lead the Japanese to the carrier task force.

These were all makeshift arrangements. Having so much aviation fuel tucked away throughout the plane was clearly hazardous. A crash on takeoff, a fire aboard ship, or a chance hit by an incendiary bullet or shell would turn a plane into a fireball instantly, but there was no way for the B-25s to reach Japan without the extra fuel.

The bomb bay still had space for bombs, but not on the original shackles. New ones had to be fabricated to carry two five-hundred-pound demolition bombs and one thousand pounds of incendiaries in two five-hundred-pound clusters. Each cluster contained 128 incendiaries.

Doolittle's next problem was armament. The B-25's top turret, with twin .50-caliber machine guns, was unreliable and subject to frequent jamming. When the guns were fired toward the rear, the barrels came so close to the top of the fuselage that the force of the blasts popped rivets and tore the plane's aluminum skin. Reinforcing plates had to be riveted behind the turrets to protect the fuselage. The top turrets were never to function satisfactorily, but without them, the planes would have been vulnerable to attack from above and from the rear.

A single .30-caliber machine gun was mounted in the nose, but it had to be moved from one gun port to another, depending on the position of the target. The gun was difficult to move in combat, but Doolittle had no time to develop anything more effective. To simulate tail guns, he had two wooden broomsticks installed and painted black to resemble machine-gun barrels. He hoped the sight of this would discourage Japanese fighter pilots from attacking from the rear. The broomsticks turned out to be highly effective.

Other modifications were necessary. Doolittle and the Wright Field engineers tried to anticipate every need. One possibility they considered was that the planes might fly to Vladivostok after the raid and be turned over to the Russians as lend-lease equipment. In that event, the pilots might encounter frigid weather conditions on their route north from Japan. Therefore, deicing equipment was installed on the leading edges of the wing and tail surfaces.

Most of the flares were removed from each plane to decrease the overall weight slightly and to reduce the danger of fire, should they ignite spontaneously or explode on impact from gunfire. Two landing flares, to provide light in case of a night landing, were placed forward of the armored bulkhead behind the pilot's seat, where they were reasonably safe from enemy fire. To use the flares, the rear gunner would have to crawl to the cockpit, unclip them, attach a static line to their tiny parachutes to ignite them, and drop them through the rear hatch.

Doolittle expected that radio silence would be maintained during the raid, eliminating the need for the 230-pound radio set in each plane. This not only reduced the weight, but it also would prevent any inadvertent transmission that might give away the bombers' location.

To make a photographic record of the results of the bombing, the lead plane and each flight leader's plane would be equipped with a small tail camera that would automatically be activated when the first bombs were jettisoned. The electrically operated cameras could take sixty pictures at half-second intervals. The rest of the planes were equipped with 16-millimeter movie cameras.

Once Doolittle was satisfied that the modifications were well under way at Mid-Continent, he returned to Washington to continue his preparations. He did not know it yet, but the planes would require even greater alterations later, and that would disrupt his plans for training the bomber crews.

While the planes were being readied, President Roosevelt was continuing to press his service chiefs about a way to bomb Japan. At a White House meeting on January 28, with Arnold, King, Marshall, Stimson, and others, the president asked Arnold if any definite plans had been made. Arnold and King were the only ones present who knew about the work of Doolittle and Duncan, and they wanted to keep it that way.

Arnold decided not to tell the president. He believed the need for security was paramount. The lives of the several thousand men of the carrier task force would depend on it. The greater the number of people who knew of the plan in advance, the greater the possibility of a leak. In all, only Arnold, King, Low, Duncan, and Doolittle were aware of the operation, and so far as Arnold was concerned, there was no need for others to know yet, not the president, the secretary of war, or the army chief of staff. Admiral King appeared to agree. He said nothing about the raid either.

Years later, in describing that meeting at the White House, Arnold wrote that he did not want the mission "to be common knowledge, so I steered clear of it and talked about bombing Japan from China and Russia; about the difficulties we had in trying to get gasoline and other supplies into our bases in those areas."

Roosevelt seemed annoyed and reemphasized the psychological benefits of bombing Japan's home islands as soon as possible. He said he had been studying a map of China and was surprised to see airfields still in Chinese hands that did not seem so far from Japan. These fields could surely be used by American planes, he added, and he urged General Arnold to consider sending bombers there. He then asked Arnold if Japan could be reached from U.S. bases in the Aleutian Islands, but Arnold said there were no planes capable of covering that distance.

At about the same time, Doolittle was being asked about bombing Japan, not by President Roosevelt, but by Roscoe Turner, an old friend from the air-racing circuit. Turner wrote to suggest that he and Doolittle form a group of hotshot pilots from their racing and long-distance flying days and undertake a mission to bomb Japan. Turner argued that because of their experience, they were the only fliers capable of the precise navigation needed to reach targets so far away. Doolittle was amused by the idea, but said they were too old for such an operation. Combat flying was best left to younger pilots.

Doolittle had asked Arnold to have his staff prepare a list of suitable targets in Japan, and on January 31, Brig. Gen. Carl "Tooey" Spaatz, Arnold's intelligence officer, brought Doolittle a list of ten cities, including Tokyo, Kobe, Nagoya, and Yokohama. Spaatz had indicated the military objectives in each—airplane factories, navy bases, oil refineries, and other essential war industries.

For Doolittle, only one major question remained. Could B-25s actually take off from the deck of an aircraft carrier?

★ ★ ★ ★

The USS *Hornet*, America's newest aircraft carrier, dropped anchor in Hampton Roads on the evening of January 31 to await a visitor from Washington. The $45-million ship, with its 809-foot flight deck (the length of a city block), four-inch armor encircling the hull, and a crew of more than two thousand, had just returned from its shakedown cruise in the Caribbean.

The *Hornet* had been commissioned three months before, on October 20, 1941. More than 75 percent of the crew were fresh out of boot camp or flying school. Most of the men were so inexperienced that they could not even find their way around a ship. During the commissioning ceremony, the *Hornet*'s navigator, Comdr. Frank

Akers, became so exasperated that he snapped to a subordinate, "Tie 'em together as best you can. If we don't watch out, they'll get lost." Now, after the shakedown cruise, the men were feeling cocky and confident, a view their more experienced officers did not share. The sailors were happily anticipating their first shore leave, but permission to leave the ship had not come. It was disappointing, and puzzling.

Their captain thought so, too. He had no idea what the visitor from Washington wanted, but he had orders to hold the ship and crew in readiness until he found out. The *Hornet*'s skipper, Marc Andrew "Pete" Mitscher, a 1910 graduate of the United States Naval Academy at Annapolis, was one of the navy's pioneer aviators. He had received the Navy Cross in 1918 for making the navy's first transatlantic flight, from Newfoundland to the Azores, and had since held increasingly important commands in naval aviation.

A tall, laconic man, he had only to look quizzically at a subordinate to express displeasure. "It was worse than a reprimand," Commander Akers recalled. Yet he was an inspiring and masterful leader of men, calm and precise, who delegated responsibility well to his junior officers. Although Mitscher revered navy tradition and ceremony on land, he ran his ship less formally. One of his first orders on assuming command of the *Hornet* was that officers would not wear neckties.

Mitscher had worked the crew hard on the shakedown cruise, convinced that the navy's newest carrier would soon be facing combat. He intended to ensure that his men would be ready for it. To imbue them with the proper fighting spirit, he had a slogan—REMEMBER PEARL HARBOR—painted in large block letters on the smokestack.

The visitor from Washington, Captain Duncan, came aboard the following day. As part of his preparations for the bombing raid on Japan, he had commandeered two B-25s that happened to be at Langley Field. It was time to find out if his and Doolittle's calculations were correct. They were convinced, in theory, that the bombers could take off from a carrier deck, but it was time to know that they had actually done so.

The pilots of the B-25s, Lt. John Fitzgerald and Lt. James McCarthy, had been practicing short takeoff runs and had been able to lift off in a distance a little longer than the length of a carrier deck. If all went well, with the forward speed of the ship and the force of the wind to help, they would be airborne before they ran out of deck.

Duncan got directly to the point with Mitscher.

"Can you put a loaded B-25 in the air on a normal deck run?"

"How many B-25s on deck?" Mitscher asked.

"Fifteen."

Mitscher went to his flight deck spotting board and, with Duncan peering over his shoulder, quickly calculated how much space the bombers would need.

"Yes," he said. "It can be done."

"Good," Duncan said. "I'm putting two aboard for a test launching tomorrow."

Duncan did not offer Mitscher any explanation for the test, and Mitscher did not ask. He knew that if it was important for him to know, Duncan would tell him. But he was certainly curious, and so were his crew, as they watched the army planes being hoisted aboard by the large dockside cranes. The bombers were lashed down, one well aft and the other far forward, the forward position being the spot from which the first plane in the group would have to take off. By nine o'clock in the morning, the carrier and an escort of two destroyers was heading out to sea. A light snow was falling, and the crew was speculating on "why army planes should squat, like awkward land birds, on the flight deck of a navy ship."

The sailors thought the idea of launching such planes was ridiculous. The largest navy plane to fly off any carrier had a wingspan of only forty feet. The B-25s had a wingspan of sixty-seven feet. They would never clear the bridge superstructure. And if by some miracle they did make it, they would never be able to land, not without a tail hook to jolt them to a quick stop.

At one o'clock that afternoon, Duncan and Mitscher, clad in foul-weather gear, waited in the wind and rain on the port wing of the bridge, overlooking the flight deck. Captain Mitscher ordered the carrier turned into the wind. One of the army fliers shouted something to Lt. Oscar Dodson, the ship's communications officer. "If we go into the water, don't run over us."

The pilot of the forward plane, Lieutenant Fitzgerald, gunned both engines and was pleased to see that his airspeed indicator showed forty-five miles per hour, the combined effect of the ship's forward speed and the wind. He would need to accelerate only about twenty-five miles per hour more to have sufficient takeoff speed.

"When I got the 'go' signal," Fitzgerald said, "I let the brakes off and was almost immediately airborne, well ahead of my estimate. One thing that worried me, though, was the projection of the island structure out over the flight deck on which the skipper stood so he could have a clear view of the deck operations. The wing of my plane rose so rapidly that I thought we were going to strike this projection. I pushed the control column forward and the wing just barely passed underneath."

Duncan was relieved to see the plane leap into the air. Theory had become reality. The mission was on.

Lieutenant McCarthy was preparing to take off when Mitscher received a report from a lookout that the periscope of a submarine had been spotted. The sighting had to be taken seriously because German U-boats patrolling off the East Coast were regularly sinking merchant ships within sight of land. The Hornet's crew raced to their battle stations, and the escorting destroyers sped toward the target area and loosed a barrage of depth charges.

Within minutes, an oil slick spread itself over the surface of the water where the charges had exploded, and the sailors shouted and cheered. It was their first time in action, and it looked as though they had sunk an enemy sub. Mitscher peered through his binoculars at the oil slick, then turned to his navigator, Commander Akers.

"Frank," he said, "it's a nice oil slick, but I can still see a foot or so of what appears to be a periscope sticking up. This is the first blasted submarine that I've ever seen like that."

A few moments later he received a message from one of the destroyers on the scene, announcing that the submarine was a sunken merchant ship whose mast was sticking out of the water.

Mitscher laughed.

"Very realistic drill," he said. "Send them a 'well done.'"

McCarthy's B-25 lifted off the deck as easily as the first one. With its mission accomplished, the *Hornet* returned to Norfolk that evening. After Captain Duncan had left the ship to return to Washington, the *Hornet* began taking on stores and ammunition. Mitscher and his senior officers discussed the significance of the day's events and speculated on what it might mean for their futures.

Duncan had said that the tests had been conducted simply to investigate the B-25's takeoff capabilities, to determine how fast it could take off and in how short a distance. The *Hornet*'s officers were skeptical about that explanation. If that was truly the case, the tests could have been performed at an airfield. Obviously, there was more to it than Duncan had been willing to reveal.

And what about the deck space? Duncan had inquired about space for some fifteen bombers. If the *Hornet*'s mission was to ferry those planes to some overseas base, there would be no need for a test launching. Cranes would put the planes aboard and would just as easily lift them off.

Mitscher decided that his ship had been chosen for an unusual and possibly dangerous mission that involved launching B-25 bombers against an enemy target. As to where that target might be, who could say? He told his staff that the less they knew the better, but he didn't feel that way himself.

The more Mitscher thought about it, the more perturbed he became that Duncan had not confided in him about the tests, particularly since, as he now suspected, they would affect the future of his ship. If the *Hornet* was slated for some secret mission, her captain should know the details as soon as possible so that adequate preparations could be made.

A few days later, Mitscher received orders to have the *Hornet* ready to leave Norfolk by March 1, a little over three weeks away. He was to proceed through the Panama Canal to San Diego, and from there to an as-yet-undesignated location in the Pacific. He was still in the dark about the operation, but he was certain they would be getting into the war.

Captain Duncan, of course, knew where Mitscher would be heading. The *Hornet*'s orders had originated with him. "I had already had the *Hornet* in mind to do this operation," Duncan said, "because she was due to finish her shakedown and go around to the Pacific coast at just about the same time everything else would be in order and the operation was ready to start. So, although nobody on the *Hornet* knew it, they were destined for the operation some time before they actually performed it. That made my friend Pete Mitscher . . . unhappy; he was not let in on the full plan until quite late in the business."

Duncan had many other arrangements to make for the navy's role in the raid. He had to investigate the weather conditions for the area east of Japan, where the task force would be sailing to reach the launch point. He sent a submarine, the USS *Thresher*, to patrol the area, to surface regularly and record air and water temperatures, barometric pressure, wind speed and direction, cloud cover, and visibility.

The bombing mission could be jeopardized by bad weather. It could force the ships to go slower than planned, prevent the launching of the planes, and obscure the targets. Severe storms could scatter the ships of the task force and damage them. Pacific typhoons could be more formidable adversaries than the Japanese navy and air force.

Duncan was also concerned about the composition of the task force. How many ships would he need, and what types? He wanted a second carrier to provide air cover, and there had to be a sufficient number of escort destroyers and cruisers, as well as oilers to provide for refueling at sea. Each ship had to be provisioned properly, with men, food, ammunition, and all the other items needed to wage war.

He had few ships to choose from, after the wreckage at Pearl Harbor. The task force would have to manage with the limited resources at hand. Yet everything would have to be arranged in less than two months. The *Hornet*, with the army planes and trained crews aboard, would have to leave San Francisco by April 1.

★ ★ ★ ★

Doolittle was also feeling the pressure of time as he worked in his office in Washington's Munitions Building. The B-25s were being modified, and now he knew that they were capable of lifting off from a carrier deck, but there were still many details to oversee for the air corps' role, and his own, in the mission. To put his thoughts in order, and to make sure he had not forgotten anything, Doolittle spent two hours methodically writing down the specifics of the raid. He gave the report the title "The B-25B Special Project."

The purpose of the project, Doolittle wrote, was to bomb the industrial centers of Japan, to interfere with war production and to lead to the withdrawal of at least some Japanese forces from the Pacific theater to defend Japan herself against future attacks. The need for the raid was clear, for the positive effect it would have on the morale of the American people and their allies, and for the negative effect it would have on the Japanese.

The navy, Doolittle added, would bring the bombers to within four hundred to five hundred miles of Japan. After the bombing, the planes would proceed to bases in China, or to Vladivostok, if the Russians agreed to accept them on lend-lease. Because the Russian field was closer than the Chinese fields, crews headed for Vladivostok would have a greater chance for survival. But Doolittle knew that the Russians would probably not permit the use of their air base. They were afraid of antagonizing the Japanese.

Next, Doolittle described the modifications being made to the bombers, noting that the work would probably be completed by March 15. Following that, a short training period for the crews would be undertaken, with emphasis on bombing, gunnery, navigation, and short takeoff runs. He suggested that each pilot be given the opportunity to take off from a carrier at least once. Training would have to be finished by April 1, by which date the crews and their planes would have to be ready to board the carrier somewhere on the West Coast.

Doolittle's plans called for a daylight bombing raid to ensure greater accuracy. The planes would be launched from the carrier at night to reach their targets at dawn, and the safe bases in China sometime that afternoon. He allowed for the possibility of a nighttime raid, should the element of surprise be lost.

He paid particular attention to the aftermath of the raid, the arrival of the planes in China at airfields in and around Chuchow, seventy miles inland. These fields had been prepared by Chennault for the bombers he had hoped to obtain for his own Flying Tigers to use against Japan. The fields were neither manned nor protected. They were simply paved runways, with no personnel, antiaircraft weapons, fighter planes, or even fuel.

Also, the fields were close to the Japanese front lines, which meant that B-25s on the ground would be vulnerable to enemy fighter attacks. It was imperative, therefore, that the army bombers refuel as quickly as possible after the raid and fly immediately to Chungking, some eight hundred miles inland, where they would be safe from air attack.

Doolittle recommended that twenty thousand gallons of 100-octane aviation fuel—the kind he had been responsible for developing while at Shell Oil—plus six hundred gallons of lubricating oil be stashed at the Chuchow fields. He detailed Harry Howze, formerly with Standard Oil of New Jersey and now an air corps lieutenant, to arrange for the fuel caches.

Chennault's cooperation was vital to the Chuchow refueling operation. Doolittle wrote in his report that Chennault should be fully informed about the arrival of the B-25s so he could arrange to have American or English-speaking Chinese personnel at each field to oversee the refueling and to provide local manpower to assist the bomber crews. Doolittle stressed that the equipping of these fields should begin at once.

He cautioned, however, against providing any information about the raid to the Chinese officials. Chiang's government was not to be told about the landing of the B-25s on Chinese soil until just prior to their arrival. Doolittle believed—and his view was shared by General Arnold and other high-ranking army and air corps officers—that information about the raid given to the Chinese would likely fall into Japanese hands. To put it bluntly, he warned, the Chinese were not to be trusted.

Unfortunately, Arnold felt the same way about Chennault. His distrust of Chennault was deep and long-standing. The man who had already become a hero to the American people was, to the air corps chief, nothing more than an adventurer and a mercenary.

George Marshall thought Chennault was dissolute and immoral. Because of this high-level suspicion, Chennault was not informed about the raid in advance, and this omission, more than any other factor, would have fatal consequences for some of the B-25 fliers.

Toward the end of Doolittle's thorough and careful analysis of the raid, he noted that he would personally take command of it. Arnold was unaware of Doolittle's determination to lead the raid himself, and Doolittle knew it was not yet time to bring the matter up.

Almost everything had been set in motion for America's first attack on Japan. Doolittle's remaining task was to select and train the crews.

★ ★ ★ ★

The men of the Seventeenth Bombardment Group were bored and restless. They had been training in their sleek B-25s and were ready for action, but it appeared as though they wouldn't be doing anything more exciting than flying antisubmarine patrols off South Carolina, not much of an improvement over their present duty—antisubmarine patrols off the coast of Oregon.

Until April of 1941, the Seventeenth, stationed at McChord Field near Tacoma, Washington, had been equipped with the old twin-engine B-18s, then B-23s. That spring, they became the first air corps unit to receive B-25s. The men thought it was "fast, hard-hitting and full of fight." Like all new planes, the B-25 had its problems, and it was the task of the Seventeenth Bombardment Group to wring out the planes to find out what needed to be changed. The men flew them cross-country to Langley Field, to test speed, armament, fuel consumption, bomb capacity, and handling characteristics.

They learned right away that the B-25 was inadequately armed. The rear gunner had a single .50-caliber weapon, the sort that had worked on older, slower bombers, but was a mistake on a ship that could reach a speed of nearly three hundred miles per hour. The force of the slipstream at top speed was too much for the gunner to handle. Air corps engineers at Wright Field tried mounting the gun farther back in the cramped tail, but that wasn't effective either. On the third try, the engineers installed two .50-caliber machine guns about three-fourths of the way to the tail, and put a power-driven

Plexiglas turret over the rear gunner's position. The turret worked only sporadically, and the gun often jammed, but it was the best protection then available.

In September 1941, the Seventeenth Bombardment Group flew to Louisiana for large-scale maneuvers. Their airfield was "bombed" by the enemy with flour sacks and "strafed" by fighters. They undertook bombing raids of their own, trying to reach their targets before being intercepted by P-38s and P-39s of the rival air force. In Augusta, Georgia, they lost a ship and her crew of five when the plane went into a slow roll on takeoff and crashed. There were several close calls, and with each one the men learned a little more about their hot planes and about themselves.

"We were whipped into shape and we were good," said Lt. William M. Bower. "Oh, it was the greatest, wildest bunch of men that I have ever been associated with. There was just something about that Seventeenth Group, about the collection of people that were in it, that I have never experienced since. We played hard, we worked hard."

They were ordered to March Field, outside of Los Angeles, and two days later were assigned to a new field, still under construction, at Pendleton, Oregon. They arrived on Monday, December 8, 1941. The temperature was minus eighteen degrees Fahrenheit, and the runways were covered with snow. Worse, the men were in a state of shock at the suddenness with which they had been plunged into war. They saw no immediate way to strike back at the Japanese for their sneak attack on Pearl Harbor, no way to give vent to the anger and frustration they felt. And like many people on the West Coast in the days just after the attack, the men of the Seventeenth expected the enemy to strike again. Lt. Ted Lawson said, "There was a helpless feeling that they *weren't* coming—that we'd have to go all the way over there to punch back and get even." "Everybody was interested in getting to the scene of action," Lieutenant Bower said, "in other words, going to war, volunteering for some mission."

Toward the end of January 1942, the outfit was ordered to South Carolina for submarine patrol duty, but some of the crews were sent first to Minneapolis to have some work done on their planes. They watched as additional fuel tanks were installed in their bombers, and assumed it was being done to give them the range for longer patrols over the Atlantic. When the planes were nearly ready, Lt. David M. Jones called the officers together in their Minneapolis hotel. He had just returned from a meeting with their squadron commander, Capt. Edward York, at Wright Field.

Jones told them that they were not going to Columbia after all. Captain York wanted to know if they would volunteer for an important and dangerous mission that would take them out of the country for a few months. Jones had no additional information about the operation but he said that it would not be held against them if they did not want to go.

At approximately the same time, during the last week of February, at the South Carolina airfield where the rest of the Seventeenth Bombardment Group had assembled, two pilots stood outside the mess hall, watching a B-25 come in for a landing. Maj. John A. Hilger, one of the squadron commanders, turned to Capt. Ross Greening.

"Damn it," Hilger said, "with all our experience, none of us can fly a B-25 like that."

The plane taxied to a stop and out stepped a lieutenant colonel any flier in the country would recognize instantly.

"For God's sake," Greening said. "It's Doolittle."

Doolittle called a meeting the next day with the group's commanding officer, Lt. Col. William C. Mills, and the squadron leaders. He told them he was in charge of a mission that involved taking off in no more than five hundred feet while carrying a maximum bomb load.

"It's strictly a volunteer operation. It'll take us away about six weeks, but that's all you can tell your men."

The next day, Mills explained the situation to his pilots. They all volunteered.

Jimmy Doolittle had his men.

# Tell Jimmy to Get on His Horse

The men crowded into the operations office at Eglin Field, not far from Pensacola, in Florida's panhandle. There were 140 of them—pilots, copilots, navigators, bombardiers, and engineer-gunners—enough volunteer five-man crews for the twenty-four B-25s parked on the field, plus twenty ground personnel. They filled the room to overflowing, sitting on chairs, benches, desks, and windowsills, waiting to find out what they had volunteered for.

It was March 1, 1942, almost three months since the Japanese attack on Pearl Harbor. The war was continuing to worsen for the United States and her allies everywhere in the Pacific. Two weeks earlier, the mighty fortress of Singapore, which the British had called impregnable, had fallen. A force of seventy thousand men had surrendered to a much smaller number of Japanese troops. The enemy had invaded Sumatra and Bali in the Dutch East Indies and defeated a combined American-British-Dutch fleet in a major battle in the Java Sea. The allies had few aircraft and ships left in the entire southwest Pacific region. Gen. Douglas MacArthur had been ordered to leave the Philippines for Australia, and everyone knew what that meant—his troops on Bataan were doomed.

The men at Eglin were excited, expectant, and ready to fight. More had volunteered than were needed. The squadron leaders of the Seventeenth Bombardment Group had combed their rosters and selected those they thought were the best. Maj. Jack Hilger, recommended by Colonel Mills, the Seventeenth's commanding officer, to be Doolittle's second-in-command, had brought the men and their planes from Columbia, South Carolina, to Florida.

They had volunteered for a straightforward reason. There was a job to do, and that was what they had been trained for. Tom Griffin, a navigator, said that "most of us volunteered simply because they were asking for trained air force personnel for an important mission, and they felt we were qualified. It just seemed that our reason for being in the air force was to take part in such an operation."

Joe Manske, an engineer-gunner, commented that "it was the thing to do. We were all young true-blooded American boys, and we were all ready to do our part." No heroics, no dramatic gestures. "We were at war," said Dick Cole, who would be Doolittle's copilot, "and it was what we were trained to do."

A short man wearing the silver oak leaves of a lieutenant colonel strode into the operations office. The men jumped to attention. For some, this was their first glimpse of Doolittle and the first they knew he was involved in the project.

"My name's Doolittle," he said, but there was no need for an introduction.

"I had read a lot about him," recalled Ted Lawson. "I was a little awestruck," Bill Bower said, "because this was my idol for years, and I had no idea that I would be associated with him." Mac McClure recognized Doolittle the instant he entered the room and whispered to those around him, "We are in for something really big."

Doolittle got right to the point. He told them he was in command of the mission they had volunteered for and that it would be the most dangerous undertaking of their lives. He made it clear that if any man dropped out, it would not be held against him.

He fell silent for a moment to give them a chance to consider his words. Several men raised their hands, and he nodded to the nearest one.

A lieutenant asked if he could tell them anything else about the mission. Doolittle said he could not, but he thought that once they began training, they would surely get some idea of what was involved.

Then he raised what he said was the most important issue: secrecy. He warned the men not to talk to anyone about the operation, not even to discuss it among themselves. The lives of hundreds of people were at stake.

"Don't start any rumors and don't pass any along. If anybody outside the project gets nosy, get his name and give it to me."

He said there was a lot of work to do on the planes, and considerable training required for the crews. The pilots would have to learn to take off in a heavily loaded B-25 in the shortest possible distance. And, he added, they had only three weeks in which to get ready.

The men found it impossible not to talk about the project among themselves, to speculate on what was in store, to wonder about those short takeoffs Doolittle had mentioned. Scuttlebutt took them all over the globe, from Berlin and Tokyo as possible targets to many points in between. There were only two things of which they were certain. First, the job was important. If it weren't, the great Jimmy Doolittle would not be in charge of it. And, second, because he was in charge of it, they would succeed. "I don't think there was any doubt in anybody's mind," said one pilot, "that as long as he was with us, whatever he wanted to do, we'd go ahead and do it."

★ ★ ★ ★

At Pensacola Naval Air Station, some forty miles west of Eglin Field, Lt. Henry L. "Hank" Miller received some unusual orders. He was told to report to Eglin to teach some army pilots how to take off from a carrier, and he had to finish the job in fifteen days. When he got to Eglin, however, he found that the base commander had no idea why Miller was there. Miller had just about decided the whole thing was a mistake when he remembered something he had been told at Pensacola. Supposedly, his job at Eglin had something to do with Jimmy Doolittle. When he mentioned the name, the commanding officer's manner changed. He closed the office door and lowered his voice to a whisper.

He told Miller he didn't know what Doolittle and his men were up to, only that they were being kept apart from others on the base. He had been ordered to give them whatever they needed, and if they needed a navy pilot from Pensacola to teach them how to fly, he wasn't about to question it. He personally drove Miller over to that part of the base where Doolittle's men were quartered.

Miller could not find anyone in charge—neither Doolittle nor Hilger was around—and he fell into conversation with three pilots. They were Capt. Edward J. "Ski" York, from Batavia, New York, Capt. David M. "Davey" Jones, from Marshfield, Oregon, and Capt. C. Ross Greening, from Carroll, Iowa. When Miller told them why he was there, they asked if he had ever flown a B-25 before. Not only had Miller never flown one, he had never even seen one.

The army fliers decided to remedy that right away. The four of them climbed into one of the bombers and took off for an auxiliary field that had been set aside for their use. When they landed, Miller gave them their first lesson in carrier takeoffs. York, Jones, and Greening were skeptical when Miller mentioned the slow speed at which they could get airborne. They were used to staying on the runway until they had run up the engines to 110 miles per hour.

Jones flew first and, following Miller's instructions, took off at an indicated airspeed of only sixty-seven miles per hour.

"Impossible," one of the other pilots said, joking that the air-speed indicator must be malfunctioning. "You can't do that."

"OK," Miller said, "come on back and we'll land and try it again."

York took the controls, and the airspeed indicator showed no higher than seventy miles per hour when the wheels left the runway. The army pilots were convinced.

Miller began takeoff training for the rest of the pilots the next day, and a competition quickly developed to see who could take off in the shortest distance with the heaviest load. More than pride was at stake. Those who did poorly would not be selected for the mission. Only fifteen of the twenty-four crews would be chosen.

White lines defining the length and width of a carrier deck were painted on the runway at the auxiliary field, and flags were spotted every one hundred feet so that the pilots could gauge the distance traveled down the field. Miller started each crew with a light load of 21,000 pounds, then an intermediate load, and finally the full 31,000-pound load they would carry to Japan. That weight, which included a full load of bombs, fuel, and ammunition, plus the crew of five, was two thousand pounds over the maximum weight for which the B-25 was designed.

At first the pilots needed about eight hundred feet of runway for taking off, three hundred more than would be available to them on an aircraft carrier. But by the time Miller had finished the training program, they were down to five hundred feet. One hotshot pilot took off in 287 feet.

Doolittle took his turn as a student with the rest, determined that even if he flunked as a first pilot, he'd fly as copilot. He needn't have worried. He was graded with the others and passed.

Doolittle and Miller got along well. "Somehow it came out that we were both old sourdoughs from Alaska," Doolittle said, "he from Fairbanks and I from Nome . . . and this was a very close bond between us." They also discovered they had both been boxers. "So we had a great deal in common. To this day," Doolittle said, in 1983, "we're very good friends."

Miller developed a standard procedure for the short takeoff runs. Wing flaps were set in the full down position, elevator trim tabs at three-fourths tail-heavy, and the wheel brakes were set. The throttles were shoved all the way forward, and the brakes released. As the plane lurched ahead, the control yoke was pulled all the way back until the tail skid was only about six inches from the runway. The instant the plane lifted into the air, the yoke was eased forward to gain flying speed, and the flaps were raised.

Miller was a thorough instructor, measuring precisely the distance and time required by each pilot on each trial to get his bomber airborne. The pilots would circle the field once, land, and taxi back for an on-the-spot evaluation of their performance. Miller also flew with each pilot at least once. "In the cockpit," he said, "I observed techniques, because you get a feel for who's a good pilot and who isn't, no matter what his takeoff distance is." It would be Miller's data and his personal recommendation that would determine who would go and who would stay.

On the last day of pilot training, Miller made a final check-flight with each crew. Dissatisfied with the performance of one pilot, he ordered the crew out of the ship and told the pilot to try another takeoff. "You fly the plane," Miller said. "Don't let it fly you. Once more around."

Miller wrote later, "He took off in a skid, he pushed into a harder skid . . . he didn't push the throttle to the floorboard, and the plane settled right back down on the runway on its belly. We came to an abrupt stop."

The plane was covered with gasoline, but luckily it did not catch fire. The pilot was not selected for the raid.

The B-25 pilots had to learn more than how to take off in a short distance. They also had to practice low-level flying. And when Doolittle said low-level flying, he meant a few feet, sometimes only inches, off the ground for a long period of time. That could be harrowing. There was no room for making mistakes or glancing around or thinking about something else. The pilots practiced again and again, dodging trees and telephone poles, hills and houses, and occasionally clipping tree branches with a wingtip or a propeller blade. They scared quite a few farmers and cows in the process.

Mac McClure, who would fly the mission as Ted Lawson's navigator, said that, at Eglin, "It was a pilot's dream to buzz people in fields, autos and buses on open highways, and fly under cross-country high tension wires. I have an 8-millimeter [film] clip showing smoke from skidding bus tires."

The pilots and the flight engineers (who also served as top-turret gunners) worked long hours to coax the best speed from the engines while using the least amount of aviation fuel. The flight from the carrier over Japan and on to bases in China would be long, and even though they would carry extra gas, it would have to be used as efficiently as possible.

According to fuel-control charts developed by the North American Aircraft Company, the pilots found they could get the best mileage by using high manifold pressures and low RPM propeller settings, around 1,275 RPM instead of the usual 1,800. Those settings were sufficient to maintain a speed of 165 miles per hour with, as Bill Bower put it, the engines "barely turning over. It worked [and] it didn't damage the engines."

They kept a close check on the carburetors as well. The manufacturer, Bendix, sent an expert to examine them. York and Greening met the man at Pensacola and flew him to Eglin, treating him to their newly acquired, breathtaking, five-hundred-foot takeoff run, which left him a bit pale. He was also irritated by the suggestion that there might be something wrong with his carburetors.

Before Doolittle could even say hello, the Bendix man was furious.

"Now what is it you want, bub? I understand you want some carburetors pressure-checked. I can tell you now they have been checked before they left the factory. As a matter of fact, we just don't send out equipment that is not in perfect condition. Furthermore—"

That was as far as he got.

"Hold it, son!" Doolittle roared. "What did the factory send? An expert or a salesman? If you're a salesman, go home, we have plenty of carburetors. If you're an expert, stick around, we need you."

The man relaxed and stuck around and soon had all the carburetors tuned to the proper pitch for maximum gas mileage.

Training for the engineer-gunners involved practice with the twin .50-caliber machine guns and the power turret. Most of the men had never fired the guns before. There was little target practice because the turrets needed frequent adjustment to keep them functioning. Breakdowns were almost a daily occurrence. In addition, some of the guns would not fire at all, and others jammed after firing short bursts.

Even when the turrets were working, there was neither the time nor the equipment to practice shooting at moving targets. The gunners would go into combat without once firing at an airborne object. They did at least practice tracking moving targets, some P-36s and P-40s from Eglin that conducted simulated attacks on the bombers. The only shooting they did was limited to firing at oil slicks in the

Gulf of Mexico and at stationary targets while the planes were parked at the field.

Time also had to be found for practice-firing the .30-caliber machine gun in the nose, although it was generally agreed that the gun's limited range, loose mounting, and the difficulty of shifting it from one gun port to another made it an ineffective weapon. The crews made strafing runs on more oil slicks to test-fire it.

One of the gunners had unusual credentials. First Lt. T. Robert "Doc" White, a graduate of Harvard Medical School, had pleaded with Major Hilger to be allowed to go on the mission. Although a doctor would be a valuable addition, there was no room for passengers. If White wanted to go, Hilger said, he would have to train as a crew member. White was delighted—he'd always wanted to be a gunner—and with no previous training he obtained the second-highest score in firing from the top turret. The mission now had not only an excellent gunner but also a flight surgeon, whose medical skills would be needed.

Considerable time was devoted to bombing practice. The purpose of the mission was to drop bombs on enemy targets, and if the men could not do that accurately, they might as well not go. The planes would be approaching their targets at near-zero altitude. They would climb sharply to fifteen hundred feet, release their bombs, and dive to ground level for the getaway.

Practice missions were carried out primarily with dummy bombs, but each crew was given the chance to drop a live one-hundred-pound bomb. It was the first time they had released a bomb from such a low level, and the pilots enjoyed making dry runs over the small Florida coastal towns, zooming across the water at wave height, pulling up sharply, and bombing the oil slicks.

They learned that the highly secret Norden bombsight was not accurate for a low-altitude mission. A simpler bombsight, dubbed the "Mark Twain," was installed in each B-25. It had been designed by Captain Greening and built at Eglin for a cost of twenty cents each. Not only was the new sight accurate, it was also easy to use.

Despite Doolittle's careful plans, the training did not proceed as smoothly as he would have liked. He had scheduled fifty-five hours of training for each crew, with the time divided among day and night navigation, gunnery, bombing, and formation flying. Additional time was scheduled for practice in short takeoff runs for the pilots, which had top priority.

Unusually bad weather and heavy fog prevented flying for days at a time. Frequent maintenance problems also cropped up, such as leaks in the auxiliary gas tanks and their fittings, and problems with the gun turrets. Because of these delays, most crews flew no more than half the number of hours scheduled.

During much of the training period, Doolittle was commuting between Eglin Field and Washington to discuss the mission directly with General Arnold and Captain Duncan. "I was a bird of passage," he quipped. He thought it unwise to report on the progress of the training over the telephone. But when he was at Eglin, he observed all aspects of the operation. Little escaped his attention.

Bill Bower remembered that whenever Doolittle would return to the base, "he'd come precisely to the point that he'd left and begin the conversation [with], 'Bill, have you done this and this and this and that?' And then he'd fly somebody's airplane and come down with a whole sheet full of discrepancies, and they were precisely what was wrong. 'Your altitude indicator is one degree off on a 360-degree turn,' or something like this, and as a result everybody was on their toes."

To keep everybody on their toes when he was absent, Doolittle delegated authority as in any air corps unit. Jack Hilger was the executive officer, Harvey Johnson the adjutant, Ski York the operations officer, Davey Jones the navigation and intelligence officer, Ross Greening the gunnery and bombing officer, Bill Bower the engineering officer, and Trav Hoover the supply officer.

Doolittle knew he could rely on these men to run the outfit while he was away. He had told them in general terms about the mission, although not the actual targets. He thought they could do their jobs better if they knew the reason for the short takeoffs and low-level flying. Overall, however, he emphasized the continuing need for secrecy.

As intelligence officer, Jones was responsible for securing maps, charts, and information about the targets. Obviously, he had to be given the names of the cities they planned to attack. He and navigator Tom Griffin went to air corps intelligence headquarters in Washington to find the necessary material. When they returned, they remained, as Griffin noted, "very closemouthed about our destination."

A small room at headquarters was assigned to them, Griffin said, "and we spent a week going over the available maps, photos, and target information. As the lowest-ranking man, it was my job each night to sweep up and make sure all notes and unnecessary papers were destroyed before locking up." One of the most difficult items to locate was an accurate topographical survey of China. After much searching, they found one at the Army War College.

"When we had assembled what we thought was the best available set of maps and target folders we could find, we asked that twenty identical sets be gotten together, crated, and sent to Sacramento for us to pick up just before boarding the carrier."

Despite the stress on secrecy, most of the men guessed correctly about their destination. "There was a lot of speculation," engineer-gunner Joe Manske recalled, "but, in general, we all were pretty sure it was to be Japan." Doolittle himself said later that most of his men "knew that we were going to bomb Japan."

Within the limitations imposed by the weather and the maintenance problems, training and preparations continued throughout the first half of March with no detail overlooked. One of the busier officers was Doc White. He taught first-aid courses, checked the immunization records of all personnel, and administered inoculations for such diseases as smallpox, yellow fever, and bubonic plague. Some of the men needed nearly a dozen shots within a three-week period.

White encountered difficulties in obtaining many of the necessary vaccines. When he sent a formal request through channels, he was told it would take up to six months to fill the order. In desperation, he brought the problem to Doolittle, who flew to Washington the next day and returned with all the vaccines White needed.

White also recorded each man's blood type on his dog tags. He assembled two first-aid kits for each plane, equipped with morphine Syrettes, sulfa tablets, a small flask of whiskey, and condoms. He prepared small personal kits for each crewman, containing morphine, sulfa, quinine, and iodine, and a medical bag for himself with additional sulfa tablets, a pocket surgical knife, and two metal catheters.

The only item White was unable to secure for the men was foot powder, something he thought would be useful when they reached China. Air corps regulations did not authorize the distribution of foot powder to its personnel, "the supposition being," White said, "that air corps troops never walk but always fly." Like Doolittle, White was trying to anticipate every contingency.

And so were the others. Before each practice flight, for example, the flight engineers calibrated the engine and flight instruments for accuracy. Out in the Gulf of Mexico, lifebuoys were placed at three-mile intervals so that airspeed indicators could be checked. During these speed runs, it was found that the propeller blades had become scratched and pitted with normal use over the last year, reducing their efficiency and, consequently, the airplane's top speed. Doolittle quickly arranged for new props to be made available in California so they could be installed before the B-25s were loaded aboard the aircraft carrier.

Life rafts for each plane had to be tested to make sure they inflated properly and did not leak. Pilots and copilots were trained to perform the jobs of other crewmen, and navigators were taught to act as bombardiers so that the mission could proceed even if some crew members were wounded or killed.

One of Hank Miller's duties, when not teaching short takeoffs, was to instruct the army men on proper behavior aboard a navy vessel. This gave away the fact that they were going somewhere by ship—probably a carrier—from which they would have to take off in a short distance, but Miller wanted them to be prepared for shipboard routines, from how to salute the flag on the stern when boarding to how to take a shower using the smallest amount of water.

In the midst of all the training and preparation, the B-25 pilots and crewmen found the time at Eglin to personalize their airplanes with names and insignia. Ted Lawson's ship, called *Ruptured Duck*, was decorated with the cartoon character Donald Duck wearing a headset and standing over a pair of crossed crutches. "We had a left engine that was always going out," Lawson said, "so we thought the name was a pretty good idea." One crew painted the chemical formula for the explosive TNT on their plane, while others chose such names as *Whiskey Pete*, *Green Hornet*, and *Bat Out of Hell*.

During the third week of March, the group took their bombers on a two-thousand-mile flight to test long-range navigation skills and their ability to get the best gas mileage from the engines. After their short, noisy takeoffs, they headed south from Eglin to Fort Myers, flew at a low altitude—skimming the surface of the Gulf of Mexico—west to Houston, and returned to base. The pilots pushed the airplanes well beyond their intended capacities as a test of both equipment and men. "That," Lawson said, "was our final exam in Florida."

The men were pleased with their accomplishments. They felt well trained, willing, and eager to go. They had confidence in themselves and, even more, in Doolittle. "There was just something about him," Bill Bower said, "his way, that made you want to do it. . . . We were going to succeed. I don't think it ever crossed my mind that there would be a failure. . . . It was just that sort of atmosphere that he'd built up amongst us—there was complete trust, complete confidence, an absolute desire to excel. And I can't explain how he did it. . . . There weren't many pep talks—he isn't one to give pep talks, he gives straight, factual, honest appraisals of things and then he does it better than you can do it."

★ ★ ★ ★

Aboard the aircraft carrier USS *Hornet*, Captain Mitscher and his men were also feeling increasingly confident about their ship and their own abilities. The *Hornet* had developed a reputation as a happy ship, one on which there was a strong sense of discipline as well as a camaraderie among officers and men. The ship had come through her shakedown cruise in good shape, and the crew was now a smoothly functioning team with a definite sense of pride. Like Doolittle's men, they were ready and eager to go to war.

As the days of March passed, however, it began to appear that they would be disappointed. Combat seemed as far away as it had when they were on the East Coast. They had sailed from Norfolk as part of a small convoy carrying troops to be sent to the South Pacific, but the Navy Department didn't seem in a hurry to order the *Hornet* any farther than California.

The *Hornet* had skirted the Florida peninsula and passed through the Panama Canal, where some of her best pilots were ordered off the ship, sent elsewhere to learn how to fly a new torpedo plane, the Grumman TBF Avenger. The rest of the *Hornet*'s torpedo plane pilots remained aboard with their slow, obsolete, underarmed TBD-1 Devastators.*

The prevailing attitude among the crew was that their magnificent ship was "destined for nothing more active than convoy service." And when they reached San Diego, their assignment was to cruise off the coast while pilots slated for duty on carriers already in combat used the *Hornet*'s flight deck to practice takeoffs and landings. Her only battle damage was sustained when the new flight deck got scorched by burning gasoline when three pilots crash-landed.

★ ★ ★ ★

While the *Hornet* sailed back and forth off the California coast, Capt. Donald Duncan was summoned to Admiral King's office in Washington. It was March 15. King had been told by Hap Arnold that the training of Doolittle's B-25 crews was proceeding satisfactorily and that they would soon be ready for the bombing mission. Admiral King had decided it was time to inform Adm. Chester Nimitz, Commander in Chief of the Pacific Fleet, and Adm. William F. Halsey, the man who would lead the task force to Japan. Duncan said he would review the mission with Doolittle and then leave for Pearl Harbor to brief Nimitz and Halsey in person.

The next day, Duncan called on General Arnold to tell him he was

---

*They would fly these planes to glory three months later in the Battle of Midway, when the world would come to know them as Torpedo Squadron Eight. Only one man would survive.

going to Pearl and that he wanted to see Doolittle first. Arnold wasted no time in ordering Doolittle up from Eglin. He opened his office door and shouted to an aide, "Get Doolittle up here right away, tonight!"

Doolittle flew to Washington through weather that had grounded other planes, but arrived in time to meet with Duncan the next morning. Duncan showed him his handwritten plan covering all aspects of the mission—the route for the task force, the ships involved, the navy procedures for launching the planes, and the weather data. This was the first time Doolittle had seen the outline for the entire operation. He read it over once, asked no questions, and said it looked fine to him.

Duncan told Doolittle he was on his way to Pearl Harbor to see Nimitz and Halsey. Doolittle said his men would soon be ready to fly their B-25s to an air corps base at Sacramento for some last-minute work, such as the installation of the new propellers, and would wait there for orders to board the *Hornet*.

Doolittle knew this was the moment to ask Hap Arnold for permission to lead the mission. The orders to leave for California could come through any day. He could not wait any longer. He believed he was the most qualified person for the job, and if he did not get this combat command, he would probably end up spending the war as a staff officer, flying a desk in Washington. That afternoon he went to Arnold to present his case.

"I know more about this mission, I know more about the aircraft, I know more about the crews than anyone else," Doolittle said. "I would like to lead it."

"Well," Arnold said, "I need you badly here, Jimmy, and I'd rather you stayed on my staff."

Doolittle launched into what may have been the most persuasive sales pitch of his career, flinging one argument after another at the air corps chief. Finally, Arnold shrugged his shoulders and interrupted Doolittle's appeal.

"I'll tell you what," he said. "If it's all right with Miff, it's all right with me."

Maj. Gen. M. F. "Miff" Harmon, Arnold's chief of staff, had his office just down the hall. Doolittle was immediately suspicious. He guessed Arnold was trying to pass the buck and that as soon as he left the office, Arnold would phone Harmon and order him to turn down Doolittle's request. Doolittle was right, but Arnold had not counted on how fast Doolittle could run.

"I saluted briskly," Doolittle recalled, "and ran as fast as I could around to Miff's office and said, 'If you have no objections, General Arnold has no objections to me leading the operation.'"

Harmon, taken by surprise, said he guessed it would be all right with him.

"Thank you very much," Doolittle said. As he got to the door, the telephone rang. Doolittle heard Harmon say, "But Hap, I just told him he could go."

"So if I hadn't run that fast," Doolittle said, "I never would have gotten on the Tokyo raid." The story still made him laugh thirty years later.

★ ★ ★ ★

While Doolittle was flying back to Eglin Field, Captain Duncan was about to be thrown off an airliner somewhere west of Albuquerque, New Mexico. In his haste to get his travel orders and make his airline reservations from Washington to San Francisco, where a military plane would take him on to Honolulu, Duncan had neglected to have his trip authorized as "top priority." And in wartime, persons with a higher travel priority could bump those with a lower one.

That was about to happen to Duncan. Asleep in his berth aboard a DC-3 Sleeper Service airplane, he was awakened by the stewardess over Albuquerque. She told him he would have to get off at the next stop because several air corps pilots with top-priority travel orders had to get to San Francisco right away. It might be several days before Duncan could get another flight.

Duncan told the stewardess he would not get off. He was under orders to be in Hawaii the following day. She said the airline had to abide by government regulations. They had no choice but to bump him from the flight.

"I'm not getting off," Duncan said.

A few minutes later the pilot came back to Duncan's berth. Duncan showed him his orders and suggested that when they landed, the pilot call Gen. Henry H. Arnold in Washington and tell him that he was about to throw Captain Duncan off his airplane. The pilot said he would talk it over with the Army Air Corps pilots who were waiting at the next stop and see if he could work something out.

"That's fine," Duncan said, "but if I leave the airplane you will have to carry me off."

Duncan went back to sleep and in the morning he was still aboard, heading for San Francisco.

He later learned that one of the army pilots scheduled to board the flight was only too happy to give up his seat and prolong his leave.

Duncan reached the U.S. navy base at Pearl Harbor on March 19 to brief the calm, soft-spoken, and decisive Admiral Nimitz. Duncan made it clear to Nimitz that Admiral King had said this was not a proposal to take under consideration, but a mission to be carried out as soon as possible.

Nimitz sent for Halsey, the brash, colorful, likable flier. When Duncan finished his presentation, Nimitz asked Halsey for his opinion.

"Do you think it would work, Bill?"

"They'll need a lot of luck," Halsey said.

"Are you willing to take them out there?"

"Yes, I am."

"Good! It's all yours." *

Halsey thought it would be a good idea if he and Doolittle could meet as soon as possible to discuss the raid. Nimitz agreed, and he

---

* That afternoon, Duncan boarded Halsey's ship, the aircraft carrier *Enterprise*, to review the plan with Halsey's operations officer, Capt. Miles Browning. He gave Browning his only copy of the plan, thinking he would not need it anymore. "I've regretted it ever since," Duncan said, "or regretted that I didn't make an arrangement with [Browning] to get it back, because I realized afterwards . . . that it would have been quite an historic document. Whatever happened to it I don't know. I simply cautioned Browning to lock it up securely, and as far as I was concerned it was Admiral Halsey's. That's the last I ever heard of it."

made arrangements for Halsey to fly to San Francisco once Doolittle arrived there. They all thought that Doolittle and his fliers should proceed to the West Coast as quickly as they could.

Duncan immediately dispatched a prearranged message to Capt. Francis Low in Washington:

**TELL JIMMY TO GET ON HIS HORSE.**

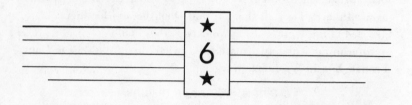

# I'll Be Seeing You

"Today's the day we move out," Doolittle announced. It was the morning of March 23, and their time at Eglin was at an end. Whatever additional training the men needed, and whatever additional work the planes needed, would have to be carried out over the next week at McClellan Field, outside of Sacramento, California. After that, they would be on their way to Japan.

Hank Miller, the pilot who had taught the men how to take off the navy way, was sorry to see the group go. It meant he would have to return to his job as a flight instructor. He was not happy with the prospect of sitting out the war in Pensacola, but his request for a transfer to a fighter squadron in combat had been turned down. He was too valuable where he was, his superiors said.

A chance conversation with Doolittle, however, gave him some hope.

"You know, I'm going to the West Coast today, and we're going to pick up another instructor out there to give us more of this," Doolittle said.

"Well, you know, Colonel," Miller said, "it's a matter of professional pride with me. I don't want anybody on the West Coast telling you, 'No, let's start all over again with this technique.' If it's possible, I'd like to go with you, if we're going to have time to do more of this practice out there."

"OK," Doolittle said. "If it's all right with Washington, you can fly out with me this afternoon."

Miller telephoned his commanding officer at Pensacola and was delighted to get permission to accompany the Doolittle Raiders to their next stop.

The men flew their B-25s across the United States in small groups, spending the first night in San Antonio. They refueled in Phoenix and stayed over at March Field, outside of Los Angeles. On Doolittle's orders, the fliers were treating the flight as part of their training, testing their gas consumption, checking their navigational skills, and hedgehopping all the way.

"One thing about that trip across the country," said Bill Bower, "I think we scattered sheep and chickens and turkeys and cattle across the breadth of the South and Southwest. We played funny little games like 'Can you race a dust cloud on the desert,' and all sorts of things like that. I suppose you could say we were irresponsible . . . but it was a release, we'd been under quite a bit of tension, so the trip from Eglin to McClellan was a release. And again, we were refining that technique of handling this airplane under fairly unusual conditions, making sure that every gallon of gas went where it was supposed to go."

From March Field they headed north to Sacramento. Some of the pilots believed their days were numbered, so they took chances, flying at treetop level like the daredevil barnstormers of the 1930s in single-engine, open-cockpit planes. They were feeling pretty damn good about themselves and thought they were hotshot pilots, until they arrived at McClellan Field to find Doolittle waiting. The Old Man had beaten them all by going directly over the Rockies from San Antonio, flying much of the time on instruments.

He gathered the men for a meeting and told them that he didn't want them "to raise hell" that night. They were to remain near the airfield and make certain that their planes were in perfect condition. Any problem, no matter how minor, was to be repaired by the base mechanics.

Then he said that the radio equipment would be removed from their planes.

"You won't need it where you're going."

★ ★ ★ ★

While Doolittle and his men were on their way to Sacramento, the USS *Hornet* was sailing from San Diego to San Francisco. The sailors were relieved to be out of the business of training pilots for other aircraft carriers, but were curious about why they were sailing north instead of west, toward the war. Their skipper, Pete Mitscher, did not have to wonder. He now knew the reason for their orders, and he could not have been more pleased.

After Captain Duncan had briefed Admirals Nimitz and Halsey at Pearl Harbor, he had flown to San Diego to see Mitscher, and, as usual, got right to the point.

"Pete," Duncan said, "you're going to take Jimmy Doolittle and fifteen army bombers to hit Tokyo."

"That's fine," Mitscher said.

Duncan briefed him on the details of the operation. Mitscher said he appreciated being personally informed by someone who had been involved with the plan from the beginning. Duncan reported later, however, that Mitscher also felt slighted because he hadn't been briefed sooner.

★ ★ ★ ★

As the date for the departure of the task force drew closer, Hap Arnold was growing increasingly concerned about the arrangements for aviation fuel and oil at the airfields in eastern China where the B-25s were expected to land. He and Doolittle had spent considerable time planning the refueling, and frequent cables had been dispatched to the American military mission to China (AMMISCA) specifying the details, but nothing appeared to be happening. American officials there failed to grasp the urgency, and Arnold couldn't risk giving away too much information because of the difficulty of maintaining secrecy in China.

Early in February, Brig. Gen. John Magruder, the head of AMMISCA, charged with supervising lend-lease operations, notified George Marshall about an experience he had had in Chungking. During a conference with a high Chinese government official, to whom Magruder had stressed the sensitive and confidential nature of their discussion, a curtain was inadvertently opened to reveal four servants who had been listening to every word. Magruder told Marshall that this situation was typical, and it demonstrated the futility of trying to keep anything secret.

Marshall passed Magruder's message to Arnold, who decided it was best not to tell any American personnel in China about the Doolittle raid, not even Lt. Gen. Joseph W. "Vinegar Joe" Stilwell, the man designated to become chief of staff to Generalissimo Chiang Kai-shek and commander of American forces in China. Arnold told Stilwell only that American bombers would arrive in China at a certain time, and that he should arrange for aviation fuel and oil, English-speaking personnel, and radio homing equipment to be stashed at several airfields in eastern China.

Stilwell left Washington for China on February 11 and did not reach Chungking until March 4. By March 16, impatient at not hearing from Stilwell about the airfield preparations, Arnold cabled him through AMMISCA. Time was running out. In another two weeks the bombers would be aboard the carrier, heading toward Japan. If the fields in China were not prepared, the bombers might all be lost. The Russians had refused permission for them to set down at Vladivostok, and there was nowhere else for them to land.

TO STILWELL. WHAT PROGRESS IS BEING MADE ON LAYING DOWN GASOLINE SUPPLIES . . . ON AIRPORTS IN EASTERN CHINA? WHAT PROGRESS ON AIRPORTS? ARNOLD DESIRES REPORT.

After waiting for two days for a reply, Arnold sent a second message.

TIME IS GETTING SHORT FOR SPOTTING GAS AT AGREED POINTS. THIS FROM ARNOLD FOR STILWELL RE SPECIAL AIR PROJECT DISCUSSED BEFORE YOUR DEPARTURE.

It took four more days before Arnold received a reply. It was later claimed by Chennault and other air leaders that Stilwell's laggardly response resulted from his lack of understanding of air warfare and thus a lack of sensitivity to the needs of the planes and crews. A simpler explanation is that Stilwell was seldom in Chungking during the time the Doolittle mission was in preparation. He spent most of March and early April 1942 in Burma, trying to save it from being overrun by the Japanese. He roamed the front lines from one isolated command post to another, and because communications were primitive, he was out of touch with events in Washington and Chungking.

Stilwell did return to Chungking on March 17 for four days, but was involved in lengthy and frustrating meetings with Chiang regarding their respective command responsibilities. Understandably, that problem (which he was never to resolve), and the rapid advance of the Japanese through Burma, took precedence over getting drums of gasoline to some airfields for a project he knew nothing about.

On March 22, Stilwell notified Arnold that the Standard Oil Company in Calcutta, India, had thirty thousand gallons of 100-octane gasoline and five hundred gallons of oil available. He requested authority to move the gas and oil to China, and asked why they were needed. Arnold immediately sent an order for ten transports from the Ferry Command to deliver the fuel from Calcutta to Kweilin, China. From Kweilin, chartered Pan American planes would distribute it to the other fields.

In a follow-up message, Arnold directed the allotment of the supplies among the various fields. He ordered that twelve ground personnel, at least one of whom should speak English, be sent to each field, along with flares and radio equipment. Everything had to be ready by midnight, April 19, the date on which the raid was expected to take place. The B-25s would arrive over eastern China several hours later.

More cablegrams were exchanged between Washington and Chungking in the following days, but no progress was apparent. On March 25, Arnold pressed Stilwell again.

THE SUCCESS OF A VITAL PROJECT WHICH I DISCUSSED WITH YOU PRIOR TO YOUR DEPARTURE DEPENDS UPON THIS MOVEMENT [of fuel from Calcutta to China] BEING ACCOMPLISHED BY AIR WITH-OUT DELAY AND IN USING EVERY POSSIBLE PRECAUTION TO PRE-SERVE ITS SECRECY.

On March 28, Stilwell was able to report to Arnold that Chiang had granted permission for the American planes to land in China. Chiang had, of course, been told nothing about their mission. But as far as the oil and gas were concerned, they were still in Calcutta. Both Stilwell and Brig. Gen. Clayton Bissell, his air officer, recommended that Chinese oil and gas, already available at some of the fields—or so they had been told—be used instead. They thought it was impossible to transfer the American fuel from India in time and in secret.

There had been no independent verification of the existence of aviation fuel and oil at the Chinese airfields by any American official. It was difficult to reach the fields from Chungking, given the limited availability of aircraft and the poor weather conditions.

By the end of March, an increasingly frustrated General Arnold had still been unable to confirm the desired arrangements for Doolittle's men. The fliers would have to rely on the Chinese fuel—if it existed—to go on to Chungking, and hope it contained no impurities to foul their engines.

★ ★ ★ ★

While Hap Arnold worried about the preparation of the airfields in China, Jimmy Doolittle, at McClellan Field, worried about whether his planes would be in any condition to reach those fields. First, not all the parts he needed had arrived. Worse, the civilian mechanics at the Sacramento Air Depot had no sense of urgency about their work, despite Doolittle's pleas, and they tended to be overly zealous about adhering to standard operating procedures, even when these violated Doolittle's specific orders. As a result, they were damaging the bombers and wrecking the raid's chances of success.

The depot routinely conducted the final checks of bombers headed overseas, to ensure that the planes met air force and manufacturers' specifications. But Doolittle's B-25s had been carefully modified to perform a special mission. The civilian mechanics could not be made to understand that. They had their orders, and they would do things their way.

Doolittle went to the depot commander to emphasize that nothing was to be altered on his planes, particularly the delicate carburetor adjustments, except what he specifically ordered. New propellers were to be installed, along with new hydraulic valves for the gun turrets, and leaks in the rubber fuel tanks were to be repaired. Beyond that, only a basic inspection was required.

"It was quite a hassle," Bill Bower said. "We were having quite a battle with the civilian force at McClellan. Our priorities weren't revealed to them evidently in such a way that we would have cooperation."

Doolittle was furious. He phoned Hap Arnold, who managed to get the depot commander's attention. The work speeded up a little after that, but the mechanics could not be prevented from tinkering. Doolittle told his men to stay with their planes and keep an eye on everything the mechanics were doing.

One day Doolittle and Hilger heard an engine backfire as a mechanic tried to start it. A huge puff of black smoke escaped from the engine. Doolittle ran toward the plane, yelling at the man to stop. The mechanic either didn't hear him or didn't care. He continued to try to start the engine, which kept backfiring. The carburetors had been so precisely tuned for maximum gas mileage that the engines had to be started in a special way. Starting them in any other manner would cause backfiring, ruining the carburetor adjustments and leading to increased fuel consumption. And that meant the plane might not make it all the way to China.

Doolittle tore open the hatch, jumped up into the cockpit, and shouted at the mechanic to stop running the engine.

"I was madder than a son of a bitch," Doolittle said, "so I said to the mechanic, 'What's going on here?'"

"We're readjusting the carburetors," the man said. "They're all out of adjustment."

"What?" Doolittle exploded. "Do you mean that somebody fooled around with these carburetors without my OK?"

"All I know is that they were checked, found way out of adjustment, and fixed up."

In addition, some special carburetors that had been installed on several planes at Eglin were replaced by ordinary ones. "We just happened to find out," Ski York said, "by looking the engines over and checking the serial numbers, that they were different. No mention was made, or notation made, to let us know that the carburetors had been changed. We accidentally found out about it." It is quite likely that this change caused York and his crew to end up in Russia.

Doc White was also having problems. The medical supply officer at McClellan was uncooperative. "In several instances," White said, "he had the desired supplies on his shelves but apparently did not want to deplete his stores and by one excuse or another refused to fill most of my requisitions." White hoped the navy doctors on the *Hornet* would be more helpful than his own air force had been.

Thus, the days at McClellan were difficult ones. Doolittle and his men became unpopular not only with the civilian mechanics and the base commander, but also with the other air force personnel. They did not socialize because they were concerned they might let something slip about their mission. They stayed together in the barracks, the mess halls, and the clubs, resisting the friendly approaches of others. They came to be thought of as aloof and snobbish, but they could not be bothered by that. They had something far more important on their minds—survival.

On March 31, Doolittle flew to San Francisco and entered the bar of the Fairmont Hotel. Several people recognized him and offered to buy him a drink, but he politely begged off and joined two navy officers at a table. They were Admiral Halsey and his chief of staff, Captain Browning. They had come to discuss the raid.

The bar was no place to talk, nor was it even a place for such well-known people as Doolittle and Halsey to be seen together, so they went upstairs to Halsey's room, where they could have some privacy.*

They talked for several hours, and Halsey and Doolittle became aware of the substantial risks each was taking. Halsey came to realize how low the chances of survival were for Doolittle's men. It seemed to him almost like a suicide raid.

Doolittle came to understand what a huge gamble the navy was taking to ferry his men and planes to within striking distance of Japan. If the sixteen-ship task force was discovered and attacked by an enemy force, the loss to the U.S. Navy and the American people, in morale and prestige, could be greater than the disaster at Pearl Harbor. The navy stood to lose two carriers—half of those available in the Pacific—plus four cruisers, eight destroyers, and two oilers. In addition, the lives of several thousand sailors would be in jeopardy, including those of Halsey and Mitscher, among the navy's most experienced leaders.

Halsey made it clear that if his task force was attacked before the carrier came within the bombers' range of Japan, Doolittle's planes would have to be dumped overboard so that the *Hornet*'s own fighters, torpedo planes, and dive bombers could be brought up on deck and launched. If they were still within flying distance of Midway, the B-25s could take off and head there, but in either event they would have to leave the carrier, one way or another. The safety of the carrier was paramount. If the task force was lost, the United States would have virtually no Pacific Fleet.

---

*In Doolittle's version of this meeting, recalled many years later, the three men discussed the mission over dinner at a restaurant; several books have used this account. In Halsey's version, related in 1946, the meeting took place in Halsey's room. Halsey's biographer, naval historian E. B. Potter, described why he thought Halsey's recollection was the more accurate. "I have preferred Halsey's version because it was recorded earlier; Halsey's memoir reveals an excellent memory, and I simply do not believe officers would discuss top-secret operations in a public restaurant." In a 1983 interview, Doolittle agreed to defer to Halsey's version.

Admiral Halsey told Doolittle that the *Hornet* had arrived that day at the Alameda Naval Air Station, across the bay from San Francisco, and was ready to take the B-25s aboard the next day. The following day, April 2, the *Hornet* would head out to sea accompanied by two cruisers, four destroyers, and one oiler. This was designated Task Group 16.2. On April 7 the carrier *Enterprise* and its force of the same composition, Task Group 16.1, would depart Pearl Harbor and join the *Hornet* group at sea on April 12. The combined group, to be known as Task Force 16, under Halsey's command, would head for Japan, taking on fuel some eight hundred miles east of Tokyo. They would make a high-speed run to the launch point, at which time Doolittle and his men would be on their own.

Halsey later described the meeting in his characteristically blunt fashion. "Our talks boiled down to this: we would carry Jimmy within four hundred miles of Tokyo, if we could sneak in that close, but if we were discovered sooner, we would have to launch him anyway, provided he was in reach of either Tokyo or Midway.

"That suited Jimmy. We shook hands, and I wished him luck. The next time I saw him, he was Lieutenant General Doolittle, wearing the Medal of Honor."

As soon as the meeting was over, Doolittle telephoned his exec, Jack Hilger, and told him to round up the men and be ready to board the carrier the next day.

★ ★ ★ ★

Sometimes, not even an admiral gets his way, and the most careful plans have to be changed for the most mundane of reasons. In Halsey's case, it was a combination of bad weather and the flu. Halsey and Browning had expected to return to Pearl Harbor on April 2, which would have allowed sufficient time for last-minute preparations for the sailing of his Task Group 16.1, but all flights from San Francisco to Hawaii, both civilian and military, were grounded because of strong westerly winds.

Every day Halsey telephoned Pan American Airways and the Alameda Naval Air Station to see if any planes were leaving, but the answer was always negative. By April 5 he was still in California, and he had to send a radio message to Mitscher on the *Hornet*, now far out to sea, postponing the rendezvous of the two task groups for twenty-four hours. Halsey was growing increasingly impatient and angry, and this probably aggravated a sensitive skin condition, resulting in an uncomfortable, itchy rash.* Then he caught the flu.

By the morning of April 6, all planes were still grounded, and Halsey was too sick to get out of bed. Browning ran across a navy doctor in the hotel lobby and brought him up to Halsey's room. The man prescribed liquids and a long rest, the last thing Halsey wanted or would submit to. At his insistence, the doctor left him a supply of what Halsey called "dynamite pills." That evening he learned that a Pan American Clipper was scheduled to depart for Honolulu in a few hours.

He swallowed more dynamite pills and dragged himself to the Pan American terminal. "When I boarded the plane," Halsey said, "I was so full of pills that I rattled, but I slept until a nosebleed woke me up as we lost altitude for our landing, and I stepped off at Honolulu with the flu licked."

He would have to hustle to make up for lost time. To keep his rendezvous with Mitscher's group on the thirteenth, his ships would have to leave Pearl in less than two days. Otherwise, the raid would have to be postponed.

★ ★ ★ ★

Navy lieutenant Hank Miller continued to drill his army pilots in short takeoff runs, right up to the time they were ready to leave. As soon as the mechanics at McClellan finished inspecting each ship, he took it and the crew to an isolated field at Willows, California, where no one would see a B-25 taking off in the length of a carrier deck.

On the morning of April 1, he was at McClellan when Doolittle stopped by to talk to him.

"Well, we'll finish up at Willows," Doolittle said, "then we're going to fly down to Alameda and go aboard. How do you think everybody's doing?"

---

* The rash would plague Halsey for two months and cause him to miss the Battle of Midway, which he followed from his hospital bed.

"Oh, I think it's no strain at all. I think everybody's doing great."

Miller's role in the mission was finally at an end, but he was determined not to be sent back to Pensacola yet. He made a pitch to go along on the next stage of the trip.

"You know, Colonel, if you want proof, I've had less time in the B-25 than anybody. You can take an extra ship along—a sixteenth airplane—and when we get one hundred miles out of San Francisco, I'll take it off. I'll deliver it back to Columbia, South Carolina, back to the army, and go back to Pensacola."

Doolittle did not answer, and Miller spent the rest of the morning checking out as many pilots as he could for their final practice run.

That afternoon the McClellan Field operations officer gave Doolittle a long form to fill out. It required his comments on the nature of the maintenance work performed on his aircraft. There were a great many blank spaces in which Doolittle was supposed to record his answers to questions about the quality of the work. Doolittle ran his eye down the form, took out his pen, and scrawled one word diagonally across the page.

LOUSY!

The operations officer was stunned, but a respect for regulations made him find his voice.

"Just a minute, Colonel. You will have to give us a detailed report. This will not do."

"I haven't got the time," Doolittle said.

"If that's the case, I won't sign your clearance. Regulations, you know."

At that, Doolittle muttered something under his breath, got into his airplane, taxied out to the runway, and took off.

The base officer was irate. He turned to Major Hilger and shouted, "Who is that guy? I can tell you he is heading for a lot of trouble."

"He sure is," Hilger said. "He sure is."

The pilots flew southwest to Alameda one at a time. It was their last chance for some free-spirited flying, and some of them took advantage of it, particularly when they saw the Bay Bridge. The temptation to fly under it was too great for some to resist.

Bill Bower recalled twenty-nine years later, with the caution born of being that much older, "I have never been able to truthfully say whether I flew under the bridge or not, but I have a sneaking hunch I did. . . . And I suppose that maybe some of the other people did too."

Ted Lawson, writing two years after the event, remembered it more clearly. His navigator, Mac McClure, had a movie camera with a roll of the new color film, and he wanted to take some footage of the bridge. Lawson's copilot, Dean Davenport, then at the controls, suggested flying under the bridge to get a good picture for McClure. Lawson agreed, hoping there were no cables hanging beneath the span. Davenport dove toward the water, leveled off, and zoomed under the bridge. McClure shouted that his camera had jammed and asked if they could do it again. Lawson wisely declined. Twice would be pushing their luck.

The first thing Doolittle's men noticed as they approached the Alameda Naval Air Station was the aircraft carrier tied up at the pier. It looked terribly small from the air.

After the planes landed at the field, Doolittle and York, the operations officer, checked with all the pilots, asking if there was anything at all wrong with their planes. Those who said no were told to taxi down to the pier. Those who said yes were directed to a hangar. When sixteen planes had assembled at the pier, Doolittle told York that those were the ones that would make the raid. If something went wrong with one of them before it was put on the carrier, a plane from the hangar could be substituted.

All the men were ordered aboard ship, whether or not their particular bomber was going. That way there would be spare crewmen, replacements for any who might have to drop out because of injury or illness. Also, taking all the men was good security. No one would be left ashore who might talk about the mission he had almost gone on. Hank Miller circulated among the men, reminding them of the proper naval procedure for boarding a ship and warning them not to say anything about their mission to the *Hornet*'s crew.

Doolittle approached Miller to say he had been aboard to talk to Captain Mitscher and several of the senior officers.

"You know," Doolittle said, "I talked to them about your idea of taking an extra plane along and they go along with it, so we'll take sixteen and launch you one hundred miles out."

"Gee, that's great," Miller said, pleased that he had talked himself into another leg of the mission. Each stretch brought him closer to combat and farther from Pensacola.

A group of sailors descended on each plane. The men drained most of the fuel from the tanks and hooked a tractor to the nosewheel. As the planes were towed out onto the pier, the army crews walked behind them, slowly and silently. They watched with apprehension as huge cranes picked up their planes like toys and hoisted them on board the carrier. Each man knew that if his plane suffered damage now, he would have to embark on the *Hornet* only to watch his buddies take off for Tokyo. But there were no accidents, and the B-25s were placed at the aft end of the deck and lashed down. The last plane aboard was Doolittle's. It was positioned first in line. The distance between it and the end of the flight deck was less than five hundred feet.

Lieutenant Miller looked on with pride as the army fliers boarded the *Hornet* displaying the best naval etiquette, just as he had taught them. Each man stopped at the top of the gangplank, smartly saluted the flag on the fantail, saluted the officer of the deck, and asked permission to come aboard. Miller thought they looked a lot smarter than some of the sailors. When he came aboard, he was bombarded with questions from the officers, wanting to know where they were going and what they were doing with army planes. Several men he had known from earlier assignments, aware that he was from Alaska, concluded that they were going there, to reinforce the American presence in the Aleutian Islands. Captain Mitscher did his best to foster the rumor that the *Hornet* was merely delivering the B-25s to Pearl Harbor.

The fliers were shown to the cramped quarters they would share with the *Hornet*'s officers and enlisted men, as appropriate to their rank. In midafternoon, tugs eased the ship away from the pier and out to an anchorage in the middle of the bay. Doolittle called his men together to announce a surprise, a shore leave that night. He delivered another lecture on the need for secrecy, on being careful about what they said and where they said it, and he accompanied them in a pitching liberty boat to the wharf at the foot of Mill Street. He was going to meet his wife, who had come to San Francisco to say good-bye.

In the hotel elevator on the way to her room, a stranger recognized him and said, "Hey, I understand you're taking off tomorrow morning." Doolittle was too stunned to speak. He stared at the man and turned away. He considered alerting the FBI, but decided the man had simply made an accurate guess. He had recognized Doolittle and had probably seen the army bombers aboard the carrier, and put the two together. Anyone who looked out to the bay could see that a carrier was taking army planes somewhere.

Indeed, most of the crowd at the popular night spot, the Top of the Mark, including several of the army fliers, could see in the moonlight the planes clearly outlined on the *Hornet*'s flight deck. Bill Bower noticed a submarine gliding past the carrier as it swung at anchor. Mac McClure sat near a window, staring at the lights of the city. "More than once," he recalled, "it crossed my mind that it would be the last time I would see it."

Tom Griffin and three of his buddies stared at the ship. "We were sure," he said, "that every spy in San Francisco was making copious notes to forward to Tokyo." But, he added, "the rest of that night is a bit of a blur."

The next morning, Doolittle said good-bye to his wife. He made it sound as casual as he could, as though he were off on a routine training flight.

"I'll be seeing you. I may be out of the country a little while. Call you when I get back."

# This Is a Breeze

The USS *Hornet* weighed anchor and got under way at 10:18 on the morning of April 2. As the huge carrier made her way toward the Golden Gate Bridge, a navy launch pulled alongside with an urgent message for Doolittle. He was to return to shore immediately for an important telephone call from Washington. Doolittle was convinced that his worst fear had come true. General Arnold was going to tell him that he could not go on the mission after all.

He was prepared to argue his case as forcefully as he could, but when he picked up the phone, he was dismayed to find that the caller was not Arnold but Gen. George C. Marshall. Doolittle knew there was no way out. He could protest all he wanted to his old friend Hap Arnold, but not to the Chief of Staff of the U.S. Army. If Marshall told him to report back to Washington, there was nothing he could do about it.

"Doolittle?" Marshall asked.

"Yes, General," Doolittle said.

"I couldn't let you leave without wishing you the best of luck," Marshall said. "Our hearts will be with you and our prayers will be with you. Good-bye and good luck, and come back safely."

"Thank you—thank you," was all a relieved and grateful Doolittle could say.

Back on board the *Hornet*, Doolittle joined Hank Miller for a walk on the flight deck. The sixteen B-25s had been arranged so that they had a full 495 feet available for takeoff, more than they had on the runway at Eglin.

"Well, Hank, how does it look to you?" Doolittle said, referring to the distance they had for takeoff.

"Oh, gee," Miller said, "this is a breeze."

Doolittle gestured to the lead airplane and suggested they get in to see how the flight deck looked from the cockpit. They settled in the pilot's and copilot's seats, and Doolittle stared down the length of the carrier deck.

"This looks like a short distance," Doolittle said.

"You see where that tool kit is, way up the deck by that island structure?" Miller asked, pointing to a spot about three-fourths of the way up the deck.

"Yes," Doolittle said.

"That's where I used to take off in fighters on the *Saratoga* and the *Lexington*."

Doolittle looked at him for a moment.

"Henry," he said, "what name do they use in the navy for bullshit?"

They climbed out of Doolittle's plane, and Miller watched Doolittle head for the bridge before going below for lunch. Before he had finished his dessert, he heard his name over the ship's loudspeaker.

"Lieutenant Miller, report to the bridge."

When Miller reached the bridge, he saw Doolittle leaving. He did not know it yet, but Doolittle had been talking to Captain Mitscher about keeping the sixteenth airplane on board and using it on the raid, instead of sending Miller back in it as a demonstration of a short-run carrier takeoff. What had persuaded them was Miller's confidence about how much room they had.

"Miller," Mitscher said, "I don't think I'll be able to give you forty knots of wind over the deck."

"Captain, I don't need that anyway, because we have 495 feet. I taught these guys how to take off from an aircraft carrier with forty knots of wind and 250 feet. We have lots of room."

"Well," Mitscher said, "do you have an extra pair of pants with you?"

"Oh, yes, sir. I brought all my baggage with me because I'm going to fly nonstop to Columbia, South Carolina."

"We'll take that extra plane," Mitscher said.

Miller was delighted and said as much to the captain. He would get his wish to see his army pupils actually take off on the mission. He felt a twinge of concern about his own position, however. He had been chasing around the United States for weeks, and would now be going almost to Japan on the strength of his original orders to report to Eglin Field for temporary duty, plus a telephone call authorizing him to Sacramento. Officially, he was probably AWOL by now. He joked with Mitscher that he'd most likely be an ensign when he got back.

Although Miller had talked confidently to Doolittle and to Mitscher about how easy the takeoff would be, he still harbored some doubts. Taking off in a short distance on land was one thing, but doing it from the heaving deck of a carrier at sea was quite another. He discussed this with Lt. Stephen Jurika, an intelligence officer aboard the *Hornet*. He talked to him about the training he had given the army fliers.

"What he really tried to instill in them," Jurika said, "and I talked to Hank many a time on this—was confidence."

"I've done everything I can," Miller told him. "They know how, it's just, will they? . . . there's nothing they don't know about short takeoffs. It's just when that deck is moving and they're taking off, will they go through with it?"

As the sun was setting on the Doolittle fliers' first day at sea, the klaxon sounded, followed by the loudspeaker announcement: "MAN YOUR BATTLE STATIONS." Two thousand sailors and their officers exploded into what the uninitiated army personnel thought was chaos. To the navy, of course, it was a time-tested, well-organized race to prepare the ship for battle in the shortest possible time. The army bomber crews had been given instructions, and they ran through the passageways and out on deck to their planes. They scrambled into the B-25s and went through the motions of preparing for takeoff. The gunners made ready to open fire.

Every day, at dawn and at dusk, the klaxon would sound and the same controlled frenzy would break out on the ship. It did not take some of the army fliers long to decide that they were not in total agreement with this practice.

"I am not sure," Bill Bower said, "whether we were completely attuned to the discipline of the ship. I wouldn't say that some of us ignored [the call to battle stations], but I suppose we did."

Some of the ship's officers found Doolittle's men to be an un-disciplined lot in all matters.

"I think *our* initial reaction," Lieutenant Jurika recalled in 1976, "most of the officers on the ship and certainly the captain's and mine, was that an all-volunteer crew like this had to be special in ability to fly and desire to do something as a group together. But in looks, in appearance, and in demeanor, I would say that they appeared undisciplined. Typical of this was the open collars and short-sleeved shirts—the weather was quite cool in Alameda—grommets either crushed or none at all in their caps, worn-out, scuffed-type shoes. They were not in flight clothing. These were people who had had a chance to stay in the BOQ and clean up and come aboard the ship. . . . our initial impression was pretty well justified by their actions during the time they were on the *Hornet*. . . . most of them were really fatalistic. It was a lark. They knew they'd get medals if they got through, they'd probably get promotions. They felt like this was a way to 'get back at the Japs.' . . . very lighthearted, except for Doolittle, who was all seriousness."

Part of this attitude can perhaps be traced to the long-standing rivalry between the army and the navy, in which each believed it was the superior service. Also, the navy had the reputation of being the more spit-and-polish outfit, more concerned with matters of appearance. In addition, most of the nonflying navy officers aboard

the *Hornet* were graduates of the United States Naval Academy at
Annapolis, and thus were career navy men. Among the army officers, only one, Captain York, was a graduate of the service academy, the United States Military Academy at West Point. Most of the
army pilots were more dedicated to flying than to military careers.
To them, form, demeanor, and social graces were not as important
as they were to the ship's officers.

But there was another source of tension aboard ship that led,
initially, to negative feelings toward Doolittle's fliers, the same problem that had plagued them at McClellan Field—the need to maintain secrecy about their mission. This caused many of the *Hornet*'s
officers and enlisted men to see them as distant and snobbish.

Capt. Ross Greening described the early contacts between the
army and navy men as "slightly strained and defensive. The army
fliers refused to give any information to the curious navy men,
which further strained the relationship between the two services.
There were no evidences of open dislike—only a defensive aloof-
ness. It was only natural that the navy men would think the army
was overdoing its part, and the army was in no mood to jeopardize
its security until it was completely safe for the navy to know the
nature of the mission."

When Ted Lawson reported to the tiny cabin to which he had
been assigned, he found it occupied by two ensigns, who made no
concession to the fact that he outranked them. They simply gestured
toward a cot and ignored him.

Mac McClure commented that at first they were treated shabbily
by the navy. "Their attitude toward us was shown by putting us at
one end of the wardroom for meals, with no silverware and no one to
serve us."

The rivalry and strained relations did not extend to Doolittle.
Captain Mitscher was a good-natured host and turned over his living quarters, a spacious suite, to Doolittle. Mitscher slept in a cabin
on the bridge.

The sailors were curious and inquisitive, and rumors ran ram-
pant. Shortly after the fliers came on board, the word got out about

the identity of their leader. Mitscher's orderly, marine Cpl. Larry Bogart, was standing at attention at his post outside Mitscher's door when he heard a ship's officer announce Doolittle's name.

"I didn't think much about it," Corporal Bogart said, "but after a while I heard our executive officer, Comdr. George Henderson, say, 'Hello, Jimmy.' Then it clicked. I knew who he was. Jimmy Doolittle! The guy who had all the flight records—speed, endurance, altitude, distance. . . . You can't blame me if I cocked an ear a little to try and hear the rest of the conversation [but] they didn't say anything worth hearing."

Jimmy Doolittle's name passed quickly around the ship and with it the feeling that they must be heading for something important. The first sergeant of the Marine Corps detachment, George Royce, called his men together and said he didn't know where they were going or what they were going to do, but he sensed an urgency in the air. His advice to his men was practical: those who had not signed up for government life insurance should do so at once.

The next morning, those of the fliers who had not already guessed learned about their destination. Doolittle assembled them all in a wardroom, gazed at them for a moment, cleared his throat, and told them what their weeks of training had been for.

They were going to bomb Japan, he said. He went on to explain about the arrangements that had been made with the Chinese government for the planes to land at airfields in eastern China, gas up, and fly on to Chungking.

Doolittle then discussed some of the other details of the operation and the additional training they would undergo, and asked again if anyone wanted to change his mind. There were enough spare crewmen to replace anyone who did not want to go, but no one backed out.

The men were glad that the long period of secrecy—and the inevitable rumors that had accompanied it—was over. Now they could talk freely and openly among themselves. Everything made sense—the extra fuel tanks, the emphasis on keeping gasoline consumption to a minimum, the low-level flying, the need for radio silence, and the long flights to practice navigating over open water. They understood at last the importance of the mission they had worked so hard to prepare themselves for. It was worth all the effort. What could be more vital at this stage of the war than striking back at Japan, exacting revenge for the losses and defeats suffered by the United States and her allies?

The importance of the mission was matched by its danger. Their lives would, in large part, depend on the condition of their B-25s. After Doolittle concluded the meeting, the men wandered out on deck to the bombers. No one ordered them there; they seemed drawn irresistibly to the airplanes that would carry them to Japan and on to safety in China, if all went according to plan. Some of the pilots paced off the deck from the nose of the lead plane to the end of the runway, measuring the distance for takeoff.

Over the next several days, singly and in pairs, the pilots and other crew members took that same walk, often shaking their heads as they thought about it. Oh, sure, they had done it on land, and Doolittle said two B-25s had taken off from that very deck off the Virginia coast, and Lieutenant Miller kept telling them it would be a breeze, but none of them—not even Doolittle—had actually done it or even seen it done.

After Doolittle had informed the men about their destination, most of the pilots told their crews to check the planes carefully and to write down anything that needed adjustment or repair, no matter how minor it seemed. Anything that was not functioning correctly had to be fixed while they still had access to the *Hornet*'s tool and repair facilities. Once they took off, they would be on their own for a long time.

That afternoon, Captain Mitscher told the crew of the *Hornet* about the mission.

"This ship," he announced over the loudspeaker, "will carry the army bombers to the coast of Japan for the bombing of Tokyo."

There was a moment of stunned silence, then the sailors broke into loud and prolonged cheering, which was echoed from the escorting ships as word of the mission was passed to them by semaphore. "The sailors I saw," recalled Mac McClure, "were jumping up and down like small children."

In his after-action report to Admiral Nimitz, Pete Mitscher wrote that "morale reached a new high, there to remain until after the attack was launched and the ship well clear of combat areas."

The news about the mission altered the feelings between the *Hornet*'s crew and Doolittle's men. Ross Greening said, "Relationships improved in a matter of seconds and immediately all hands, Army Air Force and Navy alike, joined together to accomplish all that was necessary to satisfactorily complete the mission." Ted Lawson found that his sleeping arrangements improved that night. The two ensigns with whom he shared the cabin gave him the softest bunk. And in the wardroom at meals, the air force officers received the same service as the ship's officers.

Suddenly the navy could not do enough to make their guests' shipboard life more pleasant. Navy mechanics offered help with any repair work on the planes, sailors lent extra clothing, bakers prepared special pies and cakes, and the cooks offered more than enough to eat—most of the fliers gained weight.

The navy even arranged to pay the enlisted men of Doolittle's group. They had last been paid on March 23, at Eglin Field, and their service records had not reached McClellan in time for them to be paid again before boarding the carrier. As a result, many of them had no money. Captain Mitscher and his disbursing officer waived regulations and paid the air corps men from navy funds.

The *Hornet*'s medical staff was generous to Doc White and gave him whatever he wanted from their somewhat limited supplies. They overlooked rules, regulations, and red tape governing the use of their stores, responding unselfishly to the needs of Doolittle's men.

The army crews offered guided tours through their B-25s and followed the sailors down to the hangar deck to inspect the navy fighters, dive bombers, and torpedo planes. The remaining days at sea provided one of the finer examples of interservice harmony ever witnessed. Although the navy itself would not be attacking Japan, it was determined to bring those who would as close as possible and to make sure they lacked for nothing on the way.

Still, the danger to every man in the task force, and particularly to the army fliers, was never far from their thoughts. Cpl. Jake

DeShazer, standing alone on the flight deck that night, reflected on their future.

"I began to wonder how many more days I was to spend in this world. Maybe I wasn't so fortunate after all to get to go on this trip."

In the morning, the army fliers resumed their training, this time under two of the ship's officers, Comdr. Apollo Soucek and Lt. Steve Jurika. Soucek was the *Hornet*'s air officer, and he instructed them in the carrier's flight operations. Jurika, an intelligence officer, had spent two years in Tokyo (1939–41) as an assistant naval attaché and was familiar with the city, the people, the language, and the culture. His job was to pinpoint the selected industrial and military targets in the cities to be bombed, and to teach the fliers what to do if captured. The men referred to Jurika's lectures as "how to make friends and influence Japs."

Jurika had compiled a great deal of information on worthwhile targets, the safest routes to those targets, and specific aiming points—such as rivers and bridges—in the various cities. He passed on to the fliers a wealth of personal knowledge plus information gleaned from intelligence files, such as the locations of individual antiaircraft batteries. He said the Japanese had over five hundred combat-ready planes available for defense of the homeland. That represented a formidable opposition for sixteen planes with broomsticks for tail guns, top turrets that worked erratically, and nose guns that were cumbersome to move. Jurika described the tactics that Japanese fighter pilots used in attacking bombers, certainly useful information, even for crews who could not shoot back effectively.

In addition, Jurika delivered several lectures on the histories of Japan and of China, their forms of government, and the physical and psychological differences between the two peoples. He taught the men a phrase in Chinese, *lusau hoo metwa fugi*, which meant, "I am an American," and how to distinguish a Chinese from a Japanese. That would be helpful to crews shot down in Chinese territory when the men were unsure if the area had been occupied by the enemy. "The way to tell," Jurika said, "if you didn't know the landscape or were disoriented, was simply to look at their feet. The

Chinese have all their toes together and the Japanese have the big toe separated from the others because for years they've worn a thong between them." Admittedly, this would be difficult to determine if the men encountered soldiers who were wearing boots.

Jurika, who had found the army fliers to be undisciplined when they boarded the carrier, had his opinion reinforced during the course of his lectures. "A briefing would be set up for eight-thirty in the morning, after breakfast," he said. "They would saunter in and the briefing scheduled for eight-thirty wouldn't start before nine or nine-fifteen, sometimes as late as nine-thirty. And their attention span was very short, half an hour at the most. They would be interested up to a point, and yet, from my point of view, their lives were at stake. The success of a raid was at stake. I felt that they took it very, very casually, surprisingly so."

Comdr. Frank Akers, the ship's navigator, was called on to teach a refresher course in navigation. He, too, found that some of Doolittle's men were inattentive students. "The pilots were a carefree, happy group and seemed little concerned as to the danger of the mission or what might happen to them if they were shot down over Japan." He was wrong about that.

This apparently lighthearted attitude toward their shipboard training characterized most, but not all, of the fliers. Jurika recalled that four or five of the men seemed keenly interested in his observations of the Japanese, from matters of everyday life to the capabilities of Japanese aircraft.

Navigator Tom Griffin perceptively suggested that the casual unconcern shown by many of his fellow Raiders may have been a display of youthful bravado, a feigned indifference to mask the worry and fear about the future.

"I feel that if Lieutenant Jurika had given us a test after his lectures," Griffin said, "he would have been surprised and pleased to find out how much we had heard and retained. After all, Japan and the Japanese were very much on our minds. But we must remember this group of young men found themselves living under totally alien surroundings (aboard an aircraft carrier), and they had on their minds their soon unpredictable rendezvous with the enemy over his territory. Their carefree façades undoubtedly covered many apprehensions—probably in a healthy way."

Doolittle gave the crews the choice of the city they wanted to bomb and the airfield in China they wished to land at for refueling. The crews committed to memory the physical landmarks of the overland route to the target and around the target itself. They studied photographs of their target city so they would be able to recognize quickly the key points. Memorization was necessary because although each pilot would have a map, he could not draw lines or marks on it for fear that its capture could lead the enemy back to the task force.

Each plane had to release its three five-hundred-pound demolition bombs within the shortest period and in as straight a line as possible. This would expose the planes to the briefest amount of antiaircraft fire. Their fourth bomb, the incendiary, had to be dropped as close as possible to the first three, to spread the fires the demolition bombs would start.

Doolittle was adamant in rejecting two suggestions he received from a few of his men: first, that incendiaries be dropped on residential areas—which would produce massive fires because of the wood-and-paper construction of the houses—and, second, that the Imperial Palace be bombed. Doolittle stressed that only military and industrial targets were to be hit, and he sternly forbade any deviations from that rule. Neither residential areas nor the palace were of any value to the war effort and were not worth wasting bombs on.

Some of the men argued with him about the palace, suggesting that damage to it, or even injury to the emperor, would boost American spirits and demoralize the Japanese people. But Doolittle had been in London during the Blitz, and had witnessed the outrage and the resulting unity among the British people after Buckingham Palace had been bombed. He was sure the Japanese would react similarly. An attack on the emperor would surely cause them to fight harder and more savagely. Doolittle later said that he considered that prohibition to be among the most important decisions he made during the war.

Ten planes were assigned targets in Tokyo, three were to bomb

Yokohama, and the remaining three were given Nagoya, Osaka, and Kobe. Doolittle would take off first, on the afternoon of April 19, which would bring him over Tokyo around sunset. The rest of the planes would take off about three hours later, at sunset, and arrive over their targets at night. The fires from Doolittle's bomb would serve as beacons for the other planes. Doolittle expected to reach the China airfields for refueling during the hours of darkness, while the others would arrive at daylight on the twentieth.

Maj. Harvey Johnson, Doolittle's adjutant, reported that the pilots objected to Doolittle's plan to reach Tokyo first so that he could start fires to guide the rest of them. "They felt it was too great a risk for him and did not want him to take such a risk for their benefit." Doolittle defended his plan, despite their objections, but circumstances would later force him to abandon it.

Last-minute training for the crewmen proceeded as the task force moved steadily to the north and west. The gunners were given opportunities for target practice. Auxiliary power plants were attached to the top turrets of the B-25s, and the sailors raised red kites and balloons to serve as targets. The men were also taught to recognize the silhouette of every type of Japanese aircraft. They sat in the carrier's blackout recognition room and memorized the details of enemy planes from pictures flashed briefly on a screen.

Doc White, the flight surgeon and top-turret gunner, lectured the men on personal hygiene and the sanitary measures they should concern themselves with in China. He cautioned them never to ignore any scratch or cut, no matter how minor, because of the widespread use of human feces (night soil) as fertilizer. As a result, even the smallest of scratches could harbor a potentially fatal infection. No one wanted to survive Japanese fighter attacks and antiaircraft fire only to die of disease after reaching the safety of China.

Contrary to Commander Akers's observation that the Doolittle fliers seemed unconcerned about the possibility of being shot down over Japan, some of the men were, indeed, worried about it. They talked among themselves about what to do if they faced capture, and one night at dinner, Jack Hilger raised the question with Doolittle.

The feeling was that the men would rather deliberately crash their planes on a valuable target than be taken prisoner.

"I'm an old man," Doolittle said with a grin. "I'll be damned if I am going to spend the rest of my life in some Jap jail."

He said he would order his crew to bail out, if they wanted to take the chance of being captured, and then dive at full throttle at something worth destroying.

"But," he added, "tell the men to get any ideas like that out of their heads. They are all young, they are all healthy, and even if they are captured or forced down in the China Sea, they still have a chance."

All the men had heard stories about the brutal treatment the Japanese gave their prisoners of war. Accounts of the enemy's propensity for torture and murder had been coming out of China for years, and more recently from the Philippines and Malaya. The fliers had no illusions about what they might face, particularly as the first Americans to bomb the sacred soil of the Japanese homeland. "Everybody figured that it was going to be pretty tough if they were caught by the Japanese," said Hank Miller.

Steve Jurika confirmed that conclusion, and he was in a position to know. He told them that "if they were captured dropping bombs on Japan, the chances of their survival would be awfully slim, very, very slim.

"I figured they would be, first of all, paraded through the streets as Exhibit A, and then tried by some sort of kangaroo court and probably publicly beheaded. This seemed to settle them down quite a bit."

There was little time to brood about it, however. When the fliers weren't learning about first aid for scratches or the height of a radio tower on the route to Yokohama, they were working on their planes. And there was a lot of work to be done. The planes were constantly exposed to high winds blowing across the open deck, which caused vibrations in all the control surfaces. These had to be inspected daily to ensure that nothing had been damaged. Army planes, unlike those of the navy, were not built to withstand the corrosive effects of salt water and sea air, and they had to be examined frequently for corrosion, particularly in such vital parts as control cables. The men were also concerned that the winds and thundering waves could cause a plane to break loose from its lines and be swept into one of the others, or overboard. The cables lashing them to the deck were checked several times a day.

Engineer-gunner Joe Manske recalled checking the cables one night during a raging storm. "While I was busy, the storm increased to a point that I was afraid to release my hold and go back inside the ship. Fortunately, after about twenty minutes, I was able to get the attention of the navy watch on their rounds, and they helped me back inside the ship."

The batteries ran down and had to be recharged and tested regularly. Gasoline evaporated from all the tanks, and leaked from some, so they had to be refilled periodically. The gun turret motors were found to be faulty and had to be removed for repair in the ship's workshops. The left engine of one plane had to be taken out and repaired. Generators broke down, spark plugs became fouled, brakes failed, and hydraulic systems developed leaks.

Doolittle made periodic and thorough inspections of each plane, with its crew in nervous attendance. No one wanted to find that something on his ship could not be repaired or replaced, for that would mean shoving it over the side. Doolittle was alert to every possible problem. While inspecting Ted Lawson's *Ruptured Duck*, he noticed that an intercom headset had been hung near the compass. He warned the crews to keep metal objects away from the compass and demonstrated the reason by passing a thermos bottle over it. The needle swung a full thirty degrees, more than enough to lead them miles off course.

Doolittle's men still found time to relax. They were, after all, army fliers who knew how to have a good time. Not that there was much to do aboard ship. A few engaged in wholesome activities such as watching the evening movies, getting ice cream sodas from the gedunk stand, or writing up the day's activities in their diaries. A gunner enjoyed exploring the ship, particularly the engine room, and a pilot spent his spare time tinkering in the machine shop, making a new screw for the hinge on his sunglasses.

But most of the men passed the hours gambling, at poker, craps, the navy pastime acey-deucey, and darts. "I know there were games that went on for two or three days," Jurika said. "Somebody would go to the wardroom during a meal and bring back enough to keep them from starving. I know that there was also some booze aboard."

The games were played fiercely and intensely, and the stakes got higher and higher, until a whole month's pay could ride on a single bet. The navy was ahead. "I think they took every last cent we had," Bill Bower said. "We were destitute very quickly." But they played doggedly every spare moment.

Captain Mitscher stopped in on one of the marathon poker games and looked over the shoulder of an army pilot who had a big cigar in his mouth.

"How are you doing?" Mitscher asked.

"OK, Joe," the pilot said, looking up at Mitscher without recognizing him. "Wanna take a hand?"

The navy officers present were embarrassed, but Mitscher said nothing about it.

One navy pilot had won $1,100 by the time the army fliers took off for Japan. The army got its revenge, however. On the return voyage to Pearl Harbor after the launch, the B-25 relief crews who did not go on the Tokyo raid won back the money their buddies had lost, and more.

On Sunday morning, April 5, about thirty of the army fliers crowded into the first two rows of the crew's main mess for Easter services conducted by the *Hornet*'s chaplain, Lt. Comdr. Edward Harp, Jr.

"Looking down at those youngsters," Harp recalled, "I wondered what I could say to them. I knew that some of them would not get back. However, men going into danger do not like to hear about it. Accordingly, I did not speak of the mission ahead or suggest that they 'get right with God' before embarking on it. I spoke, instead, of immortality."

After the sermon Harp played the hand organ and led the men in singing hymns. Seven of Doolittle's fliers asked the chaplain for Bibles to carry in their planes when they flew over Japan.

★ ★ ★ ★

At one-thirty on the afternoon of April 8, Admiral Halsey's task group, consisting of the carrier *Enterprise* and her escort of two cruisers, four destroyers, and one oiler, sailed out of Pearl Harbor. Since his return from San Francisco, Halsey had been meeting with Admiral Nimitz and his staff to draft Operation Plan Number 20-42, which spelled out the navy's role in the mission to bomb Japan.

As part of the operation, Halsey arranged for two submarines to patrol south and east of Japan, where they would be in position to report on any Japanese naval units that might threaten the task force. All other American submarines were ordered to stay south of the equator, well clear of Halsey's route. Thus, Halsey could be certain that any ships spotted west of the rendezvous point for Halsey's and Mitscher's group were those of the enemy.

★ ★ ★ ★

In Washington, Hap Arnold was still trying to make sure that the airfields in eastern China would be ready to receive Doolittle's men, but he was having little success. To add to his problems, the Japanese air force bombed the three most important fields during the first week of April. A broadcast from Tokyo reported that the United States had lengthened the runways and was planning to use the fields for bombing raids on Japan. The broadcast also declared, no doubt for the benefit of the Japanese people, that the raids on these fields "ended the threat of an aerial attack on Japan."

The raids did little physical damage, but they concerned Arnold and Stilwell nonetheless. On April 4, Stilwell wrote in his diary that "the three essential fields have all been bombed. Leak? Or just precaution by the Japs? Suspect talk in Washington." Stilwell had never trusted those pencil pushers in Washington to keep their mouths shut about anything.

Beginning on April 1, Arnold asked Stilwell whether transmitters with a specific frequency range, for use as radio homing devices, would be available at the eastern China airfields by April 19. On

April 5, Stilwell replied, saying that all but one of the fields were reported to have such transmitters. In his response, Arnold said that the stations should be identified to the incoming aircraft by the number 57, and that a supply of food and water be made available for the bomber crews.

Also on April 1, Stilwell requested from Arnold information on the number and types of airplanes that were coming, and the specifications of the openings of their oil and gas tanks. Refueling would have to be done by hand, the slow pouring of fuel from five-gallon cans into the airplanes' tanks. A fuel truck or tanker was a rarity in China, seen only at Chungking and a few other fields in the western part of the country. Arnold supplied the information the following day, and told Stilwell to expect at least twenty-five B-25 bombers.*

It may have appeared that preparations were well under way in China, but that was far from true. Generalissimo Chiang Kai-shek was concerned that the Japanese would find out that American planes were using his eastern airfields. The Japanese had bombed those fields already. If they believed the fields were being used as staging bases for air attacks against them, they might accelerate their land war in the eastern provinces and push to capture the airfields.

Also, there had been no American verification that fuel and oil, or even the reported radio homing devices, were in existence at the fields. Stilwell reported that Maj. Gen. Lewis Brereton, commanding officer of the newly created Tenth Air Force, in India, had been ordered to arrange for such verification, but no reply had been received from him yet.

Doolittle and his men were unaware of the difficulties in equipping the landing fields in China. They assumed everything was being taken care of. Nearly thirty-five years later, in an interview with the

---

*Historians are not certain why Arnold gave this incorrect number of planes. He knew that only twenty-four bombers had been used in the training phase of the mission in Florida, and presumably had been told that only sixteen had been loaded aboard the *Hornet*. Perhaps, in view of his concern about the problems with secrecy in China, he deliberately misstated the number.

United States Naval Institute, the *Hornet*'s intelligence officer, Steve Jurika, confirmed this view.

"Was it your impression that the Chinese were fully briefed up on this and that the landing fields would be ready? Was that the impression the Doolittle people had?"

"Yes," Jurika said, "oh, absolutely, that these fields would be there, that even if it were nighttime when they arrived there would be no problem of lighting the field through lantern or bonfire or some sort of thing, and they would be able to set down and get out."

"It didn't happen that way, though."

"No, that's not the way it happened."

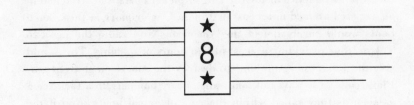

# This Force Is Bound for Tokyo

Shortly after daybreak on the morning of April 10, a Japanese navy radio intelligence unit located outside Tokyo intercepted radio transmissions between Halsey's and Mitscher's task groups. The Japanese quickly deduced the precise location of Mitscher's group and concluded that a fleet including two, and possibly three, aircraft carriers was heading for Japan. This was a staggering piece of intelligence to glean a full nine days before the attack was due to be launched.

The secret was out, but Japanese authorities saw no need to be alarmed. Tokyo and other major cities were well defended by fighter planes and more than three hundred antiaircraft guns, and those defenses would be alerted and prepared well in advance of any attack. The possibility of a surprise raid was now impossible, as far as Japanese military leaders were concerned. They knew that the range of U.S. Navy carrier planes was such that they could not be launched until they were within three hundred miles of Japan's coast.

This meant that the American fleet would have to sail a perilous three hundred miles inside the ring of picket boats that stretched in an arc six hundred miles east of Japan. One or more of these small boats would surely detect the Americans and radio the news to Tokyo, thus providing at least fifteen hours of warning. This would give the Japanese ample time to destroy the American ships at sea. Plans called for waves of long-range army bombers to attack them as soon as they sailed within the ring of patrol boats. And if the bombers failed to sink the U.S. carriers—an event that seemed unlikely to the Japanese—then torpedo planes would finish the job. The Americans would pay heavily for daring to believe they could bomb Japan.

★ ★ ★ ★

At four-thirty on the afternoon of April 12, Captain Mitscher's task group detected radar transmissions 130 miles southwest, on a bearing of 230 degrees. They came from Halsey's task group. At daybreak the following morning, the two groups met and took up formation, with the cruisers and destroyers forming a protective ring around the two carriers. Aboard Halsey's flagship, the carrier *Enterprise*, the crew caught their first glimpse of the large army bombers lashed to the *Hornet*'s flight deck.

"They're B-25s," one sailor shouted, training his binoculars on the *Hornet*.

"You're crazy," a navy pilot said. "A B-25 could never take off with a load—and if it did, it could never land aboard again."

"They won't have to carry a load," a second navy pilot said, "and they won't have to land. They're reinforcing some land base."

"Out here? Which land base?"

"I'll bet we're going through the Aleutians and deliver them to a secret Siberian base."

"Are they using army pilots on carriers? If so, our careers are over. Let's join the marines."

The men did not have to wait long to find out where they were going. Shortly after the rendezvous, Admiral Halsey made an announcement to the crews of the *Enterprise* and her escorts.

"This force is bound for Tokyo," he told them.

"Never," Halsey said later, "have I heard such a shout as burst from the *Enterprise*'s company. Part of their eagerness came, I think, from the fact that Bataan had fallen four days before."

The loss of Bataan, whose forces had fought so valiantly for more than three months, was a tremendous blow, another indication—if any was needed—that nothing seemed capable of blunting the Japanese thrust. The British continued to retreat in Burma, and American forces on Cebu in the southern Philippine Islands were being overrun by Japanese troops. Only tiny Corregidor still held, but that fortress island was as doomed as every other outpost America and her allies had tried to defend. Throughout the Pacific, the Western powers were losing, and the only chance to strike back, to regain some pride and hope for the future, rested in the men of the sixteen ships and sixteen planes of a task force now code-named "Mike."

There was no April 14 for the men of Task Force Mike. That day was lost entirely as the official calendar on each ship skipped from April 13 to April 15 upon crossing the International Date Line, shortly after the task groups merged. That was, of course, to be expected on a westward crossing of the Pacific, and was routinely taken into account in plotting arrival times. In this instance, however, navy planners overlooked the date line and failed to alter the schedule accordingly. Consequently, the army planes would arrive in China one day early, on the nineteenth instead of the twentieth. When told of the error, Doolittle professed not to be alarmed, even though the ships were now maintaining radio silence and could not notify American authorities in Chungking of the change in date. He assumed that the personnel at the airfields where the fliers were due to land would hear about the bombing raid from Japanese radio broadcasts and would therefore make preparations to receive them early. This was a risky assumption, but Doolittle had a contingency plan. He asked Halsey to request that authorities in Pearl Harbor and in Washington notify Chungking—as soon as his planes left the carrier—about the change in date. For reasons never made clear, the messages were not dispatched, and so no one in China knew, from any official source, that the B-25s were coming ahead of schedule.

On April 16, Doolittle gathered the Army Air Force personnel on the windswept flight deck of the *Hornet*, along with Captain Mitscher and some of his officers and men. They clustered around a five-hundred-pound bomb resting on a wheeled dolly to hold a special ceremony. They were going to send some Japanese medals back to their original owners.

Three months before, on January 26, Secretary of the Navy Frank Knox had received a Japanese medal from Master Rigger H. Vormstein, an ex-navy man now working at the Brooklyn Navy Yard. Vormstein had been given the medal in 1908, when his ship was part of the Great White Fleet's visit to Japan. Vormstein had asked Knox "to attach [the medal] to a bomb and return it to Japan in that manner."

Other navy men sent similar requests. Daniel Quigley of McKees Rocks, Pennsylvania, told Secretary Knox that he hoped his medal would "eventually find its way back in company with a bomb that will rock the throne of the 'Son of Heaven.'" Knox liked the idea, and he sent the medals to Admiral Nimitz at Pearl Harbor, who turned them over to Halsey. On April 16, 1942, Halsey passed them across the water in a bag from the *Enterprise* to the *Hornet*.

Doolittle tied several medals, including one contributed by Lieutenant Jurika, to the bomb's tailfin, while navy photographers recorded the scene. Some of the men chalked inscriptions on the bomb casing. Larry Bogart, Mitscher's Marine Corps orderly, wrote, "This is from Mom and Pop Bogart." Doolittle's fliers added their own sentiments: "I don't want to set the world on fire—just Tokyo," and "You'll get a BANG out of this." *

Later that day, the radiomen of Task Force 16 received a broadcast from Radio Tokyo. "Reuters, British news agency," the broadcaster reported in English, "has announced that three American

---

*After the raid, Mitscher notified Admiral Nimitz that "the medals were subsequently delivered in small pieces to their donors in Tokyo by Lt. Ted Lawson at about noon, Saturday, 18 April 1942." Secretary of the Navy Knox wrote to rigger Vormstein that "through the courtesy of the War Department your Japanese medal, and similar medals turned in for shipment, were returned to His Royal Highness, the Emperor of Japan, on 18 April 1942."

bombers have dropped bombs on Tokyo. This is a most laughable story. They know it is absolutely impossible for enemy bombers to get within five hundred miles of Tokyo. Instead of worrying about such foolish things, the Japanese people are enjoying the fine spring sunshine and the fragrance of cherry blossoms."

When Admiral Halsey was informed of the bizarre report, he was alarmed. He knew that if this news was true, the Japanese would be on the alert for a follow-up raid. They might even send out air patrols far east of Japan to search for American aircraft carriers.

Doolittle's men were also upset about the report, but for a different reason. They did not want anyone else to bomb Japan first. Now it looked as though someone had beaten them to it and they felt cheated, until Doolittle told them the report was not true.

Doolittle was certain the broadcast was false. If any other American bombing raid had been planned, Hap Arnold would surely have told him about it. To this day, this strange report from Radio Tokyo has never been satisfactorily explained.

Meanwhile, Japanese military leaders were worrying about the absence of additional radio reports from the U.S. ships whose location they had accurately plotted several days before. There had been no further interceptions of radio traffic. They were certain only that the American fleet had not come within the protective line of the picket ships. Some Japanese commanders argued that the American fleet was headed elsewhere, possibly to reinforce their position in the Aleutian Islands. Others suggested that the intercepts had been false reports or had been misinterpreted. But even if there were ships still heading toward Japan, there would be ample advance warning. Japan's military leaders remained confident that there could be no surprise raid.

As Halsey's task force continued on its westerly heading, the weather deteriorated. Heavy winds, rain, and high waves buffeted the ships, and visibility was often poor. In one sense, the rough weather was an advantage, for it helped shield the ships from any enemy observation. But it also meant the *Enterprise* could send out fewer air-reconnaissance patrols.

Scout planes took off, whenever conditions permitted, to search the seas up to two hundred miles ahead of the ships, but continuous daylight coverage had become impossible. Even when the scout planes were patrolling, they might miss enemy ships because of the cloud cover. Everyone's thoughts focused on the same thing: How much closer could they get to Japan without being detected? How much longer would their luck hold?

The pilots were growing concerned about taking off from the carrier in such rough seas and winds. One pilot climbed into the cockpit of his plane and was astounded to see the altimeter needle register a two-hundred-foot change in altitude as the carrier's bow rose and fell with the waves.

On April 17 the task force reached a position one thousand miles east of Japan. Halsey ordered the two oilers to refuel the carriers and cruisers. The weather worsened and huge swells threatened to swamp the tankers. No sooner had the fueling been completed and the hoses disconnected when the winds rose to thirty-eight knots, gale force.

Halsey ordered the cruisers and carriers to begin a high-speed run toward Japan, leaving the slower oilers and the destroyers behind. His ships held a speed of twenty to twenty-five knots, depending on the condition of the seas. If they could maintain that pace for twenty-four hours, they would arrive at the launching point, some five hundred miles off the coast, in midafternoon. Doolittle would be able to take off, as planned, three hours before sunset.

It was time to fuel and arm the bombers. The planes were spotted in their takeoff positions on the deck. Doolittle's B-25 was first in line, Bill Farrow's was last. The tail of Farrow's plane hung out over the stern. Two white parallel guidelines were painted down the length of the deck, one line for the nosewheel of the B-25s, the other for the left wheel. If the pilots followed the lines precisely on their takeoff runs, the right wingtip would clear the *Hornet*'s island superstructure by all of six feet.

Capt. Ross Greening supervised the army and navy crews in the demanding and tiring job of fueling the planes and loading them with bombs and machine-gun ammunition. The five-man flight crews of each plane began gathering their personal gear, packing B-4 musette bags, emergency rations, first-aid kits, pistols and other weapons, and unofficial supplies such as candy, cigarettes, a wind-up phonograph and records, and even extra rolls of toilet paper. Each man had his own priorities.

The planes were ready by dusk on the seventeenth. Doolittle called a meeting in the wardroom that evening for a final briefing for those going on the mission. He told them that it looked as though they would be taking off the next day instead of the nineteenth.

He reviewed the plan once more. He would take off first, about three hours before sunset. They would follow at sunset, guided by the fires started by his bombs. He told them to make sure they carried nothing that might link them with the *Hornet*—no letters, diaries, orders, not even a matchbook. He issued two specific warnings: "One, under no conditions would anyone go to Vladivostok; two, no nonmilitary targets, including the Temple of Heaven [the Imperial Palace], would be bombed."

Finally, Doolittle offered anyone who wished it one last chance to back out. No one did.

There was nothing the men could do after that but wait, and wonder, and try to win back some of their money from the navy in one last poker game. The success of the mission now depended on the carrier's remaining undetected for the next several hours and on the east China airfields being equipped to receive them.

★ ★ ★ ★

General Arnold was still trying to find out if the airfields were ready. Chiang Kai-shek—who had not yet been informed of the purpose of the mission—requested that the landing of the bombers be delayed until the end of May. He wanted time for his army to strengthen its positions around the airfields, so that the troops would be able to counter the expected Japanese attacks, once the enemy learned that American bombers had used the fields.

General Stilwell was occupied in Burma, so the responsibility for the preparations to receive Doolittle's fliers rested with his air adviser, Brig. Gen. Clayton Bissell. It was Bissell who had to deal with Chiang's unexpected request for a delay. Bissell radioed the Chinese leader's demand to Hap Arnold on April 11. Arnold passed it to

Marshall because the matter involved high-level dealings with an ally. Marshall informed Bissell that it was too late to delay the arrival of the planes. He reiterated that it was essential that the fields be ready to receive the bombers. On April 13, Arnold radioed Stilwell to repeat Marshall's message: the project could not be delayed.

Bissell met with Chiang for two days, trying to persuade him to accept the timetable. Finally, on April 15, Chiang "unwillingly agreed," as Bissell put it, to the use of all save one of the airfields, "inasmuch as no other course was possible." Chiang insisted that Chuchow not be used, for reasons he would not explain.

Bissell cabled the news to Arnold.

CHINESE AIR FORCE HAS ISSUED ORDERS TO ENSURE RAPID RE-FUELING AND THE FLARE RUNWAY MARKERS YOU REQUESTED AT ALL POINTS. HOMING RADIO AS PREVIOUSLY REPORTED WILL BE AVAILABLE AT KWEILIN, KIAN AND LISHUI. SIGNAL TRANSMITTED WILL CONSIST OF FIGURE 57, KEY HELD DOWN ONE MINUTE, FIGURE 57, KEY HELD DOWN ONE MINUTE, FIGURE 57, THEN OFF FOR ONE MINUTE. THIS SIGNAL WILL BE REPEATED CONTINUOUSLY FOR TWO HOURS ON THE DATE YOU SPECIFY. FLARES WILL BE BURNING DURING THE SAME TWO HOURS.

Arnold was gratified to receive this news, but he did not know of the mix-up with the date line. Neither, of course, did Bissell or the Chinese. Arnold radioed that "no change in plans or additional discussion of information regarding the project [is] feasible," and there was no further communication between Washington and Chungking about the Tokyo raid.

Some lingering doubts remained on one point. No American officer had been able to verify the existence of fuel and other preparations at the China airfields. Indeed, no American officer had been able to reach the fields, despite repeated attempts.

On April 3 an Army Air Force lieutenant by the name of Spurrier took off from Chungking in a C-39 (a DC-2 fuselage and wings, with a DC-3 tail) to try to reach the eastern airfields. It was raining hard, and the ceiling of only five hundred meters was the lowest ever recorded by China's meteorological service. The weather was so bad that Spurrier's commanding officer wrote that, "Neither Lieutenant Spurrier nor the C-39 [is] considered suitably equipped for the assigned mission." There is no official record of Spurrier's fate, but he never reached the east China airfields.

Ten days later, Lt. Col. E. H. Alexander, who had been sent from Karachi by General Brereton to take charge of the airfield preparations, tried to reach those fields. He and his copilot, Capt. Edward N. Backus, flew a DC-3 from Chungking to Chengtu, where they obtained two Curtiss Hawk-III fighter planes from the Chinese air force. They expected to visit the fields at Kweilin, Kian, Yushan, Chuchow, and Lishui, and issue orders to the Chinese personnel there.

Bissell gave them their instructions: "To alert the fields as of midnight 19–20 April, to supply them with landing flares and to provide for the lighting of flares at two hours before daylight on 20 April, to check on the fuel which was to have been assembled for the flight of the B-25s to Chungking, to arrange for the transmission of [direction finding] signals from these stations beginning at two hours before daylight on the morning of 20 April, and to ensure the presence of interpreters at each of the airdromes on that morning."

Alexander and Backus headed for Kweilin, but heavy rain and poor visibility forced them to turn back. They almost didn't make it. Alexander crash-landed on a sandbar in a river, and Backus was forced to bail out. Neither man was injured, but it took them four days to return to Chungking.

On April 17, as Doolittle's planes were being readied for the mission, Alexander and Backus took off from Chungking in a DC-3, accompanied by four Chinese radiomen who were to operate the homing radios at the airfields. The DC-3's radio failed while they were flying on instruments through heavy fog and rain, and they were forced down at Kunming, southwest of Chungking and farther from the air bases in the east.

The next day they tried again, but the weather was the same, and they were unable to establish radio contact with Kweilin, the largest of the eastern fields. The pilots returned to Kunming convinced that it was "impossible to make an instrumental letdown in the mountainous Kweilin area without radio aid." The following day they were ordered back to Chungking.

Thus, the U.S. Army Air Force command in Chungking had no confirmation of the status of the airfields. Even if the fields had been adequately supplied for Doolittle and his fliers, Chinese personnel at the bases were not prepared to receive them a day early. There would be no flares or homing signals to guide them. The weather forecast called for more rain, fog, and poor visibility. Without the radio signals, the pilots would be unable to locate the landing fields, and if by some miracle they did, the fuel they needed to go on to Chungking might not be there.

★ ★ ★ ★

Also on the night of April 17, Japanese civilian police called on the American and British embassies in Tokyo. Embassy personnel had been interned in their compounds pending arrangements for their repatriation. The police notified them that an air-raid drill would be held the next morning.

The American naval attaché, Capt. Henri Smith-Hutton, recalled that "there was a blackout, and we had complete blackout curtains in the embassy, the chancery, and in all buildings." This was not Tokyo's first air-raid drill, but, as Smith-Hutton said, "The drills held up to that time had not been very interesting."

★ ★ ★ ★

At 3:10 on the morning of April 18, a radar operator aboard the carrier *Enterprise* detected two ships 21,000 yards off the port bow, on a bearing of 255 degrees. Two minutes later, lookouts on the bridge spotted two lights on the same bearing. Admiral Halsey was informed at once. There was no doubt in his mind that the ships were Japanese. They probably could not see the task force because of the storm, but if they had radar, the two American carriers and their cruiser escorts would already have been detected.

Halsey immediately ordered a ninety-degree turn to starboard, course 350 degrees. The orders were transmitted to the other ships in the task force by short-range, high-frequency radio, which was difficult to detect beyond the range of the fleet itself. All ships went to general quarters, and Doolittle's men raced for their planes. Radar operators reported no change in the speed or course of the enemy ships, and no additional radio transmissions were heard. Perhaps the Japanese vessels had not discovered the task force after all.

At 3:41, blips indicating the two Japanese ships at a distance of 27,000 yards disappeared from the radar screens. Halsey reduced the state of alert, and the army fliers went below to grab some sleep. The task force maintained a northerly course until 4:15, when Halsey turned the ships westward, heading toward Japan once more. They had lost two hours and were more than forty miles farther from the launch point than they should have been. Launch time was less than eleven hours away, and they had to cover more than two hundred miles of open sea to reach it.

At 5:08, the first light of dawn, Halsey ordered three Dauntless scout planes out on morning patrol. Rain squalls, strong winds, and thirty-foot waves lashed the ships. The sky was slate gray, and the search planes quickly disappeared in the overcast.

One of the planes, piloted by Lt. O. B. Wiseman, reappeared low over the deck of the *Enterprise* at 7:15. Wiseman's rear gunner slid open his hatch and dropped a beanbag message container. It carried bad news. Wiseman had seen a ship about the size of a tugboat forty-two miles ahead of the task force. He thought the ship had spotted him.

Halsey ordered another course change, but still in a westerly direction. If the crewmen of the Japanese ship had seen Wiseman's single-engine plane, they would know it could only have come from a carrier, and they might already have reported this fact to navy headquarters in Japan. Until Halsey knew for certain that his ships had been spotted, however, he would continue to head for the launch point. The closer he could bring Doolittle's men to Japan's coast, the better would be their chances of reaching China.

Aboard the *Hornet*, Doolittle went up to the bridge to wait with Captain Mitscher. At 7:44, lookouts on the *Hornet* sighted a fishing boat at ten thousand yards. If the lookouts could spot such a small craft, surely the Japanese aboard her would have no difficulty seeing the much larger ships of the task force. As Halsey wrote in his official after-action report, "There was no doubt now that our force had been detected and almost certainly had been reported."

Minutes later, the *Hornet*'s radio operator intercepted a Japanese radio transmission. The message read: "Three enemy carriers sighted at our position 650 nautical miles east of Inubo Saki at 0630 [Tokyo time]." * The boat sending the message was Number 23, *Nitto Maru*, one of the ring of picket boats that formed Japan's early warning system. *Nitto Maru* had done her job well.

Halsey ordered the cruiser USS *Nashville* to sink the picket boat. He considered the possibility that the boat's initial radio message had not been received in Japan because of atmospheric interference, but if she was allowed to continue to transmit, the message would reach Japan eventually. The cruiser opened fire on the tiny target from a distance of nine thousand yards, but all of her shells missed.

"This was real warfare," Jake DeShazer said, watching from the deck of the *Hornet*. "The big guns were booming, and it looked as though the whole side of the cruiser was on fire."

The *Nashville* moved in closer, and her captain ordered continuous fire, but the target was too small and the sea too rough. The shells appeared to strike the tops of the waves just as the Japanese ship disappeared in the troughs.

One of the pilots from the *Enterprise* dove on the enemy, raking the target with .50-caliber machine-gun fire. He dropped a bomb, but it missed by one hundred feet. The *Nashville* fired again, closing on the picket boat.

Steve Jurika saw it all from the *Hornet*'s bridge. "There were heavy swells," he recalled, "and the picket boat was going up, it would be on top of a swell and then it could be seen, then it would be down, and you couldn't see a thing except perhaps the top of its mast. The splashes were all around it, but it was still there."

Halsey was getting angrier by the minute. He ordered the *Nash-*

* Inubo Saki, the site of a lighthouse sixty-three miles east of Tokyo, is the easternmost point of the country.

*ville* to close to point-blank range. The cruiser's skipper turned to port to bring all his gun turrets to bear. The first broadside missed. So did the second. The third salvo hit, and the *Nitto Maru*, which was nothing more than a fishing trawler outfitted with a radio and a machine gun, went down. The bombardment lasted twenty-nine minutes, and the cruiser fired 924 rounds of six-inch shells.

During those twenty-nine minutes, the situation of the task force had grown increasingly precarious. The radio transmission from the *Nitto Maru* had provided Tokyo with the first confirmation in ten days of the location of the American fleet. Several messages were dispatched to the *Nitto Maru* requesting verification, but the fishing boat did not answer the calls.

Rear Adm. Matome Ugaki, Yamamoto's chief of staff, then at the Hashirajima naval base, south of Hiroshima, responded at once to the American threat by issuing Order Number 3 [a contingency plan to repel an American fleet off the coast]. Ugaki had ample resources to attack the advancing American ships, including thirty-five planes recently returned from the Philippines, sixty-three planes from the aircraft carrier *Kaga*, ninety fighters, eighty medium bombers, thirty-six carrier bombers, and two flying boats.

The Japanese Second Fleet, consisting of ten destroyers and six heavy cruisers, under the command of Vice Adm. Nobutake Kondo, had just returned from the Indian Ocean. A five-carrier task force of the First Air Fleet, under Vice Adm. Chuichi Naguma, was on its way back from the Indian Ocean and now south of Formosa. Nine submarines were within range of the American ships, three of them only two hundred miles west of Halsey's task force. Admiral Ugaki ordered all ships to head toward the location reported by the *Nitto Maru*.

Ugaki expected the American ships to approach to within three hundred miles of the coast to launch their planes. Unaware of the *Hornet*'s cargo of twin-engine B-25 bombers, he based his calculations on navy single-engine carrier planes. He believed that by the time the U.S. ships reached the three-hundred-mile point, his ships and submarines would be waiting for them.

Aboard the *Enterprise*, Admiral Halsey had been forced to conclude that his task force had been discovered. His Japanese-language officer had intercepted and decoded enough Japanese radio traffic to report that several enemy naval units were suddenly on the move. The most alarming of these intercepts pertained to the huge carrier force of the First Air Fleet, which Halsey had thought was still in the Indian Ocean. As far as his language officer could determine, those carriers were now close to Japan. The surge of radio messages to these ships would certainly involve a change of orders. Halsey had to assume that they, and other naval units, were coming after his task force.

He had no choice. He had to launch Doolittle's men immediately, even though the launch point was 150 miles away. Halsey knew an early launch meant that the army fliers would have little chance of surviving. What had been a well-calculated risk was fast becoming, as he had feared, a suicide mission. The bombers would be able to reach Japan, but now the raid would be in daylight. And with the enemy forewarned, Doolittle and his men might well be shot down by fighter planes before they reached their targets. With the loss of surprise and the extra distance to cover, the chances of their flying on to the airfields in China were almost nonexistent. As Hank Miller colorfully put it, "We knew that the pilots really didn't have a Chinaman's chance of getting to China."

The alternative—aborting the raid and dumping the bombers overboard—was unacceptable to Halsey and to Doolittle. They retained some hope that the plan would work. What could not be risked, however, were Halsey's ships. Their safety was his primary consideration. His carriers represented half the carrier strength of the U.S. Pacific Fleet, and his cruisers and destroyers, if damaged or lost, could not easily or quickly be replaced.

Halsey could not take Doolittle any closer to Japan. They were already within range of Japanese land-based bombers, and they knew Japanese ships and carrier planes were on the way.

In his after-action report to Admiral Nimitz, Halsey termed the early launching of the B-25s "regrettable." A week later, he wrote to Doolittle: "I hated to dump you off at that distance, but because of discovery there was nothing else to do." Halsey would be criticized by some Army Air Force officers—and by some navy officers as well—for jeopardizing the success of the bombing raid by ordering the planes off early, but it was the only decision he could make under the circumstances.

Captain Mitscher of the *Hornet* agreed. "We had to launch them," he wrote. "We weren't where we wanted to be. We gave them extra gas. It was all a calculated risk. We couldn't risk [the carriers] after the fishing boats had been spotted."

At eight o'clock in the morning, while the *Nashville* was trying to sink the fishing trawler *Nitto Maru*, Halsey issued the order. It was flashed by blinker light to the *Hornet*.

LAUNCH PLANES.
TO COLONEL DOOLITTLE AND GALLANT COMMAND:
GOOD LUCK AND GOD BLESS YOU.
HALSEY.

# Army Pilots, Man
# Your Planes

When Mitscher received Halsey's message, he glanced at Doolittle and shrugged his shoulders.

"You know the score, Jimmy," he said.

Doolittle nodded. "We'll get off as soon as possible, Pete."

He shook hands with Mitscher and left the bridge. The klaxon screamed, followed by an announcement.

"ARMY PILOTS, MAN YOUR PLANES."

Pilot Bill Bower, when asked nearly thirty years later if he remembered that announcement, said, "Do I remember it? I can hear it today. I can see that little cabin that we stayed in for eighteen days. I can't tell you the way from the cabin to the airplanes, but it went past the ship's store. . . . I stopped and bought a pack or a carton of Lucky Strikes, and went up to the machine with my B-4 bag."

Sailors and airmen converged on the B-25s. Many of Doolittle's men were caught by surprise by the announcement. Some had been asleep or resting in their cabins, others just getting up or eating breakfast. Many of them were unaware of the morning's sinking of the Japanese fishing trawler, and considered the alarm to be another practice drill. They found out otherwise when they joined the frenzied activity engulfing the slippery, pitching flight deck.

Sailors tore the canvas covers from the engine cowlings and turrets, pulled the chocks away from the wheels, and unfastened the ropes that lashed the planes to the deck. The navy tractor called the Donkey maneuvered the planes into takeoff positions on the aft end of the deck, positioning them two abreast.

When the planes were in place and chocks slipped back around the wheels, sailors topped off the fuel tanks to replace any gasoline lost through evaporation. When the tanks were full, the navy men rocked the planes back and forth by the wingtips to break up any air bubbles that might have formed. With the bubbles dissipated, the men were able to add a few more quarts to each tank. They knew how desperate the need would be for fuel. They filled the ten five-gallon cans for each plane and hoisted them aboard through the rear hatches.

The *Hornet*'s control-tower personnel on the bridge hung large square cards on the side facing the planes to display in large numbers the compass heading and wind speed, which was now in excess of twenty-seven knots. Someone—no one remembers who—discovered that the five-hundred-pound bombs already in the planes' bomb bays had not yet been armed. Bombardiers attended to that while the incendiaries were brought up on deck and loaded in the planes.

The navigators converged on the *Hornet*'s navigation room to get the latest reports on the weather over Japan and China. They determined the precise location of the carrier at the moment, and the direction and force of the winds they would encounter on their flight to their targets. They found, to their dismay, that they would have a twenty-four-knot head wind all the way to Japan, causing them to burn more fuel than they had counted on.

Capt. Davey Jones discovered a serious problem with his B-25. The night before, a leak had been found in the bomb bay fuel tank. Sailors had patched it, but the tank had to remain empty overnight. By the time the fuel hoses were cut off to all planes so that the lead plane could start its engines, Jones's fuel gauge indicated that the left wing tank was still thirty gallons short. It was too late to add any more.

Pilot Harold "Doc" Watson was distressed by the haste of the mechanics as they rushed through a last-minute change of spark plugs in his ship. Watson and his crew were left to wonder whether there had been time to do the job correctly, and if the new plugs would affect their gas consumption.

As the men climbed aboard their planes, the standby crews cheered. "Lucky devils," they shouted. Some offered up to $150 to change places with their buddies who were making the raid. One copilot expressed amazement that men were willing to pay so much money for the chance to die. Ens. Don Kirkpatrick, one of the *Hornet*'s pilots, recalled that his two Army Air Force roommates wanted to go with Doolittle just to get off the carrier. They had been seasick for days.

Some of the Raiders held a less sanguine view. Jake DeShazer's pilot asked him if he knew how to row a boat, and a sergeant told him, "We just got one chance in a thousand of making it."

Jack Hilger told his crew that they did not have enough fuel to get to China. "The way things are now," he said, "we have about enough to get us to within two hundred miles of the China coast, and that's all. If anyone wants to withdraw, he can do it now." None of them took up his offer.

Gasoline was on the minds of most of the pilots. "It took some figuring," Ted Lawson said, "and the sums I arrived at . . . gave me a sudden emptiness in the stomach."

Hank Miller, who had instructed them in carrier takeoffs, went from plane to plane. He climbed into the cockpit of each one and shook every pilot's hand, wishing him luck. "I wish to hell I could go with you," he said.

Captain Mitscher turned the carrier into the wind. He told his chief engineer, Comdr. Pat Creehan, to give him as much speed as he could crank out of the engines. The more head wind Mitscher could give the planes, the better their chances of making it off the deck.

Doolittle climbed into the lead ship, settled in the pilot's seat, and began the routine preflight check with his copilot, Dick Cole. Lt. Edgar "Ozzie" Osborn, the *Hornet*'s flight deck officer, remembered that "on the way down the flight deck to man his plane, Jimmy Doolittle stopped to shake the hands of many of us and wish us luck. Imagine that."

Heavy waves rocked the ship as it ploughed ahead, plunging through them. Water broke over the deck, sending cascades of stinging salt spray over the airplanes. To the fliers, the deck of the USS *Hornet* had never looked so small.

As each plane was signaled in turn, it was time to start engines. The pilot spoke to the navigator on the interphone, asking if the battery disconnect, generator-ignition safety, and active inverter switches were all in the "on" position. When assured that they were, the pilot nodded to the copilot, who set the booster pump switch on, turned on the engine primer switch, and primed the engine for about four seconds. The copilot set the fire-extinguisher switch on, then pressed the engaging switch and the pressure energizing switch and held them in the "on" position until the engine caught. The procedure was repeated to start the other engine.

When the engines were running, the copilot kept an eye on the oil-pressure gauge. If the pressure did not reach forty pounds per square inch after thirty seconds, he would need to shut down the engine instantly and find out what was wrong. That was standard operating procedure. But here there would be no time to determine what was wrong. The plane would have to be quickly shoved overboard so that the ones in line behind it could take off.

Nobody had to shut down an engine. No planes were pushed overboard. Every engine was warmed up at twelve hundred RPM until the oil temperature gauge showed an increase and the oil pressure stayed steady as the throttle was gently advanced. The copilot set the booster pump switch off and opened the oil-cooler shutter controls to an oil temperature of forty degrees Centigrade.

The pilot, while double-checking temperature and oil pressure readings, made sure the elevator, aileron, and rudder trim tab controls were all in their proper positions. The copilot checked that the wing-flap control handle was in the "close" position. He checked each magneto at about two thousand RPM by rapidly turning each ignition switch off and on again. Next he asked the navigator to monitor the voltmeter and ammeter readings.

This was all a fast, studied routine in which few words needed to be exchanged. Pilot and copilot had rehearsed the sequence many times. So far, it could have been part of any standard training flight back at Eglin.

But when they looked up from the familiar array of dials, switches, knobs, pumps, and lights around the cockpit, and down the short length of the planked wooden deck heaving before them, with huge waves breaking over the bow as it plunged, and a man holding a checkered flag waiting for them at the far left end of the deck, the routine ended.

None of them had ever done this before. At that moment, everyone—sailors and airmen, Captain Mitscher on the bridge and Ozzie Osborn with his checkered flag—kept his eyes on Doolittle's plane.

Doolittle shot a quick glance at Mitscher up on the bridge, and waved. Mitscher saluted in return. He was worried that the plane would not get airborne and would drop off the deck, to be sliced in half by the knife edge of the bow. They all knew that if Doolittle couldn't take off, then maybe none of them could. If the other pilots saw Doolittle's plane lumber down the rain-slicked deck and disappear below the bow, they might be so unnerved that they would follow him in. The next three minutes were crucial.

It was 8:17 in the morning, April 18, 1942, four months and eleven days since the Japanese attack on Pearl Harbor.

Ozzie Osborn, whose judgment would determine when the pilots began their takeoff runs, braced himself against the wind-driven spray at his back, raised the checkered flag over his head, and waved it in a circle, the signal for Doolittle to advance his throttles. The B-25's twin engines began to roar. As the blast from the propellers hit the flat surface of the flaps, the whole plane vibrated. Osborn waved the flag faster and in a wider circle, and Doolittle pushed the throttles farther forward. The plane strained to pull ahead, and the noise of the engines drowned out the howl of the wind across the deck. Faster and faster Osborn twirled the flag, the circle getting larger and larger. Doolittle had the throttles all the way to the wall, and the plane felt as if it were shaking itself to pieces.

Osborn carefully gauged the rise and fall of the deck. When he judged that the moment was right, he brought his arm down in a brisk chop. Knowing the instant to signal the plane to start rolling was critical. Steve Jurika described it this way: "You knew how long it would take them to run down that deck . . . and you wanted to start them as the bow started down because it would take them that length of time to get to within . . . fifty or seventy-five feet of the bow, and then, as the deck started to come up, you would actually launch them into the air at least horizontal but on the upswing, in fact giving them a boost into the air."

Osborn and Hank Miller worked as a team to launch the planes. "Hank, who was more familiar with the B-25, checked the plane just prior to launching to make sure it was all in order from our viewpoint, including the sound of the engines and the flaps being down. I watched the pitching of the carrier to make sure the bow of the ship was on its way up at the time the plane reached the bow. After Hank gave me the thumbs-up and the pilot gave me the same signal, I gave the flag signal for takeoff."

When Osborn's arm came down, Doolittle took his feet off the brakes, and the deck crewmen yanked the chocks away from the wheels and threw themselves flat on the deck. The heavily laden B-25 started slowly down the deck. A navy pilot, watching it waddle forward, shouted that it wasn't going to make it. Mitscher hunched his shoulders and tensed his arms as if he were flying the plane himself.

With the nosewheel and the left wheel riding the white guidelines, the plane began to pick up speed. "I felt perfectly comfortable," Doolittle said, "because there was a thirty-knot wind. I knew that had there been a dead calm, [the carrier] could have made about thirty knots, but as it was, there was about a thirty-knot wind. In those heavy seas, the carrier was still making something over twenty knots, so we had over a fifty-knot wind across the deck. . . . That was a life saver."

A few yards before the end of the deck, the B-25 lifted into the air. Doolittle yanked the control yoke back into his stomach. "He hung his ship almost straight up on its props," Ted Lawson said, "until we could see the whole top of his B-25. Then he leveled off and I watched him come around in a tight circle and shoot low over our heads—straight down the line painted on the deck." "I didn't think he would make it," Jake DeShazer said, "and felt a lot better when I saw the wheels leave the deck in less than four hundred feet of takeoff space." In his report on the raid, Doolittle said simply, "Takeoff was easy."

The cheers from the *Hornet*'s crew were so loud they could be heard over the wind and the engines. Trav Hoover taxied his plane to the takeoff point, the sailors threw chocks around his wheels, and the tension began again. Hoover ran up his engines in response to Osborn's checkered flag and started down the runway when Osborn gave the signal. The plane picked up speed, but as the wheels came off the deck, Hoover held the nose up too long. The engines were on the brink of a stall. The plane was nose-high and tail-low, and it started to fall toward the sea.

Hank Miller remembered that Hoover "pulled that nose up just like a fighter and I thought he was going to spin in, but he just pushed it over and away he went." Hoover leveled off, climbed, and banked into a steep right turn. Like Doolittle, he roared over the deck of the *Hornet* and headed for Japan.

Flying low the length of the deck was not some grandstand play or dramatic farewell gesture, but was part of the plan for the mission. By flying past the bridge, the pilots and navigators could get a last reading on the carrier's compass heading, which was displayed on the cards hung on the control tower. The maneuver also enabled them to check their compasses and drift sights by lining up the sights on the white line on the flight deck.

The next four planes took off without incident. When it was Ted Lawson's turn, he lowered his flaps while revving the engines, but the plane shook so hard he temporarily pulled them up again. Ozzie Osborn rotated the flag over his head in faster circles. Lawson fed more gas to the engines. He was worried about the port engine, which had been slow to start.

Lawson kept his eyes on the twirling flag and his feet on the brakes as he advanced the throttles. Fifteen seconds passed, and Osborn still had not dropped the flag. Finally, after thirty seconds of full power, Osborn jerked the flag down, and Lawson and his crew were on their way—toward the left side of the flight deck. A strong gust of wind forced the plane toward the port side as soon as the brakes were released. Lawson tapped the brake pedals and yanked the wheels back on the white lines. Before he knew it, he was over the water. He banked and gained altitude and reached with his right hand to pull up the flaps. That was when he realized he had never put them down again.

"Imagine our feeling," Osborn said, "as we saw that plane going up the deck without flaps, drop over the ship's bow, and skim the tops of the waves for what seemed like an eternity before starting to climb."

The next plane was Ski York's, with Bob Emmens as copilot. "Make damned sure those throttles don't slip back," York yelled to Emmens as they raced the engines and watched Osborn wave his flag. The signal came, and the plane began to roll forward, slowly at first, then faster. "The island of the carrier was lost from sight as it passed a bare eight feet away from our right wingtip," Emmens said, "and then like a big living thing, our plane seemed to leap into the air just as the deck of the ship disappeared under us.

"Now ease up a little on the controls . . . just enough to let her nose drop and pick up flying speed. Wheels up. Now she's leveling out nicely. Airspeed up within safe limits. Now start taking off flaps, throttles back to save that precious gasoline. We adjusted our power settings and checked our compass. And then we breathed again."

Emmens chuckled as he thought about the substantial supply of razor blades, candy, and cigarettes he had purchased aboard the *Hornet* and stowed away on the plane. It was funny buying so much when he knew the mission would be over in a day and he'd be heading back to the States soon. He'd been acting as though he planned to be away for a year!

By 9:10 that morning, the fifteenth plane, piloted by Don Smith, was ready to taxi to the takeoff position. The instant the preceding plane—Jack Hilger's—had lifted off, Osborn signaled Smith to move forward. Smith nudged the throttles, but the plane stayed put. He checked the brakes and then discovered that the wheel chocks were still in place. Once the sailors removed them, it took a full three minutes to taxi into position because he could only do so when the bow angled down.

At the takeoff point, with his brakes locked and flaps down, Smith pushed the throttles forward as Osborn moved the checkered flag in ever-greater circles. The flag came down, and Smith started toward the bow. Near the end of his run, the bow dropped unexpectedly, leaving the plane suddenly airborne before it had achieved the proper altitude. Fortunately, his ninety-mile-per-hour speed was sufficient, and Smith made his turn, flew over the carrier, and sped into the mist, trying to catch Hilger, who was already out of sight.

The last plane, named *Bat Out of Hell* by Bill Farrow and his crew, had a tough time from the start. Last in line, with its tail overhanging the stern, not all of the crew could board or load supplies through the rear hatch until the plane moved forward. Just before Farrow was ready to begin taxiing, the propwash from Don Smith's plane caught the nose and lifted it in the air. The plane tilted, tail down, but there was no deck beneath it, only open water. Farrow was in danger of sliding backward into the sea.

Sailors scrambled to lash ropes to the nose hooks, but they snapped. Jake DeShazer, who had yet to board, helped the seamen grab for the nose, and they managed to force it down by hand. As they did, one of the sailors, Robert Wall, slipped on the deck and lost his grip. The wind tossed him into one of the whirling propellers, nearly severing his arm. He survived the accident but his arm was amputated later that day. George Barr, Farrow's navigator, was so upset by the accident that he wondered if it wasn't a harbinger of some greater tragedy.

Moments later, with the plane in takeoff position, DeShazer climbed into the bombardier's compartment and discovered a jagged hole about twelve inches across in the Plexiglas nose. Apparently the B-25 had at some point bumped into the rear of Smith's plane. It was too late to fix it, of course. There was no choice but to take off and fly at 150 miles per hour with a gaping hole in the plane's nose.

Farrow finally got airborne at 9:19, fifty-nine minutes after Doolittle's lead plane. As that last plane flew over the carrier and headed west, DeShazer noticed that the task force was already changing course. The navy had done its job.

★ ★ ★ ★

As soon as the sixteenth army bomber had cleared the deck, Admiral Halsey issued orders to his ships. The log of the *Enterprise* noted, "Changed fleet course and axis to 090, commencing retirement from the area at 25 knots." This fast getaway was a maneuver that had become well known throughout the Pacific. The men called it hauling ass with Halsey.

They were not running scared, but there was no need to linger. They felt reasonably safe from Japanese attack for several reasons. "First of all," said Steve Jurika, "the Zeroes wouldn't come out [approximately six hundred miles]. They'd never get back. Second, if the Japanese sent out bombers, they'd have to send some pathfinders out first, and, in the meantime, we'd be making fair speed in the opposite direction. They wouldn't know where the planes came from, so they'd really have to launch about a 180-degree search from the northeast coast of Honshu all the way round to the south. This meant that they wouldn't launch other aircraft for, oh, hours, and we'd be so far out of range that even the bombers wouldn't have a chance to get out and back. So I don't think anybody was fearful. Nobody was worried."

The Japanese were worried, however, because they had not heard any more from the *Nitto Maru* about its sighting of the American carrier fleet. At 9:45, a long-range Japanese navy patrol plane reported two twin-engine planes on a heading for Japan. Navy headquarters discounted the report. They knew that American carriers had no twin-engine aircraft. (The planes spotted by the Japanese patrol plane were the first two off the *Hornet*, piloted by Doolittle and Hoover.)

At ten-thirty, more Japanese patrol planes were ordered to scout the waters east of Japan as far as six hundred miles out. A strike force of thirty-two medium bombers, escorted by twelve Zero fighters, was also sent eastward. Before long, however, the weather between the islands of Japan and the task force worsened, resulting in limited visibility. The planes turned back to their bases before noon.

Aboard the *Hornet*, every man who could be spared, including the navy pilots, worked to prepare the carrier's planes to resume normal operations. On the hangar deck, the F4F Grumman Wildcat fighters had been lashed to the overhead, and the Douglas SBD Dauntless dive bombers and Douglas TBD-1 Devastator torpedo planes had had their wings removed and stacked together to save space. The wings had to be bolted back on and all the planes brought up to the flight deck on the elevators, an exhausting and time-consuming job.

At 12:14, a radar operator on the *Enterprise* reported an enemy aircraft at a distance of seventy thousand yards on a bearing of 20 degrees. The plane came to within 64,000 yards before disappearing from the screen at 12:28. It flew off without spotting the American ships.

At 2:10, lookouts sighted two Japanese picket boats. Planes from the *Enterprise* just returning from a routine patrol attacked the boats, sinking one and damaging the other. The cruiser *Nashville* was ordered to sink the damaged boat. She commenced firing at a distance of 4,500 yards. After twenty minutes, the five survivors of the eleven-man crew of the picket boat ran up a white flag and surrendered.

One of the captured Japanese sailors later described the moment he saw the *Enterprise* and the *Hornet*. Never suspecting the ships could be American, he awakened the picket boat's skipper to tell him that two beautiful Japanese aircraft carriers lay ahead. The skipper rushed up on deck, examined the ships through his binoculars, and said to the sailor, "Indeed they are beautiful, but they are not ours." The skipper returned to his cabin and shot himself in the head.

At 2:25, one of the *Enterprise*'s planes, apparently hit by return fire from the picket boats, crashed off the *Hornet*'s bow while she was launching planes. The pilot and gunner were rescued by the *Nashville*. During the week it took for the task force to return to Pearl Harbor, there were no further contacts with the enemy.

That night, Comdr. Stanhope Cotton Ring, the *Hornet*'s air group commander, wrote a poem for the next day's edition of the ship's newspaper, with apologies to Henry Wadsworth Longfellow. It began:

> *'Twas the eighteenth of April in forty-two*
> *When we waited to hear what Jimmy would do,*
> *Little did Hiro think that night*
> *The skies above Tokyo would be alight*
> *With the fires Jimmy started in Tokyo's dives*
> *To guide to their targets the B-25s.*

In his after-action report, Captain Mitscher wrote that "morale was somewhat lowered after danger of enemy air attack had diminished; a majority of the officers and men were quite surprised that no further action against enemy bases was contemplated, and were obviously disappointed." He went on to recommend that attacks be made as often as possible to maintain morale and what he called "action exhilaration" in a high state.

Mitscher faulted the way Doolittle and his men had left his carrier. "With only one exception," he wrote, "takeoffs were dangerous and improperly executed. Apparently full back stabilizer was used by the first few pilots. As each plane neared the bow, with more than required speed, the pilot would pull up and climb in a dangerous near-stall, struggle wildly to nose down, then fight the controls for several miles trying to gain real flying speed and more than a hundred feet altitude. Lieutenant Miller, USN, held up a blackboard of final instructions for the pilots, but few obeyed."

It was true that the Army Air Force fliers did not take off in prescribed navy fashion, but if, as the saying goes, any landing you can walk away from is a good one, then perhaps it is equally true that any takeoff you can fly away from is a good one. Nevertheless, the navy had brought the Doolittle fliers sufficiently near to Japan to undertake their mission. Without the navy's efforts, there would have been no raid on Tokyo so soon after the war began.

The task force sailed uneventfully back to Pearl Harbor, the only major problem being a lack of fresh food. The men ate lots of rice, beans, and potatoes. Jurika recalled, "They had stocked the fantail with cases and cases of potatoes, all of them were sprouting. Everything was sprouting. We'd been out of eggs for some time. Our menu was fairly limited. It was down to staples. I remember we had canned beef, lots of Spam, and all kinds of pressed meats."

It was a small price to pay for their achievements. "We felt a sense of accomplishment," Jurika said, "in getting them off, and getting off a strike at Japan."

★ ★ ★ ★

The practice air-raid drill began on schedule in Tokyo at almost the same time the sixteenth B-25 cleared the *Hornet*'s deck. It was a low-key drill, announced in the newspapers well in advance. There was not even the shriek of sirens to lend excitement or authenticity. Many such drills had been conducted in the last months, and they had become so routine that most people ignored them. There was no reason to pay attention to an air-raid drill anymore. The people had been told repeatedly that the sacred soil of the Japanese homeland was inviolable, that no enemy could ever bomb it.

The drill on April 18, 1942, was at the level of alert known as "first alarm," which meant that the citizens of Tokyo were not required to go to the air-raid shelters. Firefighting companies demonstrated their equipment in the streets and air-raid wardens stood at their posts. At the U.S. Embassy, the officials took only the most perfunctory steps required by Japanese regulations. At the British Embassy, two firefighting squads turned out with their equipment, but put it away after a half hour. By eleven o'clock in the morning, the designated air-raid warden at the U.S. Embassy had gone to play golf.

A large number of planes flew over Tokyo during the drill, but they were not connected with it. Tokyo residents had been told about the flights two days before. The planes were rehearsing for the forthcoming celebration of the emperor's birthday and the simultaneous dedication of a shrine to Japan's war dead. Fighter planes chased each other in mock dogfights. Below them, along the waterfront, barrage balloons were raised and lowered.

As the noon hour approached, all these activities came to an end. The barrage balloons were taken down, and most of the planes landed at airfields around the city. A few fighter planes circled overhead, and others were placed on alert on their runways, but these were not extraordinary precautions.

At the U.S. Embassy, one of the staff members had received permission to visit his doctor. He set out shortly after noon by streetcar. The people of Tokyo went about their ordinary Saturday activities, and the streets and sidewalks were crowded as usual. The weather was pleasant. The city was at peace.

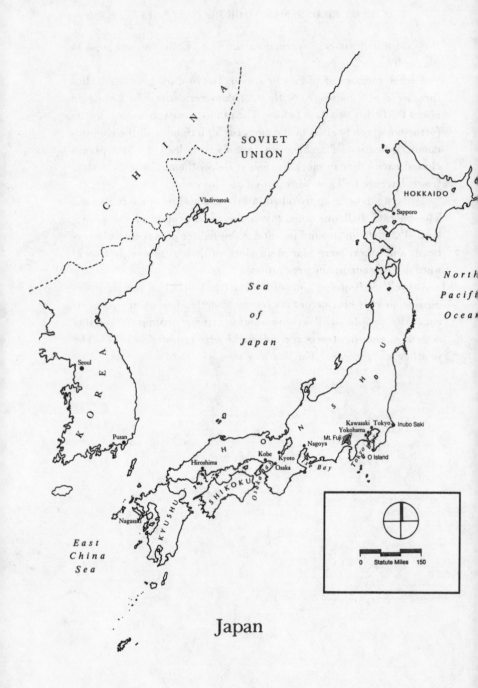

Japan

# They Were
# Shooting at Us

Doolittle and his crew flew alone for the first half hour after leaving the carrier, maintaining an altitude of no more than two hundred feet above the sea. Trav Hoover's plane joined them, keeping behind to follow them to Japan. Thirty minutes later the bombers passed a ship that Doolittle identified as a light cruiser of the Japanese navy. If the enemy did not yet know the planes were coming—if the message dispatched by the picket boat that morning had now been received—then surely the cruiser would now be radioing a warning. And that meant the enemy would be waiting for them.

Doolittle turned the controls over to Dick Cole, the copilot, and checked on the plane's position with the navigator, Hank Potter. So far, they were right on schedule, although they were bucking strong head winds, which lowered their fuel consumption. Doolittle took back the controls, and after another hour's flying, the two B-25s passed beneath a Japanese patrol plane heading for the task force at an altitude of three thousand feet. The weather was clearing and soon the sun came out. The sky was beautiful but deadly. It offered no place to hide.

Around noon, after more than four hours of flying, Doolittle spotted the coast of Japan. There were no fighters waiting for them, and that was a relief, but he quickly realized they were not where they were supposed to be. He spoke to Potter on the interphone.

"We're either fifty miles north of Tokyo or fifty miles south of it."

"I think we're about thirty miles north," Potter said.

Doolittle didn't answer. It was his job to decide which way to turn, and as they crossed the coast, he knew he'd have to make his mind up fast.

★ ★ ★ ★

About fifty miles behind Doolittle and Hoover, Brick Holstrom and his crew were having problems. Holstrom held steady to a course of 270 degrees, unaware that his compass was off by 15 degrees. As he roared over the water at seventy-five feet, he heard his engineer-gunner, Bert Jordan, trying to get through on the interphone, but Holstrom could not catch the words. Until the fuel stored in the crawl space's collapsible tank above the bomb bay was used up, there was no way Jordan could get to the cockpit. Whatever he wanted, it would have to wait.

About forty-five minutes later, Holstrom spotted a freighter. The ship immediately began to take evasive action, which puzzled Holstrom because he knew no one aboard the ship could see their insignia from that angle. There was only one explanation. The captain of the ship must have known that American planes were in the area. And if they knew, then authorities on the Japanese mainland would also have been alerted. By now they would probably have fighter planes up and antiaircraft gunners at the ready.

Holstrom and his copilot, Lucian Youngblood, discussed the idea of a course change to approach Tokyo from the south, a different direction from the B-25s ahead of them. That way, there might be less chance of running into Japanese fighters. They agreed to try it, and the navigator, Harry McCool, gave them a new course that would bring them to landfall just south of the city.

Shortly after they altered course, Jordan was able to collapse the crawl-space fuel tank and make his way to the cockpit. He had bad news for Holstrom. The gun turret was jammed, leaving their main armament, the twin .50-caliber machine guns, useless. Jordan also reported a slow leak around the gas cap of the left wing tank.

At twelve-thirty, still skimming the waves at seventy-five feet, Holstrom crossed the coast. Although they were south of Tokyo, because of the compass error they were much farther south than expected, some eighty miles off course. They would need to cover an extra 160 miles to reach their target and head south again for China, and now they had less gas than planned because of the leak. Holstrom did not hesitate. He turned toward the target.

★ ★ ★ ★

Ted Lawson was also worried about gas consumption. Shortly after takeoff, he ordered his engineer-gunner, Dave Thatcher, to fill the wing tanks from fuel in the five-gallon cans. He found it depressing to realize that *Ruptured Duck* had burned up forty gallons of gas on the flight deck of the *Hornet*, just warming up the engines and taking off. He was flying as low as he dared—about twenty feet above the water—and as slow as he could, to the point where the controls felt mushy. Although the plane was harder to fly, the low speed used less gas.

Then there was the problem with the top turret. It had stopped working the day before, and neither his crew nor the navy mechanics had been able to fix it. The twenty-four-volt generator was not functioning properly and was unable to provide power for the turret. Lawson called Thatcher on the interphone and asked him to try the turret again. An alternative was for Lawson to turn on the emergency switch in the cockpit that fed power to the turret directly from the battery. They could not maintain a constant drain on the battery, however, and it was awkward for the pilot to have to activate the switch every time the gunner wanted to fire.

Dean Davenport, the copilot, summed up the situation. "Damn, boy," he said, "this is serious."

Not long after that, Lawson spotted a small, dark object hurtling toward them. There was no time to evade it, and as the thing passed close by the left wing, Lawson recognized it as a gas can. Peering ahead, he could make out the shapes of two B-25s and realized he had almost been hit by a can tossed out of one of their own planes. Had it struck a prop, they would have crashed. They were far too low to bail out.

They passed a large Japanese freighter. Some of the men wanted to bomb it, convinced that their position was being radioed to Japan and that the raid would no longer be a surprise.

After three hours of wrestling with the sluggish controls, Lawson and his copilot were worn out. He called Bob Clever, the bombardier, and told him to turn on the automatic pilot. Clever switched it on, but when Lawson removed his hands from the control yoke, the plane veered sharply to the left. The automatic pilot was not working.

The crew wondered what else might not be working when they spotted the coast of Japan. Like many of the other planes, their landfall position was wrong. Lawson's plane was north of Tokyo.

★ ★ ★ ★

Ski York and Bob Emmens had an easy flight in the beginning. The weather cleared, and a blue sky and bright sun hovered over them. Gunner Dave Pohl called the cockpit to announce that he had emptied the last of the five-gallon cans into the auxiliary tank. It was sooner than York and Emmens had expected, but there was no reason for concern.

They reset the throttles and the propeller pitch controls to compensate for the decrease in the amount of fuel on board. Twice they spotted small boats far ahead and changed course temporarily to avoid them. They did not want to risk having their location broadcast to Tokyo, or being shot down over water. They went on without incident until eleven o'clock, two hours and fifteen minutes into the flight, long enough to check the rate of fuel consumption. Emmens took over the controls while York did the calculations on a piece of paper.

He was stunned by the results. According to his figures, they were using gas at the rate of ninety-eight gallons per hour, when it should have been no more than seventy-five gallons per hour. He passed the paper to Emmens.

"Am I screwy, or are we burning this much gas?"

Emmens looked at the numbers. They appeared to be correct.

"If that's right," Emmens said, "we're not going to get *near* the Chinese coast."

They did not know why they were burning so much gas. Perhaps one of the tanks leaked or one of the gas gauges was giving a faulty reading. Or maybe it was the new carburetors the mechanics at McClellan had installed, the ones York and Emmens had found out about only by accident. Whatever the reason, they were in trouble.

Nolan Herndon, the navigator-bombardier, checked the level in the bomb-bay tank and confirmed that it was lower than it should have been.

"We figured on the carrier," York said, "that the auxiliary gasoline should last through Japan and that we would have to go on the main tanks sometime after that. About forty-five minutes before we got [to Japan], we had to go on the main tanks."

It was definite now—it would be impossible to reach the airfields in China. They didn't want to put down in Japan, and the idea of ditching in the China Sea was not appealing. That left only one option, to head north after they dropped their bombs, north to Russia. Maybe the Russians would give them fuel to get to China, assuming they did not shoot the B-25 down first.

York asked the navigator to plot a course from Tokyo to Russia.

"I guess you guys remember Doolittle didn't exactly issue a direct order not to go to Russia,* but he made it plenty obvious that it wasn't a good idea."

Suddenly, York pulled back on the control yoke to miss a seagull. The presence of the bird meant they were nearing land. York told the crew they would check the gas again when they reached Japan and then decide what to do.

Minutes later they saw the coast on the horizon. Ted LaBan, the flight engineer, climbed atop the big bomb-bay tank to read the

---

* In a 1983 interview with the United States Naval Institute, Doolittle said of York, "He went to Russia against orders." It is unlikely, however, that York would have saved the lives of his crew had he not gone to Russia. Also, it was not unreasonable for him to suppose that upon landing in the Soviet Union, which was an ally, he would be given enough fuel to get to Chungking.

gauge. His observation confirmed the worst. With the amount of gas remaining, they would not get closer than three hundred miles to China. York told Dave Pohl, the gunner, to jettison the empty gas cans and to take up position in the turret.

A ship sailing along the coast hove into view. At first they thought it was an aircraft carrier. York swerved to port to skirt the vessel and saw it was only a freighter. He steered clear of it anyway. Even a freighter might be armed, and as low as they were flying, they made a good target.

They were near enough to land to distinguish breakers on the beach. In a minute or two they would be over Japan herself. The navigator spoke over the interphone.

"Course from Tokyo to Vladivostok, 300 degrees."

"Damn it, Bob," York said to Emmens, "I can't get over that gas consumption. . . . I guess Russia's our only out, then."

★ ★ ★ ★

Aboard Bill Farrow's plane, *Bat Out of Hell*, the last one to take off from the *Hornet*, copilot Bobby Hite crawled forward into the nose to see what could be done about the hole in the Plexiglas. He and Jake DeShazer, the bombardier, tried to stuff a coat into the opening, but it blew back in immediately. The wind whistling through the hole would slow them down and cause them to burn more fuel, but there was nothing they could do about it.

Their target was Nagoya, three hundred miles south of Tokyo. They were supposed to attack in a three-plane element, along with Jack Hilger's and Don Smith's planes, which had taken off just before them. But Farrow's plane never caught up with the others and flew on alone, one hundred feet above the water. They reached the coast about one o'clock in the afternoon.

★ ★ ★ ★

Between Doolittle's plane and Farrow's, the Raiders were stretched out in a random pattern one hundred fifty miles long and fifty miles wide. Aboard *Whiskey Pete*, pilot Bob Gray and copilot Shorty Manch (who was six feet six inches tall) opened a box of Robert Burns cigars. Despite the strong smell of gasoline in the cockpit from the collapsible tank above the bomb bay, they both lit up and smoked contentedly all the way to the Japanese coast. Theirs had been the third plane to take off, and Manch figured that by the time they got to Japan, Doolittle and Hoover would have dropped their bombs and so enemy fighter planes and antiaircraft guns would be ready to greet them.

★ ★ ★ ★

Eldred Scott was the engineer-gunner aboard *Whirling Dervish*, the ninth plane to take off. It left the *Hornet* at 8:50 in the morning, and within a few minutes, Scott knew they had problems. The gas tank that replaced the bottom turret was leaking from its corner seams, about a foot down from the top. Scott spoke to the pilot, Doc Watson, and arranged to transfer the gas to the main tank as soon as possible to keep the loss to a minimum.

Then Scott went to work on the top turret, which, like many others, was not operating properly. He traced the problem to the automatic hydraulic mechanism used to charge the guns. He removed the mechanism and found he could charge the guns by hand. It was not as fast or as efficient, but at least the guns could be fired.

Except for passing a freighter, probably the same one the other planes had flown over, *Whirling Dervish* had an uneventful flight. The bomber was in good shape. The men could defend themselves, no more gas was leaking, and their rate of fuel consumption was normal. As the plane approached the coast, Scott remarked on the beauty of the mountains. He said they looked just like the pictures he had seen in a geography book at school.

★ ★ ★ ★

Pilot Dick Joyce, taking off three minutes after *Whirling Dervish*, set a course of 270 degrees and sped away from the *Hornet* at an altitude of five hundred feet. Everything in his plane was working well, including the starboard engine, which had misfired while being run up for takeoff. Ninety minutes later, engineer-gunner Ed Horton called Joyce on the interphone to report a twin-engine Japanese patrol plane ahead. No sooner had Horton spotted it than it dove on them. Joyce rammed the throttles all the way forward and pulled away. The range was too great for either plane to open fire, and the American crew never saw the patrol plane again. Joyce decided to fly a little higher, to stay in the clouds for the next hour or so.

★ ★ ★ ★

Jack Hilger, the fourteenth to take off, saw the same Japanese patrol plane, but it was so far away he was sure his plane had not been spotted. He had a quiet, smooth flight to Japan, passing over a large number of fishing boats as he neared the coast. The Japanese fishermen waved, leading the army fliers to conclude that the enemy did not know they were coming. They expected to catch the Japanese by surprise.

★ ★ ★ ★

Don Smith and his crew saw no sign of the enemy—no ships or planes—during the flight to Japan, but Smith heard them. About three hours after leaving the carrier, he picked up a Japanese radio program, which he listened to for about an hour. Using his compass indicators, Smith determined that the station was broadcasting from Tokyo.

At 12:25 the program was interrupted by the sound of a loud bell, which rang for forty-five seconds. Three words were shouted and the bell rang again. The sequence was repeated nearly a dozen times, and the station went off the air. Smith kept the radio tuned to the same frequency, but the program never resumed, at least not by the time he reached the coast. After that, he was too busy to think about it.

★ ★ ★ ★

Most of the crews sighted at least one Japanese patrol plane, warship, freighter, or fishing boat on their flight to Japan. And most of the sightings were at such a close range that the Japanese aboard would certainly have seen the B-25s. Yet, except for the report from a patrol plane about two twin-engine aircraft—which report was discounted—no one seems to have alerted authorities in Tokyo that airplanes were heading their way. The Japanese were caught unprepared for the attack. Surprise was total.

Doolittle and his fliers enjoyed another advantage as they flew low

over the coast of Japan that warm Saturday afternoon, one that was
not planned. Indeed, at the time, the fliers were unaware of their
luck. Because of faulty compasses, a forty-knot wind that tended to
blow them off course, and the overcast that kept the navigators from
checking their positions precisely, only three of the thirteen planes
bound for the Tokyo-Yokohama area reached land where they were
supposed to. A few were south of the city; most were north of it.

As soon as each navigator ascertained his position from the landmarks, he gave his pilot a new course to take the plane to Tokyo by
the shortest route. Some planes, therefore, approached the city
from the north, some from the south, and three from the east—from
the sea. As a result, the Japanese were mystified. The bombers flew
over the city for more than an hour, and Japanese authorities were
unable to predict where they were coming from. This disoriented
Tokyo's antiaircraft forces and prevented the rapid deployment of a
coherent defense.

★ ★ ★ ★

Jimmy Doolittle flew in low over the coast and saw a large lake
ahead, which gave him his first indication of his location. He banked
the plane into a left turn and headed south toward Tokyo, barely
above treetop level. As he approached the city, he spotted nine
fighters in three flights, one thousand feet above him. He turned to
port, and they turned with him, apparently getting into position to
attack.

He straightened out and flew the last few miles to the center of
Tokyo, losing the planes in the process. He headed southwest across
the sprawling city, climbed to twelve hundred feet, and told Fred
Braemer, the bombardier, that they were approaching the target.
Braemer opened the bomb-bay doors as Doolittle held the plane
steady. They passed over the Imperial Palace and came to the target
area, the congested sectors northeast and southwest of the armory.

At 12:15 a small red light at the bottom of Doolittle's instrument
panel blinked once, then three more times, the signal that all four
incendiaries had been dropped. Doolittle knew it even without the
signal from the bombardier, because the plane was suddenly two

thousand pounds lighter. As the bombs fell, setting the buildings ablaze to provide a beacon for the rest of the planes, puffs of black smoke and flame appeared on both sides of the aircraft, about one hundred yards away. The antiaircraft fire intensified. More shells burst around and behind them.

Doolittle got on the interphone to Paul Leonard, his engineer-gunner.

"Everything OK back there, Paul?"

"Everything fine," Leonard said.

"They're missing us a mile, Paul," Doolittle said.

As he spoke, a shell exploded one hundred feet away and splattered fragments against the fuselage.

"Colonel," Leonard said, "that was no mile."

Doolittle pushed the control yoke forward, advanced the throttles, and dove as close to the ground as he dared. Eruptions of anti-aircraft fire continued to follow the plane. He saw an aircraft factory ahead, with about thirty planes lined up in a row. It was a tempting target.

Hank Potter, the navigator, recalled that they were angered by the sight of those planes. "They bothered us because we had dropped all our bombs and had nothing to use on them. They were nice red and silver training planes, lined up on a factory field. You didn't need any earphone connection with [Doolittle] to hear his roar of disappointment that a little 'Made in America' heat couldn't be turned on."

As they got closer to the coast, they flew for a while along a highway. Fred Braemer spotted a likely target for his puny .30-caliber machine gun.

"Colonel, there is either a tank or an armored car ahead. Can't I let it have a burst?"

"Relax, Fred," Doolittle said. "They probably think we are a friendly aircraft. Let them keep on thinking that."

Doolittle knew that other B-25s might be coming along that road. There was no point alerting the ground forces to the direction the bombers would be taking. Doolittle and his crew had done their job. Now they had to get to China.

★ ★ ★ ★

Trav Hoover followed Doolittle in over the coast. The plane crossed
a white sandy beach that should not have been there. They were
supposed to have made landfall at the Inubo Saki lighthouse. Carl
Wildner, the navigator, searched right and left, but could see no
sign of a lighthouse. He felt helpless, a feeling that intensified as they
trailed Doolittle inland and still recognized nothing. The features of
the terrain Wildner saw did not correspond with anything on his
map. Hoover kept asking for a course heading to the target, but
Wildner could not supply one.

After twenty minutes, Hoover saw Doolittle turn to the south, and
he followed. Shortly after that, Wildner noticed some people below.
They appeared unconcerned, assuming the plane to be Japanese. As
the B-25 got closer to Tokyo, Wildner began to recognize the check-
points. He found their position and gave the pilot a course to the
target. Hoover climbed to nine hundred feet. As Wildner was about
to tell him the target was two minutes ahead, he felt the bombs leave
the ship. It was 12:15, the same moment Doolittle dropped his
bombs.

The bombardier, Dick Miller, had been unable to identify their
target—some gunpowder factories—and had chosen a factory and
warehouse instead. Because the plane was so low, the men felt the
concussion when the bombs exploded. Had they hit the gunpowder
factory at nine hundred feet of altitude, they might not have survived the explosion. The engineer-gunner, Doug Radney, reported
seeing "half the target area covered with smoke."

Hoover dove sharply to rooftop level and headed for Tokyo Bay.
Far to the left, bursts of antiaircraft fire painted a trail of black
puffs across the sky. It was fire following Doolittle's ship. Hoover
sped low over the bay, expecting to be shot at by all the warships
they passed, but not one of them opened up. Dead ahead, a seaplane
was taking off. Hoover banked so rapidly that he almost dragged a
wingtip in the water. As he straightened out, Radney called to report that the top turret was stuck. If fighters attacked from above or
behind, they could no longer defend themselves.

Hoover flew west, making all the speed he could, to skirt Kawasaki and Yokohama, then turned south near Yokosuka. Once out over the water, he turned southwest to circle the Japanese islands and head for China.

★ ★ ★ ★

The air-raid sirens in Tokyo did not sound until 12:35, twenty minutes after the first bombs fell. Only then were the antiaircraft defenses fully alerted. The next planes were approaching a city, which, while still in a state of confusion, was beginning to organize itself for a proper defense. There was time to do so because of the twenty- to twenty-five-minute lull in the attack between the moment Doolittle and Hoover zoomed away from Tokyo and *Whiskey Pete* approached.

Bob Gray and Shorty Manch extinguished their Robert Burns cigars when they reached the Japanese coast and began scanning the skies for the fighters and ack-ack bursts they expected to see. They were off course, hitting the mainland some fifteen miles south of the Inubo Saki lighthouse.

Gray turned and approached the city from the south, across Tokyo Bay. He called the crew over the interphone, asking what they wanted to do if *Whiskey Pete* became disabled by enemy fire. They all said they would bail out and take their chances as prisoners of war. Gray said in that event he would try to hold the plane steady long enough for them to get out, then dive on the biggest target he could find.

As the plane skimmed the bay, antiaircraft fire filled the air behind and in front of them. The bursts ahead formed a path, leading them to their target. Gray took the ship up to 1,450 feet over the city and slowed as he started his bomb run northwest of the palace. In the distance, a black column of smoke from a burning oil tank rose into the sky.

The bombardier, Aden Jones, lined up the bombsight on the targets—a steel works, a gas works, and a chemical plant—and released the bombs. The pilot could not see where the first bomb hit, but he felt the concussion. The second bomb smashed into the gas works, and the third, aimed at the chemical plant, "set fire to the whole works."

Swinging away from the targets, Gray descended to one thousand feet and pushed the throttles all the way forward. As Gray retraced his course across the city and out over Tokyo Bay, Jones opened up with his .30-caliber machine gun on the crowded streets below. The navigator, Charles Ozuk, saw several buildings in flames. Jones fired at a group of workers in a factory yard, and Ozuk saw more than a dozen of them drop to the ground.

As they flew over the bay, a dozen fighter planes passed overhead, but they apparently did not see the bomber. Ships in the bay fired at them, but scored no hits. Once across, Gray turned southeast, hoping the enemy would think they were making for the Philippines. After about forty miles he turned southwest and headed for China.

★ ★ ★ ★

Brick Holstrom's crew, concerned about the inoperative top turret, spotted enemy fighters in the distance as they neared the Japanese capital from their landfall eighty miles south. Holstrom sent the co-pilot, Lucian Youngblood, aft, to transfer the remaining fuel from the bomb-bay tank to the wing tanks. The plane droned northeast toward Tokyo, seventy-five feet above the ground. Two fighter planes approached them head-on. Holstrom saw a line of tracers from one of the planes converge just above his cockpit.

He called Youngblood back at once. Two more fighters streaked across the sky at them, at an altitude of fifteen hundred feet. They seemed to be getting into position to dive. Without the twin .50-calibers in the top turret, the B-25 was defenseless against such an attack. Holstrom noticed ten fighters advancing on them from the direction of the capital, and he was still far south of the target. He had not even reached Tokyo Bay yet.

Holstrom faced a difficult choice—to try to reach the target through the swarm of Japanese fighters or to get rid of their bombs and head for China. He ordered the bombardier, Bob Stephens, to jettison the bombs, then turned and sped southward, rapidly outdistancing the enemy fighters.

★ ★ ★ ★

The plane piloted by Davey Jones crossed the coast only fifty feet above the beach. Expecting to meet Japanese fighter planes, Jones jammed the throttles forward and increased his speed to two hundred miles per hour. When he saw no signs of opposition, he dropped back to 180. He continued inland for about ten minutes and realized he was lost. He did not know if they were north or south of Tokyo. Turning south, Jones finally recognized a major landmark, the mouth of Tokyo Bay.

He turned again to head for the city, concerned about wasting fuel. There had not been time to top off the plane's gas tanks before takeoff, and that, combined with the time lost trying to find Tokyo, meant they now had less gas than anticipated.

Jones decided that instead of hitting their assigned target, which would have taken them to the far side of the city, he would bomb the first target of opportunity they saw. He pulled up to twelve hundred feet as he approached the waterfront and quickly selected some likely targets for his bombardier, Denver Truelove, to line up his sight on.

The first bomb hit dead center on an oil storage tank two blocks from the docks. The next bomb was dropped on a three-story power plant. After the bombs fell, Jones "made a turn so we could see the effect of the demolitions we dropped. As the bombs struck, the power plant assumed the shape of a barrel. The sides rounded out and the top became circular. Then the 'barrel' burst. Smoke and dust and bricks were everywhere."

Antiaircraft batteries on the ground returned heavy fire. Black puffs, up to eight feet in diameter, appeared behind and alongside the plane, and machine-gun fire from the ground followed it for a short time as Truelove released the third bomb, an incendiary cluster, on a two-story building with a sawtooth roof. The incendiary pellets set the roof ablaze before bouncing to the ground.

They dropped their fourth bomb on another two-story building, but caught only one corner of it because by then Jones had pushed his speed to 270 miles per hour to escape the ack-ack. As soon as the last bomb was gone, he shoved the control yoke forward, dove to the treetops, and peeled off to the southwest.

★ ★ ★ ★

Dean Hallmark, the pilot of *Green Hornet*, the sixth plane to reach Japan, tagged after Davey Jones's ship as it came in over the coast.

When Jones turned south Hallmark followed, but soon lost sight of him. Hallmark and his crew bombed their assigned target, a group of steel mills, amid heavy antiaircraft fire, but details of their raid are sketchy. *Green Hornet* was among the unlucky ones.

Hallmark's bombing run was the last attack made by the Raiders on the industrial and military targets in central Tokyo. Jones's unplanned strike in the harbor area coincided with a shift in the focus of the attack to the warehouse and shipping facilities along the shore of Tokyo Bay. After about 12:40, all but one of the remaining B-25s to reach Tokyo attacked the waterfront sector, leading Japanese authorities to believe that the harbor was the Americans' main objective.

The docks were the most heavily defended part of the city. Barrage balloons were suspended above vital installations strung along the north and west shores, and antiaircraft batteries dotted the banks. The next wave of planes would be flying into the heaviest concentration of defensive fire yet encountered.

★ ★ ★ ★

Ted Lawson and the crew of *Ruptured Duck* reached the coast at one o'clock in the afternoon. They swept in as low as possible over motorboats and fishing launches anchored off the beach. Fishermen on the boats waved, mistaking the U.S. Army Air Force bomber for a Japanese plane.* They roared inland over the bright green spring grass, blossoming fruit trees, and neat farms. People working in the fields also waved at them. Lawson raised the nose of the plane to clear a red-lacquered temple. Mac McClure, the navigator, had his movie camera rolling. Lawson yelled at him over the interphone to ask if he thought this was some sort of sightseeing tour.

They were heading southwest toward Tokyo Bay when they saw six Japanese fighter planes approaching at fifteen hundred feet. The first formation of three planes flew over them and so did the second,

---

* It was easy, at that early stage of the war, to confuse the American insignia with the red circle of the Japanese "rising sun" insignia. The American insignia consisted of a blue circle with a white star in its center. At the center of the star was a large red circle. The red circle was subsequently removed from U.S. aircraft because American gunners had mistaken U.S. planes for Japanese ones.

but one plane peeled off and started to dive. Dave Thatcher, in the top turret, reported that he was watching the plane. Lawson waited to hear Thatcher tell him when he needed emergency power from the cockpit, the only way the turret would operate, but no further word came. Finally, Thatcher reported that the plane had disappeared from view.

Thirty minutes after landfall, *Ruptured Duck* reached Tokyo Bay. Lawson skimmed the water at fifteen feet, maintaining his low but gas-saving speed. On their right the men saw an aircraft carrier, and ahead they spotted a B-25. It was Davey Jones's plane, climbing. A lot of little black clouds were erupting around it.

As they neared the city, Lawson pulled up to fifteen hundred feet, crossing over a jumble of wharves and flimsy buildings lining the waterfront. No sooner had he leveled out than a red light blinked on his instrument panel, indicating that the bombs were being released. One of those bombs bore the Japanese medals that were being returned. The three demolition bombs struck factories, but the incendiary fell in a densely populated residential area near the palace district.

None of the crew saw the bombs hit, but they did observe mammoth fires and towering columns of smoke over the northeast section of the city, where earlier planes had found their targets. But Lawson's men had little time to look around because just as their last bomb was released, their plane was enveloped in dark clouds of flak. The enemy gunners had their altitude, but were leading the plane a bit too much. Still, some of the bursts were close, and Lawson nosed the plane over in a steep dive to get nearer to ground level. By the time he straightened out, his speed was 350 miles per hour.

Heading southeast, so low over a railroad train that he could make out the startled face of the engineer, he slowed once they had cleared the city. Overhead, six Japanese biplanes flew by, but kept on going. Lawson was growing concerned about his fuel supply. The auxiliary tanks were empty, and they were starting to draw on the main wing tanks. Lawson skirted Yokohama and, once out over open water, changed course for China.

★ ★ ★ ★

Ski York and Bob Emmens brought their bomber in over the beach. Looking down, they saw about two hundred people in some kind of enclosure. A watchtower stood at one corner, and the people were waving frantically and jumping up and down. They appeared to be Westerners, not Orientals. York and Emmens wondered if they had passed over a prisoner-of-war camp.

The crew did not discuss the decision to go to Russia. The alternatives were not attractive. They could come down in Japan and become prisoners themselves, or drown in the China Sea when they ran out of gas.

They flew inland for thirty minutes, so low they could distinguish the happy faces of children and the details of houses built of mud and straw. They searched in vain for some landmark that might tell them where they were in relation to Tokyo, but continued to cross only farms and rice paddies. A flight of nine Japanese fighters passed high above them, and they saw the tall transmitting tower of radio station JOAK, which Steve Jurika, aboard the *Hornet,* was monitoring at that moment.

York and his crew were lost, accomplishing nothing but consuming their precious and rapidly dwindling fuel supply. He decided to bomb their first target of opportunity. He thought they were north or northwest of Tokyo, over Kawagoe, a distant suburb. He spied a factory and a power plant adjoining a railway yard and pulled up to fifteen hundred feet.

The plane shuddered as the bomb-bay doors cranked open and lightened as the four bombs were released. One of the bombs exploded in the center of a large building, but the men could not see where the others hit. York dove down to treetop level and kept his speed well above two hundred miles per hour as he weaved from side to side, alert for enemy fighters.

As they passed over an airfield lined with biplanes that appeared to be trainers, Herndon opened up with the .30-caliber machine gun in the nose.

"I wasn't going through this thing without firing this gun," he said.

York climbed to over eight thousand feet to clear the mountain range that blocked their path northwest. He skimmed the few scrawny saplings growing on the peaks, and saw the Sea of Japan some fifty miles ahead. He hugged the slopes of the mountains, barely clearing the trees and rocky outcroppings, still expecting to be jumped by fighters. The fliers were amazed they had not yet been attacked. Open water lay ahead. Russia was six hundred miles beyond the blurred horizon.

★ ★ ★ ★

Doc Watson and the crew of *Whirling Dervish* crossed the coastline thirty-five miles north of Tokyo. They swept past a long, sandy beach and suddenly found themselves over an airport where eighteen bombers lay dispersed about the field. As they passed, the engineer-gunner, Eldred Scott, spotted five biplane trainers in the air. He turned his guns on them, but the planes were no threat. They could never have caught up with the B-25.

Watson found Tokyo easily, but before they reached the city, intense antiaircraft fire bracketed the plane. "We were surprised and shocked," Tom Griffin, the navigator, recalled, "to realize that those small black clouds we were seeing were flak. They were shooting at *us*." Scott remembered that the weather was "a nice sunshiny day with overcast antiaircraft fire." He kept watching the wings, expecting holes to appear.

As they crossed another airfield, the flak grew heavier. Watson descended beneath the fire and began zigzagging over the rooftops. He climbed to 2,500 feet and kept his speed around 220 miles per hour as he began the bombing run over the target, a large complex on a spit of sand jutting into the harbor. They thought they were attacking the Kawasaki Truck and Tank Plant, but they actually dropped all four bombs on the Tokyo Gas and Electric Engineering Company. One of the bombs was seen to hit the northernmost building in the complex.

Scott watched from the top turret for the explosions. "What I saw was four streams of tracer bullets shooting up past us, real close. I looked down and there he was, a pursuit plane, coming hard. I began firing at him and he winged off. I know he was hit. Maybe we got him. Anyway, he only made that one pass at us."

Watson dropped down to rooftop level and made a long turn to the left, passing directly above the Imperial Palace, and from there he swung out over Tokyo Bay. "Going out over the harbor was when I got excited," Scott said. "We were right low on the water. A cruiser began firing at us, and one of the shells landed so near it sprayed water all over our plane. And there I was, firing back with a .50-caliber machine gun. Might as well have had a cap pistol."

Bursts of antiaircraft fire continued to follow *Whirling Dervish* as Watson headed south over Yokohama, past the Yokosuka naval base, and toward the Pacific. As they crossed the coast, a Japanese cruiser shot at them, chasing them as they set course for China.

★ ★ ★ ★

Richard Joyce, flying the tenth plane to reach Japan and the last to bomb Tokyo, made landfall precisely at the Inubo Saki lighthouse. He flew south for ten miles at 3,500 feet and then turned west, heading for upper Tokyo Bay and the city's waterfront. Over the bay, bursts of flak dogged the plane, first from an aircraft carrier steaming for the base at Yokosuka and then from land-based batteries.

He headed across the bay at 2,500 feet in a long, straight bomb run toward the target, the factories and warehouses of the Japan Special Steel Company. The first two five-hundred-pound bombs hit the main plant, destroying several buildings. The third demolition bomb and the incendiary were dropped about a quarter-mile inland, in an industrial and residential area. By then the plane was under such heavy attack that no one aboard saw what the bombs struck.

Joyce flew west along the Tamagawa River, where he was seen by a group of American civilians interned in a school building below. The antiaircraft bursts were so close to the plane that the crew expected to be shot down at any moment. A shell fragment tore a seven-inch hole in the fuselage, just forward of the automatic stabilizer, but that was the only antiaircraft hit scored by the Japanese during the entire raid.

Joyce pushed the control yoke forward and put the ship in a steep dive. As he did, nine Japanese fighters appeared overhead.* Two peeled off and dove at the B-25, closing to within six hundred yards. Machine-gun bullets struck the tip of the left wing. Diving at well over three hundred miles per hour, Joyce quickly evaded the fighters and leveled off, heading west.

They flew at treetop level toward the mountains. Three more fighters approached, but they could not catch the bomber. Near the foothills, Joyce swung south and met up with two more formations of fighters. Three planes closed in, but prompt firing from Ed Horton in the turret and George Larkin in the nose kept them at a safe distance. Another fighter zoomed in, but more rapid fire chased it away.

As the B-25 flew west of Yokosuka, antiaircraft batteries opened fire. Joyce maneuvered the ship away and prepared to throttle back, believing they were out of danger. Three fighters jumped them. Joyce made a rapid, two-thousand-foot-per-minute climb, taking the bomber into a cloud bank to lose his pursuers. He remained in the clouds at three thousand feet as he flew the length of the Japanese coast, before making the turn for China.

By the time Joyce's plane left Tokyo, large numbers of Japanese fighters controlled the skies over the city and its outskirts. On the ground, every antiaircraft battery was manned. The Japanese were prepared to respond in force to the attack. What they did not know was that the Tokyo portion of Doolittle's raid was over. The remaining American planes were going elsewhere.

---

* Joyce, and many of the other American fliers, tended to describe most of the Japanese fighter planes they encountered on the raid as the famous Zero. However, witnesses to Joyce's battle with the fighters identified them as the army Nakajima Type-97, a highly maneuverable fighter with fixed landing gear and a top speed in level flight of 270 miles per hour. Except for its landing gear, it did resemble the Zero, and may explain why so many were misidentified that day. Actually, at that time, there were few Zeros in Japan. Eleven days later, during the emperor's birthday celebrations, the Japanese public saw the Zero for the first time, when five of the planes put on a demonstration over Tokyo.

Jimmy Doolittle stands beside a painting of the Gee Bee racing plane in which he won the Thompson Trophy in 1932.
(*SMITHSONIAN INSTITUTION PHOTO NO. A2367*)

**Adm. William F. Halsey, commander of the carrier task force.**
(*NATIONAL ARCHIVES*)

Adm. Isoroku Yamamoto, commander in chief of Japan's combined fleet and planner of the surprise attack on Pearl Harbor. (*NATIONAL ARCHIVES*)

**B-25s lined up on the deck of the USS *Hornet*.**
(*SAN DIEGO AERO-SPACE MUSEUM*)

**B-25s lashed to the deck of the USS *Hornet*. The staggered arrangement of the bombers was necessary to crowd all sixteen planes aboard.**
(*SAN DIEGO AERO-SPACE MUSEUM*)

A crew member checks the lashings on the nose of his bomber. The airplane engines are protected by canvas coverings. (*SMITHSONIAN INSTITUTION PHOTO NO. 3A-03035*)

Navy and air corps crewmen stock the B-25s with machine-gun ammunition. (*SAN DIEGO AERO-SPACE MUSEUM*)

Capt. Marc A. "Pete" Mitscher of the USS *Hornet* with Jimmy Doolittle and Maj. Jack Hilger. Major Hilger served as Doolittle's second in command on the historic raid. (*SAN DIEGO AERO-SPACE MUSEUM*)

Captain Mitscher gives Doolittle a Japanese medal from an American ex-navy man who wanted the medal returned to Japan.
(*SAN DIEGO AERO-SPACE MUSEUM*)

**Doolittle wires the Japanese medal to the fin of a 500-pound bomb.**
(*SAN DIEGO AERO-SPACE MUSEUM*)

On the morning of April 18, 1942, a B-25 prepares for takeoff from the aircraft carrier *Hornet*. (*SAN DIEGO AERO-SPACE MUSEUM*)

A B-25 takes off from the aircraft carrier *Hornet*.
(*SAN DIEGO AERO-SPACE MUSEUM*)

A B-25 passes over the rigging of the *Hornet*. Each bomber flew past the bridge after takeoff to get a final compass heading.

**Yokosuka Naval Base on Tokyo Bay as seen from a B-25.**
(*SMITHSONIAN INSTITUTION PHOTO NO. 23543AC*)

**Yokosuka Naval Base with Japanese naval vessels in foreground.**
(*SMITHSONIAN INSTITUTION PHOTO NO. A23543AC*)

Doolittle sits by the wing of his crashed B-25 somewhere in eastern China (*SMITHSONIAN INSTITUTION PHOTO NO. B25758AC*)

Doolittle and his crew with Chinese civilians who helped them reach Chungking. From left: Fred Braemer, Paul Leonard, unidentified Chinese, Dick Cole, Doolittle, unidentified Chinese, Hank Potter, unidentified Chinese. (*SMITHSONIAN INSTITUTION PHOTO NO. 25757AC*)

Bobby Hite being led blindfolded from a Japanese transport plane after being flown from Shanghai to Tokyo, two days after the raid.
(*SMITHSONIAN INSTITUTION PHOTO NO. 92985AC*)

Doolittle fliers exchange smiles with Chinese soldiers under picturesque parasols. From left: Clay Campbell, Adam Williams, Mac McElroy, Bob Bourgeois, three unidentified Chinese.
(*SMITHSONIAN INSTITUTION PHOTO NO. A25759AC*)

Madame Chiang presents medals to Jimmy Doolittle and Jack Hilger in Chungking. (*SMITHSONIAN INSTITUTION PHOTO NO. 58933AC*)

Chinese natives carry Doolittle Raiders to safety.
(*SMITHSONIAN INSTITUTION PHOTO NO. A25757AC*)

Newly promoted Brigadier General Doolittle receives the Medal of Honor from President Roosevelt. Present at the ceremony in the White House are, from left, Gen. "Hap" Arnold, Mrs. Doolittle, and Gen. George C. Marshall. (*NATIONAL ARCHIVES*)

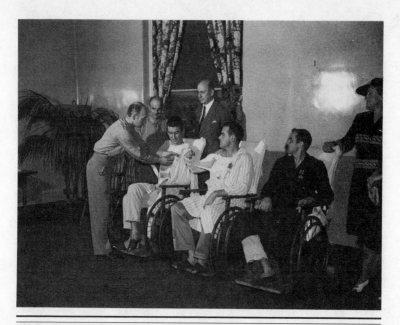

Maj. Gen. M. F. Harmon, Army Air Force chief of the air staff, awards Distinguished Flying Crosses to Mac McClure, Doc Watson, and Ted Lawson at Walter Reed Army Hospital. Looking on are Doolittle and Secretary of the Treasury Henry Morgenthau. .
(SMITHSONIAN INSTITUTION PHOTO NO. 21323AC)

62855 A.C.

At a reunion of Doolittle Raiders in Miami, Florida, April 19, 1947, Doolittle receives a plaque containing a fragment of a B-25 used in the raid from Alexander Burton of the North American Aircraft Company.

# If My Wife Could
# See Me Now

The airplane carrying Gen. Hideki Tojo, Japan's prime minister, was trying to land in the midst of the raid. Tojo had been warned about the discovery of the American fleet, but he believed, as did the military leaders, that there would be ample advance warning of any attack. He knew the American carriers would have to come within three hundred miles of the coast before launching their planes. He was so certain there could be no surprise raid that he adhered to his normal schedule for the day, which included an inspection of the Mito Aviation School, on the outskirts of Tokyo.

As his plane approached the runway, a twin-engine aircraft roared up on its right side. Col. Susumu Nishiura, Tojo's secretary, described the plane as "queer-looking." Historian John Toland reported that the bomber came so close to Tojo's plane that "the pilot's face was visible, and it occurred to Nishiura—it's American! It flashed by without firing a shot." The prime minister, the second most important man in all of Japan, had seen the enemy for the first time.

Hundreds more Japanese citizens had their first encounters with

Americans that day. At the Waseda Middle School in Tokyo, students poured onto the playground after lunch. An airplane roared overhead, sounding to them like a freight train. Kikujiro Suzuki assumed the plane was theirs until he saw an object fall from the sky. It was an incendiary. It hit one of Suzuki's schoolmates. The boy fell down and did not move.

Across the street from the school, Mrs. Ryu Aoki had just bid good-bye to her husband and son, who were off to visit an elderly relative, when she heard a terrible noise. She rushed out of the house and saw an airplane no higher than the trees. Small black canisters fell from the bottom of the plane, some of which landed on the roof of her house.

Next door, Seikichi Honjo was in such a hurry to find out about the awful noise that he forgot to put on his pants before he ran outside. He saw two incendiaries land on the Aoki house. Mrs. Aoki ran toward him, yelling, "Fire! Fire!" Honjo nimbly scaled the dwelling "like an acrobat," witnesses said, and used his shirt to beat out the flames on the roof.

In another part of the city, terrified residents watched a plane swing over their neighborhood. Incendiaries fell on the Okasaki Hospital, and the building started to burn. Orderlies carried patients out into the streets as the fire spread.

Across town, a woman found a black object on the second floor of her house. It had crashed through the roof. Smoke was pouring from it. She soaked a straw mat in water and smothered it. In another upstairs room, she found the ceiling on fire. She soaked some straw in water, wrapped it around the end of a bamboo pole, and tried to douse the flames.

Minoru Iida ran outside his father's grocery store when he heard the airplane. As it raced by, he saw several sticks tumble out of its bomb bay. He ran down the street, screaming, "Enemy plane! Enemy plane! This is an air raid!" One of the objects lodged under the eaves of a house, where it started to smoke and hiss. The boy ran back to the store, grabbed the sand bucket—something everyone kept handy in case of fire—and returned to smother the bomb. He refilled the bucket with sand and covered several more smoldering incendiaries found up and down his street.

A group of schoolboys watched from a window of their classroom as an American bomber flew past, chased by puffs of antiaircraft fire. Bombs fell from the plane and the sounds of explosions filled the air. Their teacher told them that the Americans had come from a field on O Shima (O Island), less than fifty miles from the mouth of Tokyo Bay.

Other students were walking home when they were surprised by a low-flying plane and the sound of big guns firing. Farther down the street there was an explosion. A huge cloud of smoke rose in the air. "He dropped a bomb," one boy shouted. "Let's go help." They ran toward a movie theater that was ablaze. Sirens wailed as the fire trucks approached. Volunteer fire fighters were already on the scene, but all they could do was splash buckets of water on the leaping flames.

A man stood in the street, watching an airplane pass overhead. His companion said it was an American plane, not Japanese. They walked down the street together, wondering how the plane had flown all the way to Japan.

A woman told her friend that the plane flying over their neighborhood must have come from Hawaii. More planes would come, she warned. She decided to ask her husband to build a bomb shelter for the family in the backyard.

Some residents of Tokyo were unaware that their city was being attacked. The idea of bombs falling on the capital was preposterous. Japan was winning the war. America and her allies were in retreat throughout the Pacific. The United States had no fleet left after the devastating attack on Pearl Harbor. And none of their airplanes could reach Japan.

People outside the areas being bombed assumed that the low-flying planes and the bursts of antiaircraft fire were merely a realistic end to the morning's air-raid drill. Many people on the streets waved to the pilots as they flew over. The editor-in-chief of the *Japan Times*, Iwao Kawai, looked down from his office window at the crowds who were staring at the sky. He watched the planes and listened to the guns firing, but took it all to be part of the drill. He did wonder momentarily why the antiaircraft batteries were firing live shells.

P. E. Sato was walking across a bridge in central Tokyo when he was startled by the earsplitting roar of a low-flying plane. Neither he nor anyone else on the bridge recognized the American insignia, and they did not know bombs were being dropped. The explosions they heard were thought to be the antiaircraft guns practicing. As Sato recalled, "That afternoon nothing had changed. People were living in the usual manner." Theaters were opening for matinees. Buses, streetcars, automobiles, and pedestrians filled the streets as on any ordinary day. The air-raid sirens were just part of the drill.

As explosions blanketed some sections of the city, a guard at the U.S. Embassy allowed staff members to go to the roof to watch. He assured them that Tokyo could not be bombed. One American staffer was willing to bet a hundred dollars that there had been no attack. No one took him up on his offer. It would be another hour before the guard was informed that Tokyo had been attacked, whereupon he promptly locked the door to the roof.

Joseph Grew, the U.S. ambassador to Japan, was entertaining the ambassador from Switzerland. Just as the Swiss ambassador was leaving, Grew recalled, "we heard a lot of planes overhead and saw five or six large fires burning in different directions with great volumes of smoke." They saw one plane lose altitude and fly away over the rooftops. They thought it had crashed, but decided it was maneuvering to avoid the ack-ack fire. "To the east we saw a plane with a whole line of black puffs of smoke, indicating antiaircraft explosions, just on its tail; it didn't look like a bomber and we are inclined to believe that the Japanese batteries lost their heads and fired on their own pursuit planes. All this was very exciting, but at the time it was hard to believe that it was more than a realistic practice by Japanese planes."

Capt. Henri Smith-Hutton, the U.S. naval attaché, passed the Swiss minister on his way out and asked him if there was any possibility the city was really under attack. The ambassador did not think so. Smith-Hutton joined other senior staff members at lunch in the dining room with Ambassador Grew. They saw smoke in the distance and heard another detonation.

A plane thundered over the embassy compound, barely clearing the trees, but no one suspected it was American. "We resumed our lunch," Smith-Hutton said, "and there was a warm discussion about the events of the morning. Half of our group thought it was a genuine air raid, but no one could be sure of the nationality of the planes, because there had been two or three other planes that had passed earlier which had apparently started the fires, before this last plane flew over the residence. We had not the faintest idea where they came from. The other half of our group thought it was a drill."

Later that afternoon, Ambassador Grew learned that it had not been a drill and that the planes were American. "We were all very happy and proud in the embassy," he said, "and the British told us later that they drank toasts all day to the American fliers."

Jane Smith-Hutton, wife of the naval attaché, recalled that she recognized the planes as bombers, but was puzzled because the official Japanese notice of the air-raid drill had mentioned fighter demonstrations. Nothing had been said about bombers. She considered the possibility that the bombers might be American and immediately thought of their friend—her husband's former assistant attaché—Steve Jurika. She remarked to an acquaintance, "Those are American bombers, and I bet you that Lieutenant Jurika is in one of them."

Others recognized that the raid was not a drill. The commercial attaché at the embassy of Argentina, Ramon Muñiz Lavalle, ran to the roof of the building when he heard the planes. He saw four U.S. bombers no more than one hundred feet above the streets. Bombs fell all around him. "I looked down at the streets," he said. "All Tokyo seemed to be in panic. Japs were running everywhere, pushing, shouting, screaming. I could see fires starting near the port.

"Our two Japanese interpreters in the embassy were frightened out of their skins. I sent down to get them, but they wouldn't come up to the roof. After the raid, a Japanese scrubwoman who worked for us came up to me and said, 'If these raids go on, we'll all go mad.'

"That raid by Doolittle," Lavalle added, a year after the attack, "was one of the greatest psychological tricks ever used. It caught the Japs by surprise. Their unbounded confidence began to crack."

A Polish man then living in Tokyo watched the bombs fall on a factory district. One building was gutted, and fires raged out of control in others. The local fire guards had only buckets of water to use on the flames. The regular fire fighters were busy elsewhere in the city. Hundreds of women fetched buckets from their homes. The man noticed that the antiaircraft gunners seemed confused, firing continuously, almost haphazardly, in the air.

At Sophia University, Bruno Bitter, a Jesuit priest, thought the sirens and gunfire were part of the drill. He realized it was an air raid when bombs began exploding nearby. People climbed to the rooftops and chimneys to get a good view of the destruction. "It was a thrill," Father Bitter said.

It was also a thrill for *New York Times* reporter Otto Tolischus, who was being held for questioning in a Tokyo detention prison. During the first few days of his confinement, he was disappointed when the sirens he heard turned out to be fire engines on their way to routine blazes. He wanted the Americans to strike back at Japan. On this Saturday, when the sirens wailed, he was jubilant. He saw the guards running down the corridors, double-locking the cell doors, and indicating by their gestures that this was no drill.

Florence Wells, an American teacher at Tsudo College, was permitted to travel freely, although she was an enemy alien. She was on a train at the Yokohama station when guards rushed along the platform, ordering everyone to leave the train and go down to the underpass. The passengers heard airplane engines while they waited, then the guards told them it was all right to come out.

She reboarded the train, got off at the terminus, and strolled along the Yokohama waterfront. She stopped to chat with a friend, the manager of the Grand Hotel.

"I see the Japanese fliers are practicing," she said.

"That wasn't Japanese practicing," he said quietly. "It was Americans. It was the real thing."

★ ★ ★ ★

The first plane to bomb Yokohama was *Hari Carrier*, piloted by Ross Greening, the flier who had invented the inexpensive but highly effective bombsight back at Eglin. His plane made landfall considerably north of Tokyo, at a spot on the coast that reminded Frank Kappeler, the navigator, of California. After proceeding inland for a few minutes, Greening turned south along the Boso peninsula. After crossing Lake Kasumiga, he passed over a training field. Several biplanes were practicing takeoffs and landings around the field, and as the B-25 roared over at an altitude of five hundred feet, some people on the ground waved. Others ran for cover.

Ten minutes later, Greening's plane was jumped by four fighters that looked like Zeros but had in-line engines instead of radial ones. The planes were a new type of army fighter, the Kawasaki Ki. 61, Type 3, which Americans later called the "Tony." Whatever its name, it was fast. Greening pushed his speed to 260 miles per hour, but the fighters stayed with him. "We hugged the ground as tightly as we could," Greening said, "and even flew under some power lines in the hope that some of the ships might crash into them. They didn't."

The engineer-gunner, Melvin Gardner, opened fire with his twin .50-calibers. He hit two of the fighters. One caught fire and the other wobbled off, heavily damaged, although neither was seen to crash. As Greening approached the target, more planes converged on the B-25 from all directions.

In the distance he spotted what appeared at first glance to be a thatch-roofed village. As he got closer, he saw that it was an elaborately camouflaged gasoline storage tank farm. With such a tempting target directly ahead and enemy fighters harassing him, he decided to forgo the primary target and bomb the storage tanks. Because of the hovering fighter planes, he could climb no higher than six hundred feet, dangerously low for such a potentially fiery target.

"When our bombs dropped," Greening recalled, "there were great sheets of flame and a terrific explosion that threw the copilot and me right out of our seats, even though we were belted, and banged our heads against the top of the cockpit. . . . my mind was intent on my job, of course, but I remember that I also kept thinking, Oh, if my wife could see me now."

Greening headed out over Tokyo Bay. With the bombs gone, he had no trouble outdistancing the fighters. He glanced back at the target from fifty miles across the bay and saw towering pillars of flame and smoke marking the spot. As they raced across the water, the bombardier, Bill Birch, opened fire with his .30-caliber machine gun at three patrol boats, leaving one in flames. Greening flew south for twenty minutes, then turned to follow the coast fifty miles offshore. When he reached the southernmost tip of Japan, he banked and headed for China.

★ ★ ★ ★

Bill Bower trailed Greening on the way west from the carrier. After making landfall, he realized he was far to the north of the target, perhaps as much as one hundred miles away. His navigator, Bill Pound, was lost. He could not recognize anything from his map. He suggested to Bower that they follow the coast until they reached the spot where they should have crossed, and head to Yokohama from there.

A formation of fighter planes followed them, but kept a respectful distance, never getting closer than one thousand yards, too far for either side to open fire. Bower looked down and admired the scenery. "I remember that I had the impression that, my gosh, what peaceful, pretty countryside that was . . . what do they want war with us for?"

Pound had pinpointed their location by the time they had reached Tokyo Bay, and he gave Bower a course to the target. In the distance the crew saw immense fires devouring the gasoline storage tanks Greening had hit. Bower overflew the Kisarazu naval air station and found himself in the middle of the traffic pattern. Planes circled the field in orderly fashion, and none of the pilots recognized the American bomber in their midst. Bower flew right through them.

He saw barrage balloons ahead, just where he expected, one thousand feet above the target at the Yokohama docks. As he swung north, puffs of antiaircraft smoke surrounded them, and he climbed to eleven hundred feet to clear the balloons. Once over the target, Waldo Bither, the bombardier, lined up the sight on the Ogura oil refinery and the adjacent factories and warehouses. The crew saw two of their bombs hit. One exploded at the corner of a large building and the other alongside a string of tank cars on a railway siding.

Bower immediately turned south within the line of barrage balloons, pursued by antiaircraft fire. A Japanese shell punctured one of the balloons as he raced past. Bill Pound remembered being so tense that the gum he was chewing stuck in his mouth like a wad of cotton.

Bower dove to treetop level and headed across the city, then out past O Island. On the way, Bither strafed a power station with his .30-caliber gun. Bower fixed his course for China and turned the plane southwest.

★ ★ ★ ★

The thirteenth plane to reach Japan was piloted by Mac McElroy and Dick Knobloch. They followed Greening and Bower off the *Hornet*, but when land was sighted, they went their separate ways. Neither McElroy nor the navigator, Clay Campbell, saw any landmarks that corresponded to their maps. Campbell told McElroy he thought they were about one hundred miles north of Yokohama.

McElroy turned south and skimmed along the coast. Fishermen waved to them, and Knobloch snapped their pictures with his camera. When they reached the Inubo Saki lighthouse, McElroy turned right and flew across an airfield. Antiaircraft batteries opened up on them at once. He took evasive action and flew across Tokyo Bay toward the Yokosuka naval base. As more shells burst around them, he took the ship up to thirteen hundred feet.

The bombardier, Bob Bourgeois, released the first bomb at the tip of a peninsula, but it fell short of land and made a lucky hit on a ship in drydock. It was a merchant ship being converted to an aircraft carrier, and it toppled over and burst into flames. Another bomb blew up a large crane at a loading dock and a factory that was spread over several blocks of the waterfront. The incendiary bomb landed in a congested area, starting more fires. Dick Knobloch continued to take photographs, the only ones of the raid to survive.

As Bourgeois shut the bomb-bay doors, McElroy headed out over open water for fifty miles, before turning south. The crew could still see billows of smoke over the Yokohama docks. They flew down the coast, made their turn, and headed for China.

McElroy's last bomb fell at 1:41 to mark the end of the three-plane raid on Yokohama, and the final attack in the vicinity of Tokyo. The last three planes were heading south, to targets in Nagoya and Kobe.

★ ★ ★ ★

Jack Hilger, Doolittle's second-in-command, reached the Japanese coast at the mouth of Tokyo Bay, not far from the Yokosuka naval base. He flew along the irregular shoreline at an altitude of one hundred feet for an hour and fifteen minutes, until they reached Ise Bay, which led to the port of Nagoya, 175 miles from Tokyo. He aimed for the city from the south, expecting to approach it across low, flat countryside, as indicated on his map. Instead, to his surprise, he had to climb to one thousand feet to clear a range of hills.

As they reached the suburbs, he flew over a park where a crowd was watching a ball game. Hilger thought the countryside with its little towns was beautiful, and for a moment he thought it was a shame to drop bombs on it. But he remembered the attack on Pearl Harbor. Whatever damage the Doolittle Raiders inflicted on Japan that day, the Japanese had brought on themselves. Near the target area he climbed to fifteen hundred feet for the bombing run. Flak erupted around the plane, but the shooting was inaccurate.

"It didn't bother us at all," Hilger said. "When it started, our rear gunner yelled over the interphone—'Hey, they're shooting at us'—just as if that wasn't allowed." The navigator-bombardier, Herb Macia, initially had trouble identifying their targets. The Nagoya castle was a major landmark, but it "did not stand out as had been expected, and the river just north of the castle was almost dry, whereas it had been expected to be quite conspicuous." Also, Macia and the others had been led to believe the city would be much larger.

Macia spotted the targets, opened the bomb-bay doors, lined up the sight, and released his four bombs on the military barracks at the castle, an oil and gas storage facility, an army arsenal, and the Mitsubishi aircraft factory. Ed Bain, the gunner, saw the first bomb demolish the barracks and the last bomb hit the aircraft factory. No one saw the other two bombs explode.

As soon as the bombs were dropped, Hilger dove at a pair of oil storage tanks. Bain fired thirty to forty rounds, but neither tank caught fire. Hilger recrossed the bay, and from sixty miles out, the men looked back to see a mile-high, mushroom-shaped column of smoke high above Nagoya. Hilger continued out to sea for twenty minutes, to give the appearance that they were heading due east, then turned to follow the coast to the China Sea.

★ ★ ★ ★

Don Smith, piloting the next plane to reach Japan, flew in tandem with Hilger from their landfall at the mouth of Tokyo Bay. At Ise Bay they separated, Hilger going for Nagoya and Smith continuing on for Kobe, approximately 130 miles away.

After they crossed the bay, according to their map, the terrain was supposed to be flat, but Smith saw a mountain peak he estimated at 2,500 feet. He climbed to three thousand feet and passed north of Osaka, whose sprawling suburbs joined those of Kobe. Smith and his crew began to suspect they were lost, but as soon as they crossed the mountain they saw Kobe in the distance. They skirted the eastern edge of the city and dropped to two thousand feet for the bomb run.

So far, the only other plane they had seen was a commercial airliner. Doc White, the flight surgeon and top-turret gunner, remembered that "we approached Kobe probably an hour after the raid had started on Tokyo.* But the people apparently were not aware that it had taken place. Trains were running as usual, and people placidly walked the streets." Ed Saylor, the flight engineer, said that "nobody realized we were enemies until the bombs dropped."

Smith held the speed to 240 miles per hour as they swept over the

---

* The elapsed time was closer to an hour and a half.

waterfront. Ses Sessler, the navigator-bombardier, opened the bomb-bay doors. His targets were the Vyenoshita steel works, the Kawasaki dockyard company, the electric machinery works, and the Kawasaki aircraft factory. As the bombs fell, two antiaircraft guns opened fire, and Smith dove for the bay, racing to 325 miles per hour. None of the flak bursts was close. Two fighter planes started after them but could not catch up. In their haste to get away, none of the crew saw where their bombs hit.

★ ★ ★ ★

The last plane to take off from the carrier *Hornet*—the one with the jagged hole in the Plexiglas nose and the image of the sailor who had been blown into the propeller on the minds of the crew—reached the coast of Japan just south of Tokyo. Bill Farrow, the pilot, headed on a straight run over land to Nagoya. He skimmed the ground as low as he dared, but had to climb to seven thousand feet to cross a mountain range.

In the nose, with the wind screaming through the foot-wide gap, Jake DeShazer, the bombardier, was amazed to see that people were living so high in the mountains. As the plane zoomed low, some of the people waved. DeShazer watched an old man with a gray beard and a cane glance over his shoulder at the approaching plane and fling himself on the ground. The B-25 missed him by only a few feet.

Farrow dropped to one hundred feet and held that altitude until George Barr, the navigator, spotted three fighters above them. Farrow climbed quickly and lost the planes in a cloud bank at 2,500 feet. He flew low again as they neared the city. The men saw antiaircraft fire ahead, and two columns of smoke to mark Hilger's and Smith's attacks.

Farrow climbed to five hundred feet as he started the bomb run, and told DeShazer their first target was dead ahead. Because their assigned targets included a large oil-storage facility, they were carrying all incendiary bombs. DeShazer took aim at the storage tanks and released two bombs. For some reason, three bombs dropped.

The pilot banked sharply to head for the next target as antiaircraft fire exploded around them. The oil storage tanks were on fire but had not blown up. DeShazer thought he smelled smoke, but what he was smelling was the "powder of the shells that were being shot at us instead of the bombs I had dropped. I had noticed a little black smoke cloud right in front of us, and evidently the hole in the nose of our airplane allowed the smoke to come inside."

Farrow lined up on an aircraft factory and zoomed over at five hundred feet. DeShazer dropped the last bomb. No one on board saw whether it hit, because the plane dipped into a valley on the way over Osaka.

In the nose, Jake DeShazer took hold of his .30-caliber machine gun. "I was getting ready to shoot," he said. He had read about German pilots strafing helpless French civilians and had made up his mind on the *Hornet* that he would never do such a thing, but "there is something about being shot at that makes you want to shoot back.

"I saw a man standing in a fishing boat, waving at us as we came along. He thought that we were Japanese. I thought that I would show him that we weren't. I shot a few shots near him, and the poor fellow stopped waving. I wasn't a very good shot, however, and therefore no harm was done."

When they reached the southern tip of Japan, George Barr gave Farrow their course for China. Barr was at first uncertain about his navigation. He had been watching two planes in the distance—presumably Hilger's and Smith's—and when they turned toward China, one took a more northerly course than the other. Barr had plotted a course in between, and decided to stick to it. He had guided them all the way from the *Hornet* without any problem, and he saw no reason to doubt his abilities now.

★ ★ ★ ★

As the skies over Japan cleared of American planes, the crew of the *Hornet* waited for word of the fate of the Doolittle fliers they had launched almost five hours before. Officers and men throughout the carrier kept their personal radios tuned to Japanese stations, hoping for news of the attack. Captain Mitscher asked Steve Jurika to listen to the ship's radio in the flag plot. Jurika put on the headphones and took up his vigil.

"I sat up listening to the Japanese broadcasts from Tokyo," Jurika recalled, "and when I knew that the planes should have been in Tokyo and another fifteen or twenty minutes, there was nothing to indicate from the broadcasts that there was any unusual event taking place."

The sailors knew that if the raid had proceeded as planned, the first planes would have reached their targets between noon and twelve-thirty. Because it had taken an hour to launch all the planes, the last ones would have reached their targets no later than one-thirty. But that time came and went, and the Japanese radio stations continued to carry their normal programs. There was no word of any attack.

At 1:45, a Tokyo station interrupted its program with an exaggerated, even hysterical, bulletin that had somehow gotten by the government censor.

"A large fleet of enemy bombers appeared over Tokyo this afternoon and much danger to nonmilitary objectives and some damage to nonmilitary objectives and some damage to factories. The known death toll is between three thousand and four thousand so far. No planes were reported shot down over Tokyo. Osaka was also bombed. Tokyo reports several large fires burning."

Wild cheering broke out aboard the *Hornet* and the other ships of Admiral Halsey's task force. They had done it! The war had been brought home to Tokyo, and the U.S. Navy had been part of it.

★ ★ ★ ★

Later that afternoon the people of Chungking, China, a city that had been bombed by the Japanese more than one hundred times, heard the news over Japan's propaganda radio station JOAK. As the B-25s headed for the east coast of China, the broadcaster tried to minimize the effects of the raid.

"The cowardly raiders," the announcer said, "purposefully avoided industrial centers and the important military establishments, and blindly dumped their incendiaries in a few suburban districts, especially on schools and hospitals."

It made no difference to the Chinese how the hated Japanese tried to explain away the attack. The important thing was that Japan herself had been bombed. Chinese newspapers printed extra editions, movie theaters flashed the news on their screens, and thousands of firecrackers were detonated in celebration. Harrison Forman, a reporter for *The New York Times*, attended a government briefing and heard China's war minister say, "The nightmare of the Japanese militarists can be shattered only by bombs. These raids on Japan proper are only the beginning." *

The Japanese public was told virtually nothing about the true nature of the attack. The extent of the damage was kept secret. The official survey of the consequences of the Doolittle raid listed fifty dead, 252 wounded, and ninety buildings gutted by fire and explosions.

The people were given quite a different view of the raid in the press and radio reports. The government version stressed the cowardice of the Americans in avoiding heavily defended areas and extolled the bravery of the Japanese defenders. The raid itself was called weak and ineffective. According to the authorities, the only casualties were schoolchildren and civilians, savagely gunned down on playgrounds and in city streets. The government did not mention that some of the casualties were undoubtedly caused by falling debris from their own antiaircraft fire.

"The few enemy planes that did manage to slip through the defense cordon failed to get near any of the establishments of military importance, which were too well guarded," wrote the newspaper *Japan Advertiser*. "Hence the planes were forced to fly around aimlessly over the suburbs of Tokyo, dropping incendiary bombs on schools and hospitals, machine-gunning innocent civilians and hitting at least one elementary school pupil before being brought down or driven away."

Other newspapers echoed that theme:

"Tokyo and a few districts were visited by enemy air raiders today, but the damage caused was very slight and no confusion was seen in the affected areas."

---

* It was to be two years and two months—June 16, 1944—before American bombers returned to Japan.

"The enemy's daring enterprise failed to achieve any results worth mentioning."

"Their weak attack was a sort of comic play."

"The enemy planes inflicted casualties on the public, but from an airfield, military personnel determinedly counterattacked and easily repulsed the enemy. However, casualties were kept down to an absolute minimum and our great confidence in the iron wall of our antiaircraft defenses was justified."

Mention was made of attacks on other cities, including one that had not been bombed. "One or two planes each attacked in the vicinities of Tokyo, Yokohama, Yokosuka, Nagoya, Kobe, and Niigata. There were a total of about ten planes. They dropped bombs and incendiaries at various factories, and some factories were slightly damaged. There were some casualties, but there was no damage to any military installations. The total loss was trifling."

"About 2:30 P.M., one plane dropped incendiary bombs on Kobe. No great damage. The people are going ahead with their duties as usual. It must be considered a victory for the air defenses."

The press reported nine American planes shot down, and described in detail the damage to private homes and the destruction of schools, hospitals, and a movie theater in Tokyo.* Praise was heaped on the civilians who had extinguished the fires. Succeeding editions of newspapers trumpeted the "inhuman, insatiable, indiscriminate bombing" and the "fiendish behavior" of the Americans.

Most of the Japanese people believed these reports. At the same time, however, many were shocked that American planes were able to bomb their country at all, no matter how minimal the reported damage. Some newsmen questioned the adequacy of the nation's air defenses. One writer said he could not understand why the military

---

*Historian James M. Merrill made an extensive study of the effects of the Doolittle raid. He found that six wards of a Nagoya hospital, six schools, and numerous homes were damaged. A partial list of the military and industrial targets damaged in the raid includes five electric and gas utility companies, six gasoline storage tanks, five manufacturing plants, two warehouses, a navy ammunition dump, an army arsenal, a navy arsenal laboratory, an airfield, the government communication ministry's transformer station, a diesel manufacturing plant, a steel fabricating plant, and the Nagoya aircraft factory.

had been unable to protect the city from a small number of planes attacking in daylight. Another journalist, who had learned of the warning sent by the picket boat *Nitto Maru*, wanted to know why the antiaircraft defenses had not been alerted in time. In these cases, censors struck out the accusing passages before they reached the public.

One of Japan's leading fighter pilots, Saburo Sakai, learned of the raid at his air base at Lae, in New Guinea. A cousin from Tokyo wrote that, "The bombing of Tokyo and several other cities has brought about a tremendous change in the attitude of our people toward the war. Now things are different. The bombs have dropped here on our homes. It does not seem any more that there is such a great difference between the battle front and the home front."

Sakai commented that "the attack unnerved almost every pilot at Lae. The knowledge that the enemy was strong enough to smash at our homeland, even in what might be a punitive raid, was cause for serious apprehension of future and heavier attacks."

Many Japanese came to realize that their government had lied when it promised that they would never be attacked. The Japanese homeland was vulnerable after all, and if Japan could be attacked, then perhaps she could also be conquered. Victory was no longer assured.

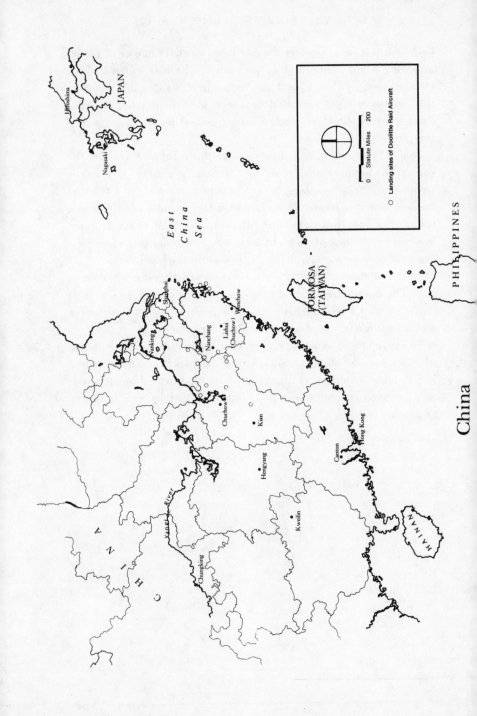

China

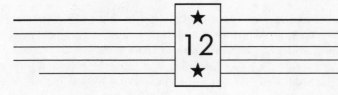

# Thanks for a Swell Ride

"**D**uring the night, fifteen of our bombers had been abandoned either over the mountains of the Chinese interior or along the seacoast of the northeast corner of Chekiang province, to the east of Hangchow." So wrote Col. S. L. A. Marshall, U.S. Army historian, in his secret report and analysis of the Doolittle raid and its aftermath the night of April 18.

Eight of the crews had made their parachute descents in the general vicinity of the eastern airfields which had been designated to receive them. Two bombers had flown much farther into China. Five had terminated their flight in the coastal area adjacent to Hangchow, which city lay within the Japanese lines. Their burned, broken, and drowned shells lay scattered across four hundred miles of Chinese land and water—some, never to be found again. One bomber survived, under internment in Siberia.

The experiences of the homing bombers were quite alike in broad outline, though differing greatly in their human and fateful detail. Night and the storm and their entry into a strange country had met them all at the same time. They had gone on as far as they dared—

and they dared greatly—until total disaster to ship and crew would have been the price of further daring. By the mercy of the thirty-mile [per hour tail] wind, which picked them up when they left Japan and blew them across the East China Sea, they made the mainland with some little gasoline to spare. Some had put down in or near the shoreline waters, whether because they had trended too far north and their fuel was running out, or because the strain of fourteen straight hours of operation was beginning to tell on the engines and they would not lift over the mountains which flanked the seashore. Those who dared this barrier did so blind. Its slopes were enveloped in mist and its peaks were lost to their vision. They estimated the heights by guess (since no maps record the true elevations of the mountains of China), gained altitude, and went on through the swirling grayness as the dark closed in on the planes. . . . An occasional ground light, blinking at great distance through a break in the fog, was all they saw of China. Some of our bombers actually flew over Chuchow [one of the fields the fliers thought was ready to receive them]. Not only was the field totally without homing arrangements, but when the planes were heard overhead, an air-raid alarm was sounded, and all lights were turned off.

The [homing] signal for which they listened did not come. For want of it, they groped their way forward. They had not been able to recognize any landmarks where they made entry into the Asian mainland, and some had not seen the coastline at all, being on instruments when they crossed it. So they could not know except in a most general way whither they were heading. Yet if these circumstances laid extraordinary stresses on the morale of the crews, it did not reflect itself in the conduct of a single member. The weather being what it was—altogether prohibitive of a landing—they had no feeling that the Chinese arrangements had failed them but only a sense of bitter disappointment that they had to abandon the ships which had carried them through. It is conspicuous in the detailed reports from the pilots that they knew the weather had balked them and that *nothing* could have ensured the safe arrival of the mission at the Chinese bases.

The time came, as the fuel supply neared exhaustion, when each crew captain had to make his decision.

The distance from Tokyo to the fields in eastern China at which the men expected to land—where, they had been told, radio homing signals, flares to mark the runways, and enough gas to get them to Chungking would be waiting—was over twelve hundred miles. At their gas-saving cruising speed of 150 to 165 miles per hour, that meant at least eight more hours of flying time from their targets, most of it over open water. The fifteen planes heading for China were strung out in a stream over 150 miles long. The day began to darken. Rain, mist, clouds, and fog encircled each ship. The winds of a storm hammered at them, forcing exhausted pilots and copilots to fight the controls to keep their ships level and on course. Visibility had been reduced to zero. The crews could barely see the wingtips.

Apprehensive pilots watched the gas gauges and anxious navigators watched their maps, hoping the lines they plotted on them represented their true position. Their lives depended on those lines, on how much fuel they had left, and on whether their engines would continue to run.

By five o'clock in the afternoon, Doolittle, flying the lead plane, was still three hours from the China coast. Some seven hundred miles to the north, another B-25 had already made landfall—the coast of Russia.

★ ★ ★ ★

Ski York and Bob Emmens, guided by the calculations of Nolan Herndon, the ship's navigator-bombardier, flew along the rugged shoreline for about ten minutes. It took that long to ascertain that they were really off the coast of Russia and not Japanese-occupied Korea. They turned inland to approach Vladivostok from the interior rather than from the seacoast, which, they reasoned, might be heavily defended against intruders. And there was no question in their minds that they would be considered intruders.

Suddenly they found themselves directly above an airfield with some forty planes lined up on the runway. York dove to pick up speed before anybody saw them and decided to shoot first and ask questions later. By then, both York and Emmens had concluded that overflying a country at war was probably not a good idea, and they decided to land as soon as possible. A few minutes later they spotted a small airport with a few buildings and some men dressed in long black coats who were watching the B-25. The field was at Primorskiy, a town thirty miles across an inlet from Vladivostok.

As York lined up on the runway, a biplane fighter appeared on their right. He lowered the wheels to let the fighter pilot know their intentions. When they landed, the fighter was on their tail. It was 5:45. They had been flying since eight-thirty that morning and had covered more than fourteen hundred miles.

The men who met their plane were Russians, but none of them spoke English. Since none of the crew spoke Russian, they all sat for a while in a room at the headquarters building, smiling at one another. Presently, a man brought a large world map into the room and nailed it to the wall. York and his crew realized they were expected to show the Russians where they had come from, but they did not yet want to give away anything about the bombing raid on Japan.

York walked over to the map, pointed to the Aleutian Islands, and traced a route to the vicinity of Vladivostok. There was no response. The Russians talked among themselves, played records on a phonograph, and offered the Americans water and the opportunity to join in a game of chess. None of the fliers knew the game. After about an hour, another Russian entered. He was dressed as a pilot, in flying jacket, helmet, and goggles, and he gestured for York to tell his story on the map. York traced the fictitious route from the Aleutians, whereupon the Russian pilot smiled, shook his head, and pointed to Tokyo.

At nine o'clock that evening, a Russian army colonel arrived with an interpreter. He welcomed the Americans to the USSR, and asked where they had come from. The colonel listened politely, congratulated them on completing the long flight from Alaska, and told them they would spend the night here. But first there would be dinner, with a great many toasts of fiery vodka.

By the end of the meal, York decided to tell the colonel about the raid on Tokyo. The officer commended the fliers for the service they had rendered the United States. "You are heroes in the eyes of your people." Glasses were refilled. The colonel proposed a toast to their flight and shook hands with each of them. Although the Russians could not have been friendlier, Emmens noticed that they evaded the Americans' questions about providing fuel so that they could fly on to Chungking. They also tactfully turned aside inquiries about seeing the American consul. The men were told to rest first. Everything would be taken care of in due time.

The next morning, April 19, York and his men were awakened at nine-thirty and told they would eat with the colonel at ten o'clock. The meal began with water glasses full of vodka and sumptuous offerings of caviar, fish, cheeses, butter, and black bread. Soup followed, along with roast goose, fried potatoes, and a whole roast pig. They ate until three o'clock that afternoon and drank more toasts than anyone could remember. At the beginning of the meal they asked about gasoline for their plane, but the colonel refused to discuss business during the meal. All decisions would be made in due course.

The crew gave the Russians a tour of their bomber, and by four o'clock they were escorted back to their room and told to rest. A half hour later they were roused and bundled aboard a DC-3. Questions about their destination were ignored. They landed at Khabarovsk, 375 miles north of Vladivostok, and were interrogated by a Russian army general about their mission. The officer was particularly concerned about whether Japanese planes had followed them to Russia. The Americans noticed that the mood of their hosts was considerably colder than at the first base where they landed.

When the general had finished with his repeated questions, he announced their fate through his interpreter. They were to be interned in quarters outside Khabarovsk until such time as "further decisions" were made. York asked to see the American consul general and was told only that the man was in Vladivostok. The Russians did not indicate that they would contact him. The fliers were led to large black cars and driven an hour away to a house inside a fenced and guarded compound.

★ ★ ★ ★

Jimmy Doolittle crossed the coast of China at 8:10 on the evening of April 18, somewhat north of his expected landfall. The sky was overcast, but there was enough visibility to make out the low islands off the coast and the hills just beyond it. Doolittle tried to pick up the homing signal that was supposed to be broadcast from Chuchow on 4495 kilocycles, but nothing came through. He continued inland, but the weather worsened, and as visibility dropped to zero, he climbed to eight thousand feet and went on instruments.

Occasionally the crew spotted dim lights on the ground through the almost solid clouds. Doolittle continued to monitor the radio receiver for the homing signal, but it seemed they were on their own. He calculated that they were probably no more than fifty miles from the Chuchow airfield, but he knew the field was ringed by mountains four thousand feet high.

He called the crew on the interphone to explain their predicament.

"In this weather, we can't get a better fix than we've got now. If we keep going in any direction, we'll just be getting farther away from Chuchow. I'm going to circle as long as we have any gas left. If the weather breaks, we'll go down and take a better look. If it doesn't, we'll have to jump."

The weather did not improve over the next fifteen minutes, nor did it show signs of breaking. The gas gauge indicated empty, and Doolittle knew the time had come to bail out. He read their position as 30°15'N, 119°E. It was 9:15. He told the crew the order in which they would jump; as pilot, he would go last.

Paul Leonard bailed out first, followed by Fred Braemer and Hank Potter. When Dick Cole, the copilot, tried to get up to take his turn, something held him back. The straps of his parachute were caught in the seat. Doolittle reached over to untangle them, and Cole made his jump, dropping through the hatch in the navigator's compartment. The time lost untangling his straps would mean that he and Doolittle would land several miles from the rest of the crew.

It was Doolittle's turn. He activated the automatic flight control equipment to keep the ship level, shut off both gas cocks, adjusted his parachute, and lowered himself through the hatch. He had no idea if he was over a lake or dry land, a marsh or a mountain peak, and he braced himself for the impact. What worried him was that if he landed too hard he might break his ankles, as he had done in

Santiago, Chile, in 1926, when he had fallen from the balcony demonstrating his gymnastic skills.

He need not have been concerned. Doolittle made a soft landing in the middle of a rice paddy liberally fertilized with night soil. He scrambled out as fast as he could, unhooked his chute, and headed for the lights of a farmhouse about one hundred yards away. He knocked on the door and called out the Chinese phrase that Lieutenant Jurika had said meant "I am an American." The reaction inside the house was swift. The lights went out and a bolt on the inside of the door was snapped into place.

Shivering from the wind and rain, he pounded on the door and repeated the phrase, but the house remained dark and silent. It was obvious he would receive no help there. He wandered along a path for about a half-mile, looking for shelter from the biting wind. He came upon a large box covered with wooden planks that was resting atop a pair of sawhorses. Doolittle thought it was not much, but it was the best shelter he was likely to find. He removed some of the planks and crawled inside the box.

He quickly learned he was not alone. An elderly man lay stretched out on his back, with his hands folded across his chest. Doolittle was in a coffin. The wind whistled through cracks in the sides and there was little room to move around. Doolittle climbed out to find the rain coming down harder, but at least it rinsed some of the night soil from his uniform.

He continued along the trail in the dark until he came to a watermill, which provided some protection from the rain but not the cold. He spent much of the night exercising his arms and legs in a vain attempt to keep warm and maintain some circulation.

Dick Cole, meanwhile, slept in relative comfort some miles away. He had decided to stay wherever he came down. "Landing in a tree," he said, "I stretched my chute between it and another tree, making a hammock, and proceeded to go to sleep." Paul Leonard landed on a mountainside shrouded in fog. "Crawled about twenty feet down hill," he said tersely. "Got no place. Went up hill twenty feet past chute. Got no place. Came back to chute. Rolled up in it.

Put arm around bamboo tree and went to sleep." Hank Potter also bedded down under a tree.

By morning, Doolittle was in despair over the fate of his men, not only his own crew, but also the seventy-five men in the other fifteen planes. He was their leader, he was responsible, accountable for their safety, and he did not know where they were. He might be the only one of them alive. Nor did he know if the raid had been a success. He knew he and Trav Hoover had reached Tokyo, but what of the others? And if they had reached Japan, were the antiaircraft defenses alerted by his attack so strong that they had been shot down?

Cold, tired, hungry, and dirty, Doolittle wandered up the trail, tormented by concern over his men. He came across a farmer who showed no sign of understanding Jurika's handy phrase, or anything else Doolittle tried to indicate in pantomime. Doolittle drew a sketch of a locomotive, hoping the man would lead him to a railroad. The man smiled at the picture and motioned for him to follow. He led him not to a railroad but to a Chinese army unit, which regarded Doolittle with considerable suspicion. The officer in charge wanted Doolittle to surrender his .45-caliber pistol, but Doolittle shook his head and tried to explain who he was and where he had come from. The officer seemed to comprehend some English but appeared unconvinced by Doolittle's words.

Three Chinese enlisted men kept their tommy guns trained on Doolittle, who began to suspect he was about to be shot. He told the officer he would take him to where he'd left his parachute. Surely that would persuade the man of the truth of his story about bailing out of an airplane. But when they reached the site, the parachute was gone.

He asked the officer to speak to the occupants of the farmhouse. They would certainly remember someone banging on the door and shouting the previous night. They might even have heard his airplane. When they reached the house, the officer spoke to the farmer, his wife, and their two children.

"They say they heard no noise during the night," he told Doolittle. "They say they heard no plane during the night. They say they saw no parachute. They say you are lying."

Doolittle knew he was in trouble. He had no identification and could not prove he was a pilot who had jumped from his airplane after a bombing raid on Japan. To the Chinese army officer, he was an unkempt foreigner with a gun and no verifiable explanation for his presence. Doolittle continued to reason with the man, but his explanation was simply dismissed.

Two of the Chinese soldiers entered the farmhouse to search it. They came out grinning and carrying a large white bundle. It was Doolittle's parachute. The officer's attitude changed instantly. He shook Doolittle's hand, dispatched search parties into the countryside to hunt for the crew, and took him to see the provincial governor. By afternoon the rest of his crew had been located, and the five men were reunited at the governor's house. Two had been captured by thieves intent on robbing them until a boy who spoke some English convinced them that their prisoners were Americans. They were released and shortly met up with Paul Leonard, who had survived a shootout with four bandits and gotten away unscathed.

All the men were in good condition except Hank Potter, who had hurt his ankle on landing. Doolittle was pleased to have his men back with him, but still, by nightfall the day after the raid, he was no closer to learning the fate of the others.

★ ★ ★ ★

Trav Hoover followed Doolittle's plane across the China Sea, but lost it as the weather deteriorated when they neared the coast. Clouds extended down to sea level, and visibility was poor along the shoreline. Carl Wildner, the navigator, saw enough of the coast to recognize that they were close to the Japanese lines, and he gave Hoover a heading to the southwest.

Hoover had started to climb above the clouds and the mountains he knew were not far inland when the left engine stopped. The plane staggered and shook. He reached down with his right hand, flicked on the fuel booster pump switch, and pushed the control yoke forward. The engine started up again and Hoover began to climb, but the engine quit once more. He quickly dove to allow the gas in the rear tank to flow forward, and the engine roared to life.

Three times he tried to climb, and each time the engine cut out. It was apparent they would not be able to clear the mountains or even maintain level flight much longer. They were almost out of gas and too low to bail out. On one engine, Hoover could not gain enough altitude for them to jump. That left one option—a wheels-up crash-landing. Hoover and his copilot, Foggy Fitzhugh, scanned the ground ahead and saw a long flat stretch of rice paddies. It was almost dark, and a light rain was falling. Hoover crossed the paddies, looking for obstructions. They saw none.

He went around one more time, lined up on the watery fields, and began his approach. Fitzhugh called out the decreasing speed and lowered the flaps while Hoover adjusted the trim tabs. He turned off the ignition switches seconds before the plane touched down and made a smooth landing. The plane slid almost gently in the mud and came to a stop, suffering only minor damage.

The men piled out, taking everything they might need—guns, flashlights, knives, compasses, canteens, emergency rations, and clothes. They set fire to the plane, with the incendiary provided for that purpose, aware that the flames could give away their location, but they didn't want the B-25 to fall into Japanese hands. Above the crackling of the blaze, they could hear high-pitched voices. They might be Chinese, but it was too risky to stay around to find out.

The crew headed west in the dark and climbed part way up a mountain. Finding no shelter from the rain, they spent the night shivering in a trench. The next morning they stumbled on a hut and decided to stay there, out of sight, during the day. At night they headed west again. They had seen no people since their landing. All they could do was keep walking and hope the Japanese did not find them.

★ ★ ★ ★

Bob Gray's plane, *Whiskey Pete*, crossed the Chinese coast in the dark and rain. He could not see the shoreline, but he did notice scattered blinking lights and what he took to be a city through the overcast. About an hour after the navigator, Charles Ozuk, calculated they had crossed into China, they dropped two flares, hoping to see enough level ground to land on, but they saw nothing.

By ten o'clock that night they had no choice but to bail out. There was not enough gas to keep flying. Aden Jones and Ozuk jumped through the forward hatch. The copilot, Shorty Manch, shined his flashlight into the rear of the ship to make sure the engineer-gunner, Leland Faktor, had gone. It seemed empty back there, so Manch outfitted himself with his survival gear—a box of cigars, Baby Ruth candy bars, an ax, a knife, a Winchester rifle, two .45s and a .22, and his phonograph—and prepared to jump.

His parachute opened with such a jolt that he lost everything but a .45 and the handle of the phonograph. The impact was so great that the candy bars were sucked from their wrappers. He landed on a hillside and tumbled seventy feet before coming to a stop. It would be foolish to wander over such steep terrain in the dark, so he wrapped himself in his parachute and lay down to sleep.

Jones, the bombardier, landed high up in the mountains close to the peak, where he chose to spend the night. He dug his heels into the dirt so he would not slide downhill and went to sleep. He remembered hearing a plane pass low overhead, but he could not see it. Ozuk landed on the same mountain, but his chute caught in a tree, and he was slammed back against some rocks, cutting his left leg badly. He tried to free himself from his chute throughout the night, but without success. Leland Faktor's parachute failed to open after he jumped. He was the first casualty among the Doolittle Raiders.

In the morning, Shorty Manch searched for the gear he had lost during the jump but found none of it. He started down the hill toward a village and met an old woman carrying a bundle of sticks.

"Pardon me, madam," he said, in his thick Texas drawl.

She did not seem to hear him, so he stepped closer.

"Lady," he said.

She looked at the six-foot-six foreigner in a military uniform, ran away to her house and slammed the door. Manch followed her and knocked on the door. The house was empty and when he went through it and glanced out the back, he saw the villagers running into a nearby bamboo thicket.

He walked on and came across a Chinese man who was more curious about Manch than afraid. The man invited him home. "First," Manch recalled, "he drew a Japanese flag and pointed to that. I didn't know whether he wanted to know if I had bombed Japan or was a Jap myself. I decided the last was the idea so I held my nose and waved the picture away. The Chinese grinned and then brought out a clipping of an old Blenheim [bomber] and pointed to the English insignia. I shook my head again. Then he brought out a copy of *The Saturday Evening Post*, about four years old. On the cover was a picture of President Roosevelt. I grinned and pointed to Roosevelt, then to me. He got the idea and everybody in the room laughed and we shook hands."

His new-found Chinese friends accompanied Manch as he continued making his way west, but by nightfall they had not found any other members of his crew.

Charles Ozuk managed to cut himself out of his parachute harness in the morning. His left leg was mangled. He made a crutch out of a tree branch and hobbled along as best he could. Aden Jones also walked inland, looking for his crewmates. At intervals he fired his .45 in the air hoping to attract their attention. Late in the day he found a village where the residents took him in for the night.

★ ★ ★ ★

Dean Hallmark's plane, *Green Hornet*, ran out of gas four minutes before it reached the coast. At an altitude of only one hundred feet above the sea, Hallmark had to ditch. He told the crew to strap themselves in and make sure they had their Mae West life vests on. He held the ship straight and level until both engines quit. The plane bounced off a wave, plummeted into the sea, and broke apart.

The left wing hit the water first and sheared off. The fuselage split open, and the sea rushed in violently. Bill Dieter, the bombardier in the nose, screamed in pain from the impact. Hallmark was thrown through the windshield.

Chase Nielsen, the navigator, hit his head against the back of the copilot's seat and was knocked unconscious. When he came to, the water was up to his waist. His nose was broken and he was bleeding. He climbed out on top of the plane and found Bob Meder, the copilot. Hallmark scrambled up to join them, despite deep cuts on his knees. Dieter hauled himself atop the right engine, and Don Fitzmaurice, the engineer-gunner, pulled himself out through a side window. Dieter and Fitzmaurice were badly hurt.

Fifteen-foot waves lashed the wreckage, pushing them into the icy water as the bomber sank. Meder tried to inflate the life raft, but the lanyard on the $CO_2$ cartridge broke. They would have to swim for shore. It took them four hours.

Fitzmaurice lost consciousness, and Meder grabbed him and tugged him ashore, only to realize he was dead. As Meder pulled himself up on the beach, he discovered Dieter's body, brought in by the tide. He tried to revive both men, but it was no use. Hallmark and Nielsen floundered ashore separately, unaware of what had happened to the others.

All three survivors knew that their stretch of coastline was territory occupied by the Japanese, and they tried to get off the beach as quickly as they could. Nielsen climbed some rocks and fell into a ditch, striking his head. When he awoke the next morning, he saw two vultures perched above him, watching and waiting. He eased himself up and looked around. He saw Chinese fishermen, working on their boats, and a small village about a half-mile away. Then he noticed what they all feared—Japanese flags on the small motor launches at the dock.

Nielsen moved cautiously along the treeline to a path that led to the village and the waterfront. He watched several Japanese soldiers board their boats and head out into open water. He spied other soldiers wearing a different uniform and thought they might be Chinese, but he had no way of knowing. Then he noticed a crowd of Chinese people on the beach. They were standing around two bodies lying on the sand. The bodies were wearing life preservers. Nielsen crawled toward the sand dunes to get a better view. A pair of black, split-toed, rubber-soled canvas shoes appeared in front of him and a voice ordered him to stand up.

Nielsen rose to face a man carrying an ancient rifle, wearing the uniform he took to be Chinese. In broken English, the man asked if he was Japanese or American. Nielsen replied that he was American.

Dean Hallmark wandered into the village Nielsen had seen near the shore, and was taken by Chinese soldiers to a house and given tea. They tried to hold a conversation, but none of them spoke English. Suddenly, one of the soldiers gestured that someone was coming. Hallmark assumed it was the Japanese, and he picked up a large club. Raising it above his head, he moved over by the door. The door opened and a man entered. It was Nielsen.

The two Americans were conducted to a Chinese army garrison about an hour away and reunited with Bob Meder. When Japanese troops came through the area on a patrol, the Chinese soldiers hid them. The Chinese belonged to the puppet government forces, which the Japanese left alone, as long as they caused no trouble. The Chinese soldiers promised to help get the fliers into unoccupied China, but warned them it would be a dangerous trip.

After dark, some Chinese troops led the Americans to the spot where the bodies of their fellow crewmen had been hidden. Coffins had been built, and twenty-nine-year-old Sgt. William J. Dieter, from Vail, Iowa, and twenty-three-year-old Sgt. Donald E. Fitzmaurice, from Lincoln, Nebraska, were buried.

★ ★ ★ ★

Ted Lawson flew *Ruptured Duck* low over the beach, looking for logs or any other obstructions that might prevent him from using it as a landing strip. It was getting dark and rain was spattering against the windshield, but the beach appeared clear and clean. They had flown over a series of islands for about ten minutes, looking for landmarks or for a field in which to land, and had given up finding either one. Lawson was climbing to head inland when he spotted a hole in the clouds over a long, curving beach. He decided to put down there, spend the night in the plane, and take off for Chuchow in the morning.

He approached the beach over the water and lowered the landing gear and flaps, while Dean Davenport, the copilot, called out the decreasing airspeed. Just as Davenport said, "one-ten," both engines quit. Lawson jammed the throttles and the propeller pitch controls forward with his right hand and pulled back on the control yoke to keep the nose up with his left. It was too late. The main landing gear struck the crest of a wave, and the plane slammed into the sea. It was like hitting a wall.

Lawson and Davenport, strapped into their armor-plated seats, were thrown through the windshield. Bob Clever, in the bombardier's position in the nose, was tossed through the Plexiglas headfirst. Mac McClure, the navigator, had been kneeling behind the pilots' seats with his shoulders braced against the backrests. He, too, was catapulted through the windshield into the water.

Dave Thatcher, the engineer-gunner, remained inside the plane. He was stunned for a few minutes, and when he revived, water was pouring into the fuselage. He inflated his Mae West and tried to escape through what he thought was the rear hatch, but he could not seem to get out. Then he realized the plane was upside down—he had been trying to get out through the top turret. He crawled onto the wreckage of the belly of the ship and saw the beach about one hundred yards away.

When Ted Lawson came around, he was strapped in his seat under ten feet of water. He unbuckled his seat belt and shot to the surface, but found it difficult to move. He felt paralyzed and unable to think coherently. The waves pinned him against one of the bomber's wings and spun him around. He remembered facing the twin rudders, which were sticking up out of the water. They looked like tombstones.

The tide brought him onto the beach, and he found he could barely walk. His injuries were extensive. The bicep of his left arm hung loose, as though neatly sliced through with a carving knife. His left leg was cut so deeply from upper thigh to knee that muscle and bone were visible. His front teeth were missing, and his face was bloody.

Dean Davenport also found himself strapped in his seat underwater. He got to the beach, but had trouble walking because of deep cuts in his right leg.

When Mac McClure surfaced, he reached out with his right arm to start swimming to the beach. Pain shot through his shoulder. The same thing happened when he tried to move his left arm. Both shoulders were broken, and his arms were swollen to the elbows. He slowly plowed his way through the surf to the beach.

Before he reached the shore, Bob Clever called out to him.

"Is that you, McClure?"

"Yes," McClure said.

"Come help me."

"I'm not sure I can," McClure said. "I've got two broken arms."

"You son of a bitch! Help me," Clever yelled.

"When I came upon him," McClure remembered, "he was sitting crossed legs and holding his head. I could see blood oozing down his forehead. He said something like, 'I'm bleeding to death.'"

Clever had sustained severe cuts around the head, and his eyes were swollen shut. Half his hair was gone. He had sprained his back and hips and could not stand upright.

Dave Thatcher came through with only a slight gash on his head and a few cuts and bruises. As the five men came together on the beach, Davenport walked up to Lawson and looked him over.

"Goddamn," he said. "You're really bashed open. Your whole face is pushed in."

Lawson noted blood running down Davenport's forehead and asked if he was badly hurt.

"I think so," Davenport said.

The men sprawled on the sand for a half hour, unable to move despite the continuing rain. Thatcher noticed two men standing on a rise just beyond the beach. He took out his .45, aimed it, and asked Lawson if he should shoot. Before Lawson could answer, McClure looked up at the men and shouted, "Don't shoot! They're Chinese fishermen."

"How do you know?"

"Haven't you ever read *National Geographic?*" McClure said.

The men wore black blouses and pants and flat bamboo hats, just like the pictures McClure had seen. The fishermen came down to the beach and were soon joined by six others. They regarded the Americans carefully, making mournful sounds, and asked, through gestures, if anyone else was on the plane.

They helped the fliers to a hut a half-mile away. Lawson wondered if they would turn them over to the Japanese. Once inside, Thatcher did what he could for the others, bandaging wounds with dressings from his first-aid kit, with his handkerchief, and finally with dirty rags the fishermen gave them. There was nothing Thatcher could do for their terrible pain. They would need to find a doctor if they were to survive.

In the morning, Thatcher returned to the plane to hunt for additional first-aid kits and the morphine supply, but he could not locate them. He saw a Japanese patrol boat offshore, but its crew did not see him or the wreckage.

That afternoon, a procession formed up at the fishermen's hut. Four seriously injured Americans, in great pain from their untreated wounds, were wrapped in blankets and toted on wooden stretchers over a hill to the far side of the island. There they were placed on a boat that would take them to the Chinese mainland. By nightfall of the nineteenth, when the boat came to rest on a sandbar, they fell asleep. It would take almost twenty-four hours to reach the coast, and they would still be forty-five miles from the nearest hospital.

★ ★ ★ ★

Dick Joyce had to go on instruments one hundred miles before he reached China. When his navigator, Horace "Sally" Crouch, told him they should be over the coast, he started to climb. It was dark, foggy, and rainy. Aside from one brief glimpse of land—which reassured them they were indeed over China—the men saw nothing else.

They reached the point at which they expected to receive the homing signal from Chuchow, but they did not pick up any radio transmissions. They flew fifteen minutes beyond, wanting to be certain they were well beyond Japanese lines. Joyce climbed to nine thousand feet, and when he estimated there was only fifteen minutes' worth of gas remaining, he told the crew to prepare to bail out. Ed Horton, the engineer-gunner, would jump first.

"OK, fellas," Joyce said, "I'll see you in Chuchow. Let me know when you're ready, Horton."

"Horton to pilot. All ready, sir."

"Go ahead, Eddie, and good luck."

"OK, Lieutenant, here I go, and thanks for a swell ride."

"I laughed when he said it," Joyce said later, "and it sure made me feel good. You can't beat men like that."

Roy Stork, the copilot, stuffed his pockets with candy bars and cigarettes before he jumped.

"Those bars were flying in every direction, my parachute gave me such a flip," he said. "It was pouring rain and in no time my chute was soaked with water and I was falling very fast. I couldn't see anything in the dark and so I was in a completely relaxed condition when I hit the ground. Otherwise I might have been hurt. I must have been knocked unconscious, as I don't remember anything until I found myself lying against a tree. I lay in the rain until morning before starting out."

When he was sure all the others had gone, Joyce rolled the stabilizer back so the plane would not pick up too much speed. As he tried to get out of the cockpit, he found it difficult, with his parachute on, to squeeze between the seats. He had to lean back and push on the control yoke to keep the plane from stalling while edging himself through the narrow space. He reached the escape hatch and paused long enough to grab some food before dropping into the darkness. When his chute opened, one of the leg straps broke, and he nearly fell out of the harness. He slipped down, and the chest buckle smacked him on the jaw, stunning him. His .45 flew out of its shoulder holster, and he spun crazily as he heard the plane crash below him.

Joyce and his crew were lucky. None of them was injured in landing, and by the night of the nineteenth, they were being led to safety by friendly Chinese.

★ ★ ★ ★

Ross Greening, piloting *Hari Carrier*, gave the order to bail out. The plane was at 9,500 feet, and the crew had seen enough of the terrain below to know they were jumping into mountains. The engineer-gunner, Mel Gardner, went first. His parachute opened with a vicious snap, and he felt he was floating sideways rather than down. He shone his flashlight below him, hoping to see the ground, but could distinguish nothing through the clouds and fog. He made a hard landing on a bluff, clambered up until he found a secure spot, and wrapped himself in his parachute.

Ken Reddy, the copilot, also made a rough landing, cutting his head and bruising one knee. He started down the mountain, shouting as he went, but he got no answer. He fired a shot, but there was no signal in return. Finally he made a shelter out of his chute and tried to sleep.

The navigator, Frank Kappeler, jumped with a lit flashlight and a load of candy bars, all of which he lost when his chute jerked open. He watched the beam from his flashlight get smaller until it disappeared. His parachute shroud lines caught in the top of a tree, breaking his fall just as his feet touched the ground. He fell backward and kept slipping every time he tried to get up. He decided to stay put, and he remembered it as the longest night of his life. In the morning he was able to free himself from the lines.

The next day, Greening's crew headed west, assisted by Chinese farmers and soldiers. By ten o'clock that night they had all arrived safely in Chü-hsien, where they were given tea, milk, and crackers, and put up in a hotel. By then they were well beyond the danger of the Japanese lines.

★ ★ ★ ★

Most of the other crews were also out of danger, or at least on their way to safety, by the night of April 19. Brick Holstrom's crew bailed out at six thousand feet, twenty minutes after crossing the coast of China. They landed on the side of a mountain and waited for daylight. They made their way separately to the west, aided by friendly Chinese who passed them on from one village and army garrison to the next.

★ ★ ★ ★

Davey Jones's crew jumped in the vicinity of Chuchow. Joe Manske, the engineer-gunner said, "My bailout was a very frightening experience. We were out of gas in closed-in weather conditions. I was first out of our ship and didn't realize how far each of us would be separated on the ground. After my chute opened, I panicked, being a small frame person, weighing about 110 pounds. With the weather socked in, I had nothing to compare my descent with. Being so light, I thought I was suspended and not falling."

No one was hurt and the next day Jones and copilot Ross Wilder ran into each other and were taken by train to Yushan where the Chinese gave them a hero's welcome. The citizens cleaned their uniforms, fed them, and ceremoniously washed their feet. Later in the day they were reunited with the rest of their crew.

★ ★ ★ ★

Bill Bower figured he had enough gas for twenty more minutes of flying, and he told the crew to get ready to jump. They were well inland from the coast at nine thousand feet, somewhere near Chuchow. It was eleven-thirty at night. Waldo Bither, the bombardier, crawled out of the nose into the navigator's compartment and accidentally snagged his parachute, causing it to spring open. They had no extra chutes, so he had to stop and repack it, which he did calmly and efficiently on the navigator's table. At thirty-six, Bither was one of the older men on the mission. "Those old sarges," Bower said, "they could do anything."

Bither jumped and landed on a steep slope. He decided that the first thing he should do was smoke a cigarette. When he finished, he flicked the butt away and was astounded to see the tiny red flare fall for a very long time. He realized then that he was on the edge of a precipice. Undaunted, he thought it wise to spend the night without moving, and, "in spite of rain and cold, was able to sleep very well."

Omer Duquette, the engineer-gunner, fractured an ankle when he landed, but his was the only injury among that crew. Bower jumped wearing the .45 his father had carried in World War I, and it stayed with him when his chute was yanked open. "I landed on top of a pretty high hill," Bower said, "and immediately rolled up in the parachute and went to sleep. At dawn I looked, and I was right on the edge of a cliff, so I landed in the right place really."

Four of the crewmen found a village the next day. They received word that Duquette was being carried there and would arrive in the morning. "We stayed in this particular village and house overnight," Bower said. It was an uncomfortable night. "The place was full of lice and the people boarded it up, and they used the bucket in the corner." But they were all safe and soon on their way to Chung-king, riding part of the way in a 1940 Plymouth.

★ ★ ★ ★

Doc Watson's plane flew over the coast of China through thick clouds, fog, and rain. Tom Griffin, the navigator, recalled that "our plane flew inland approximately three hundred miles before we ran out of gas. After fifteen and a half hours in the air we bailed out, still in the storm. We were farthest inland of any of the others."

Eldred Scott, the engineer-gunner, jumped first, after helping himself to a pint of whiskey and some cigarettes. Before he had time to accept fully the fact that he had actually jumped from an airplane at ten thousand feet, his parachute hooked the top branches of a tree and deposited him gently in the fork of another one. He smoked a cigarette, tossed the butt away, and had the disturbing experience of watching it fall a great distance. He settled back in the branches, took a sip of whiskey, and went to sleep.

Tom Griffin was astonished at the silence he noticed after his chute opened. "I seemed to be suspended in a blank, silent void with no feeling of movement . . . I could just see my parachute canopy and it seemed to have a life of its own. It would descend to a level with me and start to collapse—I was afraid it would spill all of its air—then it would fill and swing overhead and descend to the other side, where it would once again collapse.

"I was, of course, in a great pendulum with no feeling of move-ment at all. Fortunately, the great air currents causing the action subsided after a time, and when a branch of a tree struck my face, my shroud lines lowered me to the ground in what must have been one of the gentlest landings a jumper could possibly experience. I was not able to pull my chute out of the trees above, so I unbuckled my harness and moved off, leaving my chute hung up above."

The next morning, Griffin found Scott and James Parker, their copilot, and the three fliers slogged westward in a driving rain through one rice paddy after another. Late in the afternoon they persuaded a farmer to let them dry their clothes in front of his stove. While they waited, the house was surrounded by soldiers pointing rifles through every door and window. Griffin repeated in Chinese the phrase Jurika had taught them—"I am an American"—but it was in a different dialect and was not understood. The men were taken prisoner and led away to the walled city of Ihwang, where two American Catholic priests confirmed their nationality. Griffin, Scott, and Parker were freed, and the Chinese residents welcomed them as heroes.

Wayne Bissell, the bombardier, had been captured by bandits, but he managed to escape and join his fellow crewmen in Ihwang.

Doc Watson had a difficult jump. His right arm became entangled in the shroud lines above his head. When he was able to work the arm free, it flopped uselessly at his side. The shoulder was badly dislocated, and he was in considerable pain. He fashioned a sling from his parachute and temporarily eased the pain with a morphine injection from his medical kit.

He walked a mile before being taken in by some peasants. They dried his clothes, gave him hot water and rice, and wrapped him in a blanket. Watson slept for eighteen hours, until late on the twentieth, when he was taken to Ihwang and reunited with his crew.

The fliers began their journey west. It would take them until May 14 to reach Chungking.

★ ★ ★ ★

The crew of Mac McElroy's ship shook hands and bid one another good-bye while they waited at the open hatch in the navigator's compartment. Their altitude was 6,300 feet, and they were not sure whether they were over China or open water. One by one they dropped through the hatch, relieved to find they were over land. Dick Knobloch, the copilot, landed in a rice paddy and turned on his flashlight, hoping the others were close enough to signal back. Seven lights answered his, three more than there were crewmen. He did not turn on his light again.

He wandered for an hour and stopped to try to sleep, but it was too cold. He spotted another light. It was McElroy. At dawn they came to a village, where a boy led them to a Chinese army unit. They learned later that Japanese soldiers had been only two miles away from the village.

The officer in charge of the Chinese army detachment took them to another village. They were given eggs and tea. Doors were placed on sawhorses for them to sleep on. The next day the rest of the crew joined them—all in good shape—and they began a trek to Chungking by foot, sedan chair, ricksha, donkey, boat, bus, and train.

★ ★ ★ ★

Pilot Jack Hilger was the last to jump from his ship. When he looked around and discovered that he was the only one still aboard, he was overwhelmed by a terrible feeling of loneliness. The others in the crew had landed safely. When Hilger's parachute opened, he was jolted by a fierce pain in his groin. The right leg strap of the harness had come unfastened, and he slipped down so far that the chest buckle hit him in the face, drawing blood.

He dropped near the peak of a mountain and was knocked unconscious. When he revived, he found he was hanging on a steep slope, held by his parachute, which had caught in a tree. His left wrist and hand were sprained, his back was wrenched, and the wind and rain threatened to drown him. He cut the chute down, made a tent of it, and went to sleep.

When he awoke, he was startled to hear the sound of surf. His first thought was that his crewmen must have landed in the sea, but eventually the fog lifted and he saw that he was sitting between two raging mountain streams. A village lay below him in a valley. He made his way there and was treated with great kindness. He was the first Westerner the villagers had ever seen. A boy led him to a Chinese army unit, but the sentries almost shot him before an officer recognized Hilger's insignia.

The soldiers took him in a ricksha to Kuang Feng. He was offered food and drink, cleaned up, and reunited with his crew. They slept that night on straw pads and set out for Chungking. The trip took two weeks.

★ ★ ★ ★

The mountains loomed out of the fog in front of Don Smith's plane. He jammed the throttles all the way forward, climbed to the right, and headed back out to sea to avoid them. The port engine was backfiring and the starboard one began to misfire. It was obvious they would not have enough power to keep flying much longer. He told the crew to prepare for a crash-landing at sea. They were five hundred yards off the coastal island of Tantowsha Tao. Visibility was almost zero as Smith glided in at 120 miles per hour.

He held the ship in the air until the speed dropped to ninety, and set it down so gently that no one aboard suffered so much as a bruise. The Plexiglas nose shattered, however, and water poured into the fuselage. The men gathered up every bit of equipment they could carry. Doc White took his medical supplies and surgical kit. The others hauled their first-aid kits, rations, guns, and even parachutes out of the plane. The bomber remained afloat long enough for them to load the life raft. Only then did it begin to sink beneath the waves, with its bright navigation lights casting an eerie glow under the water.

Jammed in the raft, the men paddled toward the coast. The small rubber boat sprang a slow leak, and a wave swamped it, dumping men and supplies into the water. Four of them struggled to right it and get back aboard, but Ses Sessler, the navigator-bombardier, struck out on his own for shore. The crewmen on the raft struggled for an hour and a half before reaching land. There was no beach, and they had to climb over rocks and an eighty-foot cliff.

They rested for an hour and decided to head for a light they saw inland. It was a farmer's house. He took them in, sat them by the fire, and brought them hot food. The neighbors came in to stare at the strangers. Through sign language, Doc White got them to search for Sessler, who was found the next day.

Smith and the crew studied a map and determined that they were on the only offshore island in the area that did not have a Japanese garrison stationed on it. The Chinese promised to get them to the next island, called Nandian, and from there to the mainland, on the following night. The men did not know it yet, but they were not far from the four badly injured fliers from Lawson's plane, which had crashed off Nandian Island. The men who so desperately needed Doc White's skills were no more than a few miles away. It would take five more days for him to reach them.

★ ★ ★ ★

"We're in a tough situation, fellas," Bill Farrow told the crew of *Bat Out of Hell.* They had crossed the Chinese coast an hour before and had been flying on instruments at eleven thousand feet, trying, unsuccessfully, to pick up the radio homing signal from Chuchow. The darkness and the overcast prevented them from finding a place to land. Farrow decided to push on to the west in case the weather cleared enough for them to set down.

George Barr, the navigator, thought they should hold that course only fifteen minutes more, then turn south to make sure they wouldn't be over Japanese territory when they ran out of gas. Farrow and his copilot, Bobby Hite, disagreed with Barr, and they continued west until 11:45, when the fuel warning lights came on. At that moment the crew spotted a break in the clouds, and through the hole they saw the lights of a city. Barr identified it as Nanchang, which was behind Japanese lines. It was too late to do anything but jump.

All five men landed safely. Jake DeShazer, the bombardier, came down in a cemetery. He fired his .45 several times, hoping for an answering shot, but he heard nothing over the sound of the rain. He walked for a long time and stopped at a little shrine to sleep.

Barr landed in a rice paddy and made his way in the dark across a river. He heard a shout behind him and felt the muzzle of a rifle at his back. The man summoned several other soldiers. They tied Barr's hands and led him to a town. Barr was still not sure whether they were Chinese or Japanese. He found out once he was taken to a room with more than a dozen Japanese army officers. He was a prisoner.

They offered him something to eat and drink, which he refused, and began their interrogation. Barr responded only with his name, rank, and serial number. They did not question him long, and he was put in a room and allowed to go to sleep. During the night he was awakened when the door opened, and soldiers led Bobby Hite into the room.

The next morning, DeShazer continued to make his way on foot along a path, passing several people who seemed uninterested in him. He began to believe he had landed in free China. He stopped a few people to ask if he was in Japanese territory, but either they did not understand him or were unwilling to say. He walked for several hours and passed some soldiers, but could not tell from their appearance if they were enemies or allies.

Some time later he came upon more soldiers. He pointed to himself and said, "America," then pointed to them and asked, "China or Japan?" One soldier answered, "China," but DeShazer did not believe him. About a dozen other soldiers confronted him and also said, "China," in response to his question. He felt a bayonet at his back and saw ten rifles aimed at him. He was taken to an officer who began to question him through an interpreter.

DeShazer refused to answer any questions and pretended that he did not know his interrogators were Japanese. He was given some hotcakes and apple butter, and after he had eaten, the officer told him he was in Japanese hands.

"Aren't you afraid?" the interpreter asked.

"What should I be afraid of?" DeShazer said.

The following day, the five men of *Bat Out of Hell* were brought together, handcuffed, and placed in separate cells, with four guards on each cell. Individually, the American fliers were taken from the cells, interrogated, and warned they would be shot for refusal to answer the questions. The men dutifully repeated their names, ranks, and serial numbers, and even made up fanciful replies to the questions. Barr said he had hit his head when he bailed out and could not remember anything about his mission. Hite claimed he was a fighter pilot.

That afternoon they were blindfolded and placed aboard a plane, handcuffed to the seats, and flown to Shanghai. At midnight on April 19, two guards came to Bobby Hite's cell and yanked him to his feet. They led him to a room where a Japanese officer and an interpreter were sitting behind a table. The interpreter gestured to a chair in front of them.

"You will please to sit down," he said.

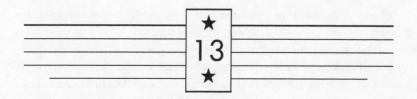

# We Lost Some
# of the Boys

On Saturday, April 18 (Sunday, April 19, in China), Americans were shocked by newspaper headlines such as this one in *The New York Times:*

JAPAN REPORTS TOKYO, YOKOHAMA BOMBED BY "ENEMY PLANES" IN DAY-LIGHT; CLAIMS 9

The report came not from the U.S. government but from a Tokyo radio broadcast picked up by a listening post of the Columbia Broadcasting System.

"Enemy bombers appeared over Tokyo for the first time in the current war," said the article, quoting the Japanese source, "inflicting damage on schools and hospitals. Invading planes failed to cause any damage on military establishments, although casualties in the schools and hospitals were as yet unknown.

"This inhuman attack on these cultural establishments and on residential districts is causing widespread indignation among the populace."

According to the Japanese announcer, nine of the attacking

planes were shot down and the rest repulsed by heavy antiaircraft fire.

The report presented American military leaders George Marshall and Hap Arnold with a dilemma. They had received no communication from Stilwell or Bissell in China, or from Doolittle, and thus had no confirmation about the success or failure of the raid. If the Japanese claim of nine kills was true, then the raid would have to be viewed as less than a triumph. To lose more than half of an attacking force on a mission that might have caused only minimal damage was not the sort of news to bolster American morale.

If this was the case, then detailed information on the planning and execution of the operation would have to be withheld from the public. Japan was not the only country interested in producing an altered version of the facts. Until Marshall or Arnold heard from American military authorities in China, they would say nothing to the press, and they cautioned Stilwell and Bissell in Chungking to do the same.

The first official air force documentation on the Doolittle raid, dated July 18, 1943, states: "Marshall directed Stilwell to maintain an atmosphere of total mystery regarding the bombing. No publicity was desired for the project, and Stilwell was to deny any connection therewith, insofar as public information was concerned. Marshall desired also that the Generalissimo [Chiang Kai-shek] observe the same policy."

At home, Americans were informed that "the war department and the navy department said early today that they had no confirmation of reports that [Allied] airplanes had bombed Tokyo. The reports, however, created no surprise in official circles, and there was no denial of the possibility that American planes might have participated in an attack upon the Japanese capital."

To absolve those in Washington of any culpability for what might be a disaster, press spokesmen for the military told reporters that "such an attack could have been made without direct orders from Washington. Even if plans for a raid on the Japanese capital had been worked out with the assistance or at the instigation of Washington strategists, the fact that the raid was undertaken at a specific

time would be the concern chiefly of the army and navy officials
entrusted with the task of carrying it out." In other words, if the
raid had failed and become a public-relations nightmare, the heads
that rolled would not belong to anyone in Washington.

By the following day there was still no word from Doolittle, but
Bissell forwarded a confusing message he had received from the Chinese air force.

"Three crew members are at Chuchow. According to crew members, sixteen planes started, the formation being disrupted by bad
weather. Crew members say they flew twenty-one hours."

Later that day, Bissell sent another message stating that he had
received many conflicting reports about casualties, and that it was
impossible to verify the number of men killed and wounded. That
was disturbing news, indeed.

Although the American military personnel in China knew no more
about the raid, the Japanese were supplying details that made the
front pages of American newspapers. On April 19 they reported that
the cities of Kobe and Nagoya had been bombed, and that the fires
there had burned for an hour and a half. The attacking force was
said to consist of sixty planes bearing U.S. insignia. This was the
first published indication of the nationality of the attackers. The
articles repeated the claim that nine planes had been shot down and
that the only damage sustained was to civilian targets—schools and
hospitals.

The intercepted radio broadcasts from Tokyo called the raids
a "Yankee joke and propaganda stunt for home consumption in
America," but they also noted that Emperor Hirohito was "greatly
concerned."

American newspapers speculated on how the planes might have
reached Japan. Most journalists suggested they had probably flown
off an aircraft carrier stationed in the Aleutian Islands. The Chinese
government was quick to deny reports that the bombers had come
from air bases in their country. They knew the Japanese would ex-
act a terrible vengeance if they thought that to be the case. The
White House and the war department continued to maintain silence
about the bombing. This puzzled the press corps. If American

planes had bombed Japan, why was no one taking credit for it? The only government official to comment on the reports from Tokyo was Stephen Early, President Roosevelt's press secretary, and all he said was that he knew absolutely nothing about any air raid.

On April 20 the American public received the first confirmation of the raid from a neutral source. The Swiss telegraphic agency had learned from its Tokyo bureau that numerous fires had been started in Tokyo and that several factories had been destroyed. They quoted a Tokyo newspaper claim that 140 schoolchildren had been killed by bombs and fires, and another thirty machine-gunned to death. And still American government officials—civilian and military—refused to confirm that a raid had even taken place.

By April 21, Marshall and Arnold were desperate for word from Doolittle. They could not deflect inquiries from Congress or the press much longer. Finally they received a note from T. V. Soong, China's minister for foreign affairs. Doolittle had sent a telegraph message through the governor of Chekiang province. It had been routed through Chinese communications facilities to T. V. Soong in Washington instead of through the U.S. Army radio transmitter in Chungking directly to Arnold. It had taken two days for the message to reach him.

MISSION TO BOMB TOKYO HAS BEEN ACCOMPLISHED. ON ENTERING CHINA WE RAN INTO BAD WEATHER AND IT IS FEARED THAT ALL PLANES CRASHED. UP TO THE PRESENT ALREADY FIVE FLIERS ARE SAFE.*

COLONEL DOOLITTLE

Arnold's worst fears were confirmed. All sixteen B-25s were missing and, so far, seventy-five of the eighty men were unaccounted for. This was an unacceptable casualty rate. If word of it leaked, the damage to air force prestige and public morale would be incalcula-

---

*The communication Doolittle sent said that five *crews* were safe. By the time Soong and Arnold received it, however, the message had been translated from English into Chinese for transmission to Washington, and then back into English. In that process, "five crews" became "five fliers."

ble. And Arnold's own reputation would be clouded; after all, he was the one who had authorized the mission.

After he had received Doolittle's message, he wrote a memorandum to President Roosevelt: "Subject: Recent Attack on Japan."

For the past few days we have had very little positive information as to what happened to Colonel Doolittle's squadron after it took off for its attack on Japan. Information now being received is slowly but surely clearing up the whole operation. It is quite evident that his squadron attacked with a considerable amount of success the targets located in the Tokyo-Osaka area. It is also quite evident that the attack came as a distinct surprise. Sixteen B-25s left the carrier for this purpose.

Arnold went on to tell the president that he did not know the number of planes forced down or shot down over Japan, and he pointed out that "foul weather gave this squadron a bad break over China," apparently forcing some crewmen to bail out. He tried to be optimistic about the number of casualties, noting that additional crew members might still be found, but he did not flinch from considering the possibility of heavy losses.

"From the standpoint of damage to enemy installations and property, and the tremendous effect it had upon our Allies, as well as the demoralizing effect upon our enemies, the raid was undoubtedly highly successful. However, from the viewpoint of an air force operation the raid was not a success, for no raid is a success in which losses exceed 10 percent and it now appears that probably all of the airplanes were lost."

The Doolittle raid gave Marshall and Arnold another worry: the possibility of Japanese retaliatory raids on the United States. That such a prospect was given serious attention attested to the impact of Japan's early successes in the Pacific on the minds of American military leaders. If the enemy could wreck the U.S. Pacific Fleet at Pearl Harbor and capture Wake Island, Bataan, Hong Kong, Singapore, and the Dutch East Indies, all in four months, they could do anything. In mid-April of 1942, then, the fear of a Japanese attack on the West Coast of the United States was real.

On April 19, the day after American newspapers carried the first reports of the Tokyo bombing, the director of the Office of Civil Defense, James Landis, kicked off the campaign to prepare Americans to cope with an enemy bombing raid. Speaking in Chicago to 21,000 civil defense air-raid wardens, Landis said they must "prepare their communities for possible revenge as a result of our attack on Japanese cities." The bombing of Tokyo, he added, "puts aside, once and for all, the conception that the United States can go through this war unscathed."

Within hours of his warning, air-raid sirens screamed throughout San Francisco. Traffic on the Golden Gate and Bay bridges was halted. Radio stations from Sacramento to Monterey were ordered off the air so as not to serve as homing signals for enemy bombers. The state of alert lasted for three hours. The cause was apparently the appearance of what the Fourth Interceptor Command called an "unidentified target" off the coast. It was never identified.

Newspapers from Seattle to San Diego undertook a campaign to prevent panic and what they called "undue excitement" in case of a raid. Influential citizens voiced their fears to Washington, demanding better defenses for the West Coast. Those emotions were heightened when it was learned that the war department had anticipated that the enemy might drop poison gas on coastal cities. The army rounded up all the gas masks used for training—more than 600,000 of them—and shipped them to the Western Defense Command, with orders to issue them to police, air-raid wardens, and other civilian officials considered important enough to be kept alive in the event of an attack.

On April 20, at his office in Washington's Munitions Building, the deputy chief of staff for the Pacific and Far East, War Plans Division, Dwight Eisenhower, asked his intelligence officers for an assessment of the Japanese capability of bombing targets in the United States. The answer he received was distressing. Not only were the Japanese equipped to attack the U.S. mainland, but their national character demanded that they retaliate for the bombing of Tokyo.

To save face, the report to Eisenhower said, the Japanese would have to attack a target more important than any they had hit before.

Another assault on Pearl Harbor, for example, would not serve as sufficient retribution. Eisenhower was advised that the only target the enemy would consider important enough was the capital, Washington, D.C. Secondary targets were thought to be the Panama Canal and the defense operations along the West Coast—the naval bases, shipyards, and aircraft manufacturing plants.

The next day, Secretary of War Stimson, concerned about a possible revenge raid on the U.S., summoned Marshall and Arnold to his office, "for a few earnest words." He told them he was "very much impressed with the danger that the Japanese, having terribly lost face by this recent attack on them in Tokyo and Yokohama, will make a counterattack on us with carriers; the West Coast is still very badly undermanned, and the trouble is that it has been very hard to get any bombers to help in that."

Apprehension about such an attack in response to the Doolittle raid continued for two months, until the Battle of Midway, and vigorous attempts were made to send reinforcements to the western states. General Marshall visited likely targets on the coast and sent all the antiaircraft units and barrage balloons that could be spared.

In addition, more fighters and bombers were supplied. The demand for extra aircraft was so great, and the number of available planes so small, that the initial transfer of the Eighth Air Force to England was suspended. One of its bombardment groups, equipped with B-17s, was hurriedly moved from New England to bases in California and Washington State. A fighter group was sent from Maine to North Carolina, with orders to proceed to California. By then, however, the Japanese fleet had been defeated off Midway. The perceived threat to the American West Coast that resulted from the Doolittle raid was thus eliminated by the sea battle initiated by the Japanese in response to that raid.

Hap Arnold eventually received more news from Chungking about the survivors of the Doolittle raid. The number of fliers safe was up to nineteen. By the twenty-first Bissell (acting for Stilwell, who was in Burma) cabled Arnold to ask how many planes and crewmen he should be searching for. He reported that the rescued fliers had been found over an area encompassing thousands of square miles of eastern China. Locating other survivors and transporting them to Chungking would not be quick or easy.

On April 22, war department officials received a secret cablegram from William Standley, the U.S. ambassador to Russia reporting on the B-25 that had landed near Vladivostok. Standley listed the names of the crew—five more men accounted for—and noted that they were in good health but were going to be interned. He passed along a request from the Russian government: "The Soviet military authorities would like to have this information kept secret and especially do not wish that the press should know that a United States Army plane has landed in the Soviet Union." Two days later, however, the Russians themselves released this information, stressing that, in accordance with international law, they had interned both the plane and its crew. This was the first confirmation by an ally that the planes that had bombed Japan were American. The war department refused to comment on the Russian announcement, or to answer any other questions about the raid. By then, six days had elapsed since the first public report of the bombing.

The number of fliers accounted for gradually increased, but the more information Arnold received, the clearer it became that part of Doolittle's first message was correct—all the B-25s were lost. Wreckage and debris of the bombers, crashed and burned, was being sighted almost hourly throughout eastern China. Then came a report that one plane had crashed in Japanese-occupied territory. The crew had been captured.

The story continued to be front-page news every day, even though the government maintained its silence, still not admitting officially that a raid had occurred. Finally, one man did say something about it, a comment that delighted the American people and confounded the Japanese. It came to be one of President Roosevelt's favorite stories. He had asked his close friend and speechwriter Judge Samuel I. Rosenman, what he should say when reporters asked where the bombers had come from.

"Mr. President," Rosenman said, "do you remember the novel of James Hilton, *Lost Horizon*, telling of that wonderful, timeless place known as Shangri-La? It was located in the trackless wastes of Tibet. Why not tell them that that's where the planes came from? If you use a fictional place like that, it's a polite way of saying that you do not intend to tell the enemy or anybody else where the planes really came from."

Roosevelt called Stephen Early, his press secretary "and told him that if anyone wanted to know where the bombers originated he was going to say 'Shangri-la.'" And that was exactly what Roosevelt did at a White House press conference on April 21.

★ ★ ★ ★

In Kunming, China, Claire Lee Chennault—the square-jawed, aggressive leader of the famous Flying Tigers, and a tactical genius at air warfare—was furious when he heard about the raid on Tokyo and the number of planes lost over China. On orders from Marshall and Arnold, Chennault (like Stilwell and Bissell) had not been informed about the mission, despite the fact that he had established a broad and effective network of aircraft spotters throughout eastern China, linked by radio and telephone. The spotters served as his early-warning system and had allowed his group to take a heavy toll of enemy planes.

Chennault was convinced that, had he known the bombers were coming, his warning net, plugged into one of the Flying Tigers' radio stations, could have guided all the planes to safe landings. Arnold believed Chennault was too close to the Chinese leaders, and did not trust him to keep information about the raid confidential. Chennault believed that Doolittle's planes were lost needlessly by "that bit of bungling" and he remained bitter about it for years.

★ ★ ★ ★

On April 22, Hap Arnold prepared another memorandum for the president. This time the news was more encouraging.

Eight airplanes and about forty crewmen have been located in China. Three of the forty were dead.

Piecing together all the information available, if the Chinese information . . . is reliable, then eleven [planes] have been accounted for. Five apparently then are the maximum that the Japs could have shot down.

Everything points to Doolittle having accomplished a most remarkable flight. He knowingly and willingly took off twelve hours ahead of time, which put him over Japan at the worst possible time of day. He also knew that this would put him over China at night where, if the weather broke against him, the chances of getting in safely were very, very poor. Thus, he had the breaks against him on the takeoff, at the time he did his bombing, and also at the time of landing in China.

Arnold also sent a message to Bissell in Chungking, authorizing him to award the Distinguished Flying Cross to each of the men in Doolittle's command. He cautioned Bissell against allowing any publicity about the decorations. Half of the men were still missing, and the government had not officially admitted to the raid. Bissell was instructed to award the medals privately.

General Marshall dispatched his congratulations to Doolittle in a message sent to Chungking:

"The president sends his thanks and congratulations to you and your command for the highly courageous and determined manner in which you carried out your hazardous mission and for the great service you have rendered to the nation and to the Allied cause. Your nomination as a brigadier general [skipping the rank of colonel] goes to the Senate this morning. To me, your leadership has been a great inspiration and fills me with confidence for the future."

The medals could not be presented, nor could Doolittle be apprised of his promotion. None of the men had arrived in Chungking, and Bissell had no idea where they were.

★ ★ ★ ★

Doolittle and Paul Leonard, his engineer-gunner, inspected the ransacked wreckage of their airplane. It was April 20. Doolittle had wanted to see the plane again, and he and Leonard had hiked twelve miles from the provincial governor's house where they had spent the night, to the hillside on which the bomber had crashed. As he stared at the debris, Doolittle confided to Leonard his fear that the mission had failed, that he had failed, and that his hope of seeing more active service in the war was doomed. He wondered if he might be court-martialed for losing all his planes and an untold number of his men.

Leonard, an old-timer, an eleven-year veteran of the air force at the age of thirty, demonstrated that he may have understood how the military worked better than Doolittle did. He listened to Doolittle express his despair about the failure of the mission and about his own future, and gently placed his hand on the colonel's shoulder.

"I want to ask you a favor, Colonel," Leonard said. "After we get out of here, I don't know where they'll assign you, but no matter where they send you, I want to be a member of your crew."

Doolittle was deeply touched.

"The tears came to my eyes," he recalled. "I said, 'Son, if you want to be my mechanic, you can be forever.' " *

Doolittle continued to insist, however, that he would never be given another command, much less an airplane.

"Colonel," Leonard said, "you know what's gonna happen when we get back? They're gonna make you a general and give you the Congressional Medal of Honor." It turned out that the sergeant was much better at predicting the future than the lieutenant colonel was.

Doolittle and his crew had to get to Chungking. Eastern China was a region of rugged mountains, and its cities, towns, and villages were separated by miles of distance and days of travel time. The land was primitive, most of it locked in the ways of the nineteenth century, and communications and transportation were difficult and time-consuming.

What roads did exist were muddy in the rainy season and sandy the rest of the time. Because of the hilly terrain, a road might meander for twenty miles to cover one mile as a plane would fly. The state of the roads made little difference, however, because there were few modern vehicles to travel in. Cars and buses were rare.

There were few railroad lines and fewer locomotives. If one came across some tracks, there was no guarantee that a train would pass in the direction one was going. The airfields were subject to Japanese aerial attacks, which had disrupted any passenger service. Add to that the dismal weather and the treacherous mountain

---

* Doolittle kept his word. Leonard remained his crew chief until he was killed in North Africa during a German air raid on January 18, 1943. Doolittle called Leonard's death his greatest personal tragedy of the war.

peaks, and one can understand why planes flew infrequently. Further, the limited number of Chinese aircraft were needed in the west to ferry supplies from India over the Himalayas.

Telephones were as rare as automobiles and planes, and even more difficult to keep functioning. Telegraph service was almost nonexistent. Eastern China was a vast wilderness that imposed isolation on its inhabitants and on the Doolittle Raiders who landed there that April. Even the provincial governor, at whose house Doolittle was staying, was often out of contact with the rest of the country.

The governor could not order up an airplane or a train, or even a car, to whisk Doolittle and his crew off to Chungking. They and the other crews would have to improvise travel arrangements as they went, covering up to one thousand miles by donkey and ricksha and every other form of conveyance imaginable. Doolittle and his men reached Chungking on May 3; others did not arrive until almost a month after the raid.

They would not have made it without the help of the Chinese people, from peasants and farmers to businessmen and army officers, all of whom risked their lives to spirit them along, sometimes one step ahead of the Japanese. Every day, in villages, farmhouses, and settlements, the Chinese offered food and shelter and guides, and in some instances carried the wounded from town to town. Left on their own, some of the men might have died of hunger or exposure. But wherever Doolittle's men passed, the Chinese honored them as heroes, with dinners, parades, and lavish entertainments. They willingly assisted their allies who had bombed the hated Japanese. In the end, they paid a terrible price for having done so.

★ ★ ★ ★

Among the hazards on Doolittle's journey to Chungking were a pig and an ill-tempered donkey. The men were asleep in a farmhouse when he was awakened by deep guttural noises. He reached out in the darkness and touched sharp bristles. The sounds turned to squeals. It was the family's pig, rooting about at the strange objects that were occupying its stall. Doolittle pushed it away and went back to sleep.

Later, exhausted from hiking so long up and down the mountains, Doolittle told the Chinese officer who was guiding them that he would have to stop to rest. At forty-five, age was catching up with him.

"I will see if I can find a donkey for you to ride," the officer said, and he returned with one a half hour later.

"Doolittle, ready for anything," recounted Ross Greening, "walked around the rear of the animal to mount. Just as he passed the south quarter the donkey kicked him savagely in the chest, sending him sprawling down the hill. The colonel sat gasping for a few moments and held his injured chest. The little officer watched the scene complacently, then walked over to the colonel and said, 'He bites, too.'"

Doolittle and his fliers made part of their journey in a cramped cabin on a riverboat. They were startled by a loud banging on the cabin door, followed by a Southern drawl asking if there were Americans inside. They glanced at one another, uncertain whether to respond.

They opened the door to find a young American missionary by the name of John Birch, who had been brought to the boat by a Chinese man. Birch volunteered to help them, and he accompanied them part of the way to Chungking as a guide and translator. Later, at Doolittle's request, Birch would assist the Raiders by arranging the burial of Cpl. Leland Faktor, the twenty-year-old engineer-gunner from Plymouth, Iowa, who was killed when his parachute failed to open.

Doolittle was impressed with Birch and grateful for his help. Birch told him he wanted to join the American army in China and help defeat the Japanese. When Doolittle reached Chungking, he mentioned Birch's name to Bissell and others. Shortly after, Birch was given a commission in the Army Air Force.*

---

* John Birch spent the rest of the war as a field intelligence officer for Claire Chennault's Fourteenth Air Force, operating for long periods behind Japanese lines. On a mission for Chennault in August, 1945, just prior to Japan's surrender, Birch was shot and killed by Chinese Communist troops, thus becoming what some have called the first American victim of communism.

On Sunday, April 26, Doolittle and his men arrived in Chuchow where the Raiders had expected to land and refuel. He was delighted to find several of his pilots there—Jack Hilger, Ross Greening, Bill Bower, and Bob Gray—and many of their crewmen. Hilger had word of other crews who were on their way west. Doolittle was greatly relieved to learn that the number accounted for had risen to fifty-six.

Hilger also had bad news. Dean Hallmark's crew was in the hands of the Japanese-dominated puppet Chinese forces in the vicinity of Nanchang. Doolittle urged the military governor to send troops to the area where Hallmark's men were being held, but the governor said it was impossible; he did not have enough troops to take the offensive. Doolittle suggested the governor try to negotiate for the release of his men or even offer to pay a ransom.

But there would be no negotiations, no ransom, and no freedom for the men until the end of the war.

★ ★ ★ ★

The day before Doolittle arrived in Chuchow, a section of Bill Farrow's plane, *Bat Out of Hell,* was brought to Tokyo and put on public display. There were only a misshapen wing with the manufacturer's name, "North American," stamped on it, struts from a landing gear, and a parachute. The chute was draped over a tree so that people could see the words "U.S. Army Air Corps" on the harness.

Some two million Japanese filed past the exhibit, to the pleasure of Japanese propaganda officials, who wanted the people to see that they did not have to worry about future air attacks. Here was tangible proof of the strength of the nation's air defenses. And this was the wreckage of only one American plane. There were eight others, the government said, scattered over Japan.

★ ★ ★ ★

At about that same time, Admiral Halsey sat down in his cabin aboard the *Enterprise* to write a letter to Jimmy Doolittle.

The hats of the task force are on high to you. Superb! The takeoff was splendid. The conditions were trying for our trained carrier pilots, and for men who have never taken off from a carrier deck before [it] is little short of marvelous.

I stated to my staff, that on landing you should have had two stars pinned on each shoulder, and the Medal of Honor put around your neck. I am highly honored in having had you, the very gallant and brave lads with you, serve under my command for a short period of time. I do not know of any more gallant deed in history than that performed by your squadron.

God knows when or where this will reach you, but if and when it does, I would appreciate hearing of your experience. This, of course, at your leisure. Again my hearty congratulations. Keep on knocking over those yellow bastards.

★ ★ ★ ★

Doolittle would have liked nothing better, but at the time he was still out of touch with Washington. Although the trip by air from Chuchow to Chungking would have taken only a few hours, authorities could not risk sending a plane that far east to pick him up, not even for a new brigadier general who would be going home a hero.

The next day he boarded a train at Chuchow, taking several of the fliers with him. The overnight train trip was followed by a 210-mile bus ride over bumpy roads to Yintan. Another bus took them 120 miles through pine-forested mountains that reminded them of the Rockies. Flooding forced them to leave the bus and walk three miles to Taiko. There the residents threw a banquet in their honor and provided the most welcome luxury—a real bathtub.

After another all-day bus ride, they arrived at Hengyang, 410 miles from Chungking. The town was far enough west and sufficiently accessible for a plane to be sent for the two-hour flight. Bissell met them at the Chungking airport with the news of Doolittle's promotion. Half of Sergeant Leonard's prediction had come true.

Because there was no post exchange in Chungking, no place for Doolittle to obtain the silver stars he was now entitled to wear, Bissell, who himself had been promoted to brigadier general a few weeks before, gave Doolittle his.*

---

* On his way back to the States, Doolittle stopped in Kunming to call on Claire Chennault, who had also been promoted to the one-star rank. He had not been able to get

The men were invited to stay on the grounds of Chiang Kai-shek's compound during their time in Chungking. "We lived there for a number of days," Bill Bower said. "We milked [Madame Chiang's] cow and drank the milk from the cow and just moved in, and they accepted us and kept us."

The Chiangs graciously hosted a lavish luncheon for the Americans, awarding them Chinese medals and scrolls certifying their membership in the Chinese Order of the Clouds. Chiang made a speech, but no American understood it because no translation was offered.

Madame Chiang also sent a letter of thanks to each of the Doolittle fliers in Chungking.

To the Valiant American Airmen who bombed Japan:

It is with mixed feelings that I write these words. I have looked forward to the pleasure of seeing you for you represent America where I have so many friends, and to tell you what your gallant exploit in braving unknown dangers to bring war to Japan has meant to my people.

We have for five years suffered the inhumanities and barbarities of the Japanese military, not only on land and sea, but also from the skies. The lion heart of your great President must have throbbed with grief at the distress of millions of my countrymen who have endured uncomplainingly but none the less painfully the agonies of remorseless Japanese aggression. I feel certain that this must have largely influenced his decision to send you on a mission which would put an end to inhuman warfare. The entire Chinese people are grateful to you and to him for your brave deeds. I venture to think that you have even helped to lay the myriad ghosts of cities, villages, men, women and children, who have been the innocent victims of Japanese bombs.

---

his own stars either. Since Doolittle was going home and could easily get some more, he gave his stars to Chennault. Tactfully, he did not tell Chennault the stars had belonged to Bissell; he knew there was a long-standing, deeply-rooted animosity between the two men.

I was glad of the opportunity to thank you on behalf of my compatriots. The Generalissimo and I both were happy to see you. We hope for days to come when you will revisit China in happier circumstances. Our Chinese people will always welcome you with friendship and admiration.

Meanwhile may all be well with you. May you continue to vindicate freedom and justice so that by your efforts a happier and more unselfish world society will evolve when victory is ours.

> May Ling Soong Chiang
> Headquarters of the Generalissimo
> Chungking, Szechuan
> China

Many years later, in 1983, navigator Tom Griffin returned to China and wanted to visit the place where he and his fellow Raiders had been honored. "I asked my guides in Chungking to take me back to this house so I could take pictures of this place that had so many memories. They refused—very diplomatically." The Chiangs are not in favor with China's present leaders.

When Doolittle received his medal from Madame Chiang, he questioned her rather brusquely about the efforts being made to free the men being held by Chinese puppet troops in the Nanchang area. She assured him that her government was doing everything possible to secure their release, but Doolittle had no way of verifying that. He could not pursue the matter himself, because on May 5 he received orders to proceed to Washington.

Although he no longer expected to be court-martialed on his return, he retained a sense of failure about the mission. "As to whether the results were worthwhile," he said, discussing the raid twenty years later, "at that time I was very skeptical. . . . It, for me, was a very sad occasion because, while we had accomplished the first part of our mission, we had lost all of our aircraft, and no commander feels happy when he loses all of his aircraft. And of course, we lost some of the boys."

★ ★ ★ ★

"I stood up on my two legs for the last time in my life at about dawn on [April] 20," Ted Lawson wrote. He and the other injured men of his crew—Davenport, McClure, and Clever, along with Thatcher, the only one among them in good health—were trying to reach China's mainland by boat from Nandian Island, where they had crash-landed. When they got to shore late that afternoon, the Chinese boat crew seemed wary of landing and waited almost two hours before pulling up to a rickety wharf. Japanese troops and Chinese puppet forces were not far away.

A group of coolies carried the four injured Americans five miles inland to a village where Chinese nurses fed them and bathed their wounds. The nurses could offer little else. They had no medication for the pain, not even aspirin. The next morning, Dr. Chen, a physician, arrived with twelve coolies to transport them twenty-six miles inland to his hospital at Linhai. They had to leave immediately, Chen said, because Japanese troops were searching the coast for the Americans.

At ten o'clock on the night of the twenty-first, they arrived at the hospital and were met by an English missionary couple, Mr. and Mrs. Parker. They told the Americans that Linhai was safe but that little medical treatment could be offered. The hospital had few supplies—only antiseptic, chloroform, and bandages.

Nonetheless, Dr. Chen and his staff did what they could, performing minor surgery on Lawson's leg and pulling his loose teeth. He remained in considerable pain and had to be fed intravenously. The others were not quite so critical, but they, too, needed more medical attention than Dr. Chen's facility could provide. But Lawson could not be moved, and there was no better-equipped hospital within a reasonable distance.

Two days later, Mr. Parker brought some news. He had received word that another American crew, which had crash-landed off the coast, was making its way to Linhai.

"One of them is a doctor," he said.

Don Smith and his crew, which included Robert "Doc" White, the flight surgeon, had hidden in a Buddhist temple through the twenty-first, while Japanese soldiers searched the area. At one point the crew had heard the clomping of their boots overhead. They were on the island where Lawson's crew had come ashore. Five Chinese guerrillas stood guard to protect them with a motley collection of antique weapons that the Americans doubted would even fire. That night, they put the Americans aboard a junk and sailed them to the mainland, evading two Japanese patrol boats.

The men were in a hurry to reach Linhai. The Chinese had told them about the wounded fliers who had been taken there. But making good time over that harsh, barren terrain was difficult, and they did not reach the hospital until the morning of April 24, six days after the raid.

Dr. White examined Lawson and the others and was appalled by the extent of their injuries. Lawson's left knee was fractured, the leg dangerously infected, and there were deep cuts on his face and jaw. Davenport's right leg was infected; Clever showed deep cuts on his head, scalp, and right hand, plus a sprained ankle; and McClure had a fractured right shoulder and an injured nerve in his left arm.

White gave Lawson a blood transfusion, using whatever medical equipment was available, in this case an old, leaky syringe. The donor was Smith's copilot, Griff Williams. White fashioned splints for Lawson's leg and McClure's left hand and sprinkled sulfanila-mide on Lawson's and Davenport's wounds. Twice a day he had to scale the dead flesh off Lawson's leg, a procedure so painful that Lawson said he could no longer bear it. White said he had to bear it or lose the leg. Lawson told the doctor to go ahead and amputate. White scraped only once a day for the next several days, but the infection spread and there was growing concern for Lawson's life.

On April 27, Don Smith and the rest of his crew, and Dave Thatcher from Lawson's crew, set out for Chungking. They traveled for three days in sedan chairs, transferred to rickshas, then to automobiles, and finally to a train that took them to Chü-hsien. There they met up with Trav Hoover and his crew, along with Davey Jones, Charles Ozuk, and Brick Holstrom.

While they were at Chü-hsien, the missionary, John Birch, led a funeral service for Leland Faktor, who had been a close friend of

Thatcher's. The service was held in an air-raid shelter where the men were forced to spend part of each day anyway during Japanese bombing raids. On May 3 they boarded a bus and rode for three days to the airfield at Hengyang, where a plane was sent to take them to Chungking. Another thirteen U.S. fliers were safe.

★ ★ ★ ★

But at the hospital at Linhai, Lawson's condition was getting worse. Dr. White administered another transfusion, with Clever and McClure as donors, but he showed no improvement. By May 3, White knew he would either have to amputate the left leg or watch his patient die. Lawson sensed what was coming and asked White directly if he was going to lose the leg. When White said yes, Lawson told him to go ahead. "All I could think of now," Lawson wrote, "was getting rid of that damned thing."

The hospital had some Novocain, which had been smuggled out of Japanese-occupied Shanghai, and this was used as a spinal anesthetic. There was only a small amount, and before the operation was finished, Lawson reported that he was beginning to get twitches in his other leg. White worked faster. Once the anesthetic wore off, there was nothing left to give him to block the pain.

A few minutes later, Lawson noticed more feeling returning to his right leg. Two Chinese nurses held his wrists as White went to work with a silver saw. The nurses picked up the severed leg, and Lawson watched them carry it out the door. As White sewed up the stump, Lawson saw his arm move rhythmically up and down, and he felt the needle every time it pricked his skin.

About two weeks later, Chinese orderlies gave him a pair of crutches. He looked at them for a long time, remembering how he liked to ski, then one agonizing step at a time, he began to learn to walk on them.

An elderly Chinese man visited the hospital, bearing beautiful black silk slippers he had made for the courageous Americans. He proudly presented a pair to each man. As he handed the slippers to Lawson, his gaze shifted to the pilot's one good leg. The man was mortified. He hurriedly backed out of the room, bowing in embarrassment and shame. The incident did little to boost Lawson's spirits, but he did wear one of the slippers.

McClure developed carbuncles because of the awkward way he had to lie with his injured shoulder and arm on the coarse jute sacking that covered the springs of his bed. The inflammations were deep and painful. On May 16, White had to lance them. "The knife he used was so dull," McClure said, "he had to exert so much pressure, that when it did break through the skin, it went in very deep, enough to cause blood to run down to my heels before he could stop it."

McClure was reacting poorly to the sulfathiazole Dr. White had managed to obtain through the Chinese. The drug seemed to be inducing depression. During one of his low periods, on a Sunday afternoon, the English missionaries were conducting a service on the veranda. Mr. Parker asked if McClure wanted to attend. McClure at first said no, but then changed his mind.

Parker helped him outside and placed him on a chaise longue so he could sit up. "I was really feeling terrible and I said to myself, 'What the hell are you doing here?' I'd rather be in my bed where it's more comfortable.

"I was handed a hymnal book. The service began and within a half hour with words from the minister and a few songs I was feeling at peace and no pain in my body could I feel. For the rest of the day I thought of that transformation. I could—and still do—believe God put his hand on me."

Forty-five years later, McClure said, "I can still remember vividly how I changed that Sunday on the veranda."

★ ★ ★ ★

The Americans had to evacuate Linhai on May 18 because the Japanese were less than forty miles away. Chinese army troops and bank officials had already fled. Lawson said it seemed as though he could feel the hot breath of the Japanese on his neck as they were carried out of the hospital in sedan chairs. Three Chinese soldiers guarded the column, expecting to be ambushed by enemy troops around every bend.

They traveled all day, while the Japanese closed in behind them. Japanese troops also threatened to cut off their escape route ahead. They had to make several detours, but no matter which path they chose, the men faced two constants—pain with every jolting step, and warm welcomes from the Chinese in every village. Banners hailed the "American air heroes" in every town, and the best food and accommodations were provided. One young, English-speaking Chinese official addressed Lawson.

"I know all about you, Lieutenant," he said. "Thatcher came through here about a month ago. He told me everything. The other boys were with him."

When Lawson asked how they were, the man smiled and said, "Fine. We beat them."

Lawson asked him again, certain he must have misunderstood.

"We beat them," the man repeated. "Our church basketball team challenged them and beat them by two points. A wonderful game."

"Good Christ," Davenport muttered, as they all breathed sighs of relief.

After four days of rough handling in sedan chairs, some of the men were transferred to a 1941 Ford station wagon with bullet holes in the body. Others, including Lawson, were placed aboard a Chinese truck that ran on charcoal. The truck had no springs, and Lawson had to hold his stump with both hands to keep it from banging on the floor with every bump in the road.

They heard explosions behind them. Japanese troops were so close that the Chinese army forces were blowing up the bridges as soon as the Americans had crossed each one. On May 22 the men learned they would not be able to get to Chü-hsien—the enemy was in the way—so they turned south to Lishui, which also had an airfield. Maybe a plane could be sent there to pick them up. It turned out, however, that the Chinese had been forced to destroy the field to prevent the Japanese from using it.

At two o'clock on the afternoon of May 24, they reached Nanchang. They could talk of nothing but getting to Chungking, and from there home. But the Chinese had destroyed Nanchang's airfield. In the wreckage they found a supply of iodine. White painted them from head to toe, dabbing the antiseptic on all their welts and sores.

The little convoy moved on across raging rivers, through mountain passes, from one village to the next, with the grateful Chinese continuing to pay them homage. Tires blew, carburetors clogged, Japanese planes menaced overhead. Bedbugs attacked at night and mosquitoes by day. Lawson's stump became infected, Davenport developed a skin inflammation, and they all wondered if they would ever reach safety.

The next day they made Kian, where the Flying Tigers had an auxiliary field and radio station, but that field also had been blown up. The Flying Tigers' hostel was intact, offering hot showers and American food, but the fliers had no choice but to push on to Hengyang. That airfield, which they reached on the twenty-seventh, had been barricaded to prevent Japanese planes from landing.

From Hengyang they traveled by train to Kweilin, arriving at the Flying Tigers' field early in the morning. The plane that was supposed to have been sent for them that day would not come until the following day. But the following day brought Japanese bombers instead. Dr. White got hold of a Thompson submachine gun and lay in wait in case a plane flew low enough to shoot at. None did.

On the afternoon of June 3 Lawson and the others saw an Army Air Force DC-3 come in for a landing. The copilot was Mac McElroy. Davey Jones had come along to bring medical supplies.

They took off at five o'clock in the morning and had been in the air no more than an hour when they received a radio message that Kweilin, the field they had just left, was under attack. They landed at Kunming, headquarters for the Flying Tigers—"great guys with plenty of dough," Lawson said—and Lawson had a runway reunion with two of his classmates from flying school.

Lawson, McClure, and Clever were not sent on to Chungking. On Dr. White's recommendation, they were to be flown as quickly as possible to Walter Reed Army Hospital in Washington, D.C. A month and a half after the Doolittle raid, they were finally going home.

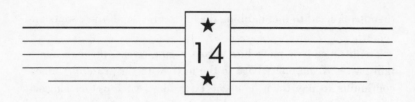

# Days of Stark Horror

They called their keeper "Mike." His full name was Mikhail Constantinovich Schmaring, and he was an officer in the Russian army. Two other officers and two enlisted men also lived in the house near Khabarovsk with Ski York and his crew, but Mike was the only one who spoke English. Beginning on April 20, the first day of their internment, he became their only link with the outside world.

He translated the news from the radio—the "reproductor," he called it—and it was depressing. Tokyo had announced that eleven American bombers had been shot down. The men were shocked. It meant that most of their buddies were either dead or prisoners of the Japanese. It looked as though the mission had been a failure.

They did not know if the American embassy had been informed of their presence on Russian soil. Every time they asked Mike, he gave an evasive answer. He was vague about most of their questions, replying in one of two ways—either it was time for them to rest, or they would be told at some indefinite time in the future. The only information he provided was about their location. He told them they were on the bank of the Amur River. The land on the opposite side was Japanese-occupied Manchuria. It was unsettling to the American fliers to be so close to the enemy. The Russians might decide to hand them over to the Japanese at any time.

On the second day of their internment, Mike told them the Japanese were reporting that only seven planes had been shot down, but they did not know which story to believe, if either of them. On the third day, their baggage from the plane was brought in, minus their guns, cigarettes, and candy. Mike said the weapons were being held for safekeeping.

The Russians seemed friendly and certainly offered them plenty of food. Eggs, black bread, butter, red caviar, and tea for breakfast. Soup, meat, vegetables, sweet rolls, and chicory coffee for other meals. There was a continuous supply of vodka and *Ducats*, the Russian cigarettes.

It was the boredom and the uncertainty about their future that were so hard to bear, and wondering if their families thought they were dead or prisoners of war. They had a lot to time to focus on these depressing thoughts. Their only activities were eating, sleeping, listening to the radio news broadcast at midnight, whittling pieces of wood, and making halfhearted attempts to learn the Russian language. They had little motivation for the latter because they believed they would not be held for very long.

On their ninth day of confinement, Mike translated a report from Tass, the official Soviet news agency, stating that one of the American bombers that had attacked Japan had landed in Russia, and that both plane and crew had been interned. The men were glad to hear that, for it meant that the U.S. Embassy was aware of their existence. They were certain now that they would not have to stay in Khabarovsk much longer and, indeed, the next day Mike told them they were leaving. He would not say where they were going, but the Americans hoped they would be placed in the custody of the embassy. From there, of course, they would quickly be flown home.

Mike, the five fliers, and two other Russian officer-guards boarded a third-class car of the Trans-Siberian Railroad, their home for the next three weeks. They were allowed to get off only once, for a bath after two weeks. During the trip, they were shocked by the poverty they saw through the grimy train windows. People dressed in rags begged for food at every stop. Mike had stocked their compartment with enough food for the journey, and at one station the Americans passed some bread out the window to hungry children. Mike was furious. He slammed the window shut and drew the curtain.

"You must never give food away," he said, "or let them know that we have food in here . . . food is difficult to get with the war going on. . . . It must be given only to those who deserve to have it."

A few hours later, while they were enjoying black bread, red caviar, and vodka, and watching the passing scenery, someone threw a stone through the window, giving Mike the opportunity to say, "I told you so."

After seventeen days they neared Kuibshyev, the city to which all foreign embassies had been relocated when the Germans threatened Moscow. York and his crew were delighted with this news, although Mike said they would not be allowed off the train. It was for their own good, he said, to protect them from the Japanese embassy personnel in the city.

This did not bother the Americans. They were sure that U.S. Embassy officials would come to the station to meet their train. They shined their shoes, polished their brass, and put on their best uniforms. When the train halted at Kuibshyev in the morning and Mike got off, they reminded him to be sure to tell the embassy people where they were.

They waited all day, locked in their compartment and guarded by two officers armed with submachine guns, but no one came for them. At five o'clock, Mike returned. He had not contacted the U.S. Embassy and it was clear he had no intention of doing so. The men were disappointed, then angry, and finally they realized the truth about their status as prisoners, no matter how kindly they were being treated by their jailers.

The train trip ended at the village of Okhuna, three hundred miles southeast of Moscow. Mike and the other guards escorted them to a house with many gables and eaves, and a wide porch wrapped around three sides. The rooms were comfortable and reasonably well furnished. A staff of six was there to cook and clean for the

Americans and their guards. The food was plentiful—more fresh meat, vegetables, butter, cheese, red caviar, black bread, and vodka. Obviously they were being fed better than the majority of the Russian people.

Mike kept them supplied with Russian films and even an American movie, *One Hundred Men and a Girl*. He produced a phonograph and Russian records. The men were allowed baths every other day, and the Russians were astounded that they wanted to bathe so often. Their days settled into another boring routine until June 9, when they finally had visitors from the U.S. Embassy, a civilian identified only as "Page," and the military attaché, Col. Joseph Michela.

The first thing the embassy officials said was how well they were living compared to most of the people in Moscow, to which the foreign embassies had, by then, returned. They brought Emmens a telegram from his wife, announcing the birth of their first child, a son, and said they were working on a plan that might free the fliers within three weeks. Because the Russians were concerned that the Japanese would take offense if they openly released the Americans, York and his crew were advised to be patient a little while longer.

Page and Michela had no additional news of the Tokyo raid. They could not tell the men anything about survivors that they did not already know from the Russian news broadcasts. They did bring two boxes of gifts—cigarettes, shirts, socks, and seven American newspapers—and promised to be in touch every week. No longer need York and his crew feel forgotten, isolated from the rest of the world.

Their situation had definitely improved, although they did not expect to be released within the next couple of weeks. They were sure it would take somewhat longer.

★ ★ ★ ★

Dean Hallmark, Chase Nielsen, and Bob Meder lay in the tiny compartment below decks on a sampan, gagging and retching. They covered themselves with filthy rags and mats, and lay in bilge water and human waste, listening to the footsteps of the Japanese search party overhead. It was April 20, the day after the Chinese puppet forces who found them had buried their crewmen, Bill Dieter and Don Fitzmaurice. The Chinese troops were trying to help the American fliers reach the mainland so they could get to free China.

The door to their compartment was shoved open, and a Japanese soldier poked about inside with a stick. It struck Nielsen, but he forced himself to remain quiet. The Japanese troops left, and the sampan reached shore at Wenchow. Captain Ling, who was in charge of the Americans, went ashore and returned with the news that Japanese troops were searching for them up and down the coast.

Ling took them into the city after dark, turning them over to a Mr. Wong, an elderly Chinese man who had been educated in England. Wong treated them to a delicious meal and a lengthy description of the brutality of the Japanese. His stories were horrifying, especially to those who were facing the possibility of capture. Later that night, Wong received word that Japanese soldiers were undertaking a search in their part of the city. They would have to leave.

Wong led them through a maze of alleys, sometimes within sight of Japanese patrols, but the enemy had surrounded the area. They could not get out. Wong took them to a room that offered few hiding places. Hallmark backed into a corner and sat covered with blankets and sacks. Nielsen and Meder climbed up into the rafters. Wong settled cross-legged on the floor and worked at trying to light a charcoal burner while hobnailed boots rang on the paving stones outside.

The door swung open and a Japanese soldier strode into the room. He looked at the old man sitting on the floor and at the pile of rags in the corner, and left. A few minutes later, Captain Ling, who had brought the fliers by sampan, entered the room, accompanied by a Japanese officer and two soldiers. Ling spoke sharply to Mr. Wong, who shrugged his shoulders in reply. Ling slapped him across the face. One soldier blocked the door and aimed his tommy gun, and the other headed for the corner where Hallmark was hiding. He kicked at the blankets until he uncovered the American.

The Japanese officer said, in English, that if Hallmark did not get up he would be shot. When Hallmark stood, the officer asked him where the others were. Hallmark said he had no idea what the man was talking about. The officer yelled at Wong and started to beat him. The old man fell against the wall, below the spot where Nielsen was perched in the rafters. The Japanese officer stepped back from Wong and happened to look up, spying Nielsen. At the same instant, one of the soldiers cried out and pointed his weapon at Meder, in another corner of the ceiling.

The Americans climbed down and the officer announced that they were prisoners of Japan, but they had nothing to fear so long as they did what they were told. While the soldiers tied their hands behind their backs, the Japanese officer and Captain Ling began to argue. Nielsen thought Ling may have been trying to keep them in his custody. After several minutes of shouting, the Japanese officer pulled out his revolver and pointed it at Ling. The Chinese captain looked at the Americans, holstered his gun, saluted the Japanese officer, and left without a word.

As the fliers were led through the streets of Wenchow, Nielsen started to speak to the officer. A guard kicked him viciously in the side, sending him sprawling on the pavement. He was jerked to his feet and told to say nothing except when questioned by his superiors. Nielsen recalled the stories of the sadistic treatment prisoners received at the hands of the Japanese. This was only a sample. He thought his future might be a lot shorter than he expected.

★ ★ ★ ★

Bill Farrow and his crew were blindfolded and placed aboard an airplane at Shanghai. It was April 20, the day after they had been brought to Shanghai and questioned. They had been roughed up and threatened with execution, but had revealed nothing beyond name, rank, and serial number, despite being confronted with evidence that their interrogators already knew a great deal about them. Jake DeShazer recalled that he was asked specifically about the aircraft carrier *Hornet* and about Doolittle.

After two and one half hours, the plane began its descent. DeShazer could see a bit around his blindfold and recognized Mount Fuji. They were being taken to Japan! Bobby Hite managed to recognize the city of Tokyo, which the Raiders had bombed only two days before. After they landed, the men were driven to a military barracks and placed in separate cells. They were stripped and their clothes were searched and returned to them. They learned they were in the hands of the Kempei Tai, the army's military police, the Japanese version of the Nazis' Gestapo, professionals trained in the practice of brutal interrogations. In the refinements of their sadistic techniques, the Kempei Tai had no master.

One at a time, the Americans were led into a room with a table and chair, an officer, an interpreter, and three or four guards. At first, they were beaten with *gunto* sticks, long bamboo poles, for refusing to answer the questions. This was just the first stage in the interrogation process. The next stage began at nine o'clock that night.

Again they were brought to separate interrogation rooms. Cuffs had been placed around their ankles and baskets over their heads. A different Kempei Tai team prefaced the session with the remark that they did not wish to hurt the Americans but would do so if their questions were not answered. The queries were more specific this time, most of them relating to the *Hornet*. Apparently the Japanese had found something to link the men to the ship, either in the wreckage of one of the planes or in their clothing.

George Barr, Farrow's navigator, recalled how surprised he was at "the knowledge they had concerning the raid, even in the first questioning. Did we know . . . Doolittle?" He even thought they had lists of the men on the raid. Although the Japanese may have had such information, they needed to have it confirmed by the prisoners. Also, they found it hard to give credence to the idea that the bombers had taken off from an aircraft carrier. They may have suspected that the evidence they found linking the Raiders to the *Hornet* had been planted to mislead them about the launching site for the raid.

The Japanese interrogators asked the fliers how it was possible to have taken off from a carrier deck in a B-25. They wanted to know the length of the flight deck, the number of bombs the planes carried, and the number of aircraft and crewmen involved.

The questions were repeated, and with each evasive answer, the beatings grew more severe. Much harsher treatment was promised if they continued to hold out. Each session lasted about two hours, and they were renewed every few hours around the clock for several days. None of the men was sure how long this period of torment lasted, for time soon lost all meaning.

Between the questioning and the beatings, the men were fed a starvation diet of rice and tea and were not allowed to sleep. The intensity of the beatings progressed in carefully calculated stages of increasing pain. The subsistence rations, lack of sleep, and constant pain were wearing down the will to resist.

Dissatisfied with the Americans' answers, the Kempei Tai proceeded to the next stage, beyond beatings to precisely formulated methods of torture. Barr remembered that his torturers boasted that "Japanese methods [were] scientee-fic." The water treatment was first. The men were tied and stretched flat on their backs on the floor with guards holding their legs. Water was forced into their mouths and noses until they passed out; it was not unlike drowning. The Japanese would force the water out, usually by jumping on their stomachs. When they revived, brought back from the point of death, they were stretched out again and the process was repeated. The Kempei Tai knew exactly how far to go before reviving them. And then the questioning would resume.

The men were also subjected to a form of torture called the "knee spread." With their hands tied behind their backs, they were forced to kneel. A pole about three inches thick was placed behind their knees. Guards jumped on their thighs, forcing the knee joints to spread. The pain was so excruciating that the men almost lost consciousness. After a few times, blood circulation was disrupted and their legs went numb. At that point the Japanese dragged them upright and released them, laughing as they collapsed on the floor.

The third torture the Kempei Tai used on Farrow and his men was finger-bandaging. The fingers of one hand were bound tightly, and a stick was forced between each pair of fingers. One guard squeezed the fingers while another slid the sticks back and forth. In addition to creating intense pain, this technique frequently caused fractures or swellings that lasted for days.

And always there were the questions. The Japanese received some answers that seemed to satisfy them. The men could tell when they had given a correct response because the torture would stop for a while. But after the interrogators had compared notes, another line of inquiry would begin, bringing renewed torture.

Most of the questions focused on the raid, but others were of a more general nature, such as the attitude of the American public toward the Japanese people or toward President Roosevelt. Other points involved the location of vital defense installations such as factories and airports. The prisoners quickly learned not to say that they had never visited a particular city. That was a wrong answer and only led to pain. They fabricated answers they hoped sounded plausible.

In between the interrogation sessions, they were kept in solitary confinement, denied the chance to communicate with one another. Their diet and lack of sleep continued to weaken them, and they were not allowed to bathe or shave. To counteract the growing stench of the unwashed bodies, the Japanese who questioned them took to wearing a strong-smelling cologne. Kept under such conditions, the fliers were gradually reduced to the level of subhumans, barely capable of functioning, lacking all hope of ever getting home, much less of ending the pain.

★ ★ ★ ★

Hallmark, Nielsen, and Meder were taken in handcuffs by boat from Wenchow to Shanghai, arriving on April 24. In Shanghai they endured the same treatment at the hands of the Kempei Tai that Farrow and his men were undergoing in Tokyo. In addition, they were subjected to a modern version of the medieval rack, in which their bodies were stretched nearly to the breaking point. As with their other methods of torture, the Japanese had refined the technique so that the victim was brought only to the edge of endurance, not to death.

The torture continued throughout the day. At dusk, Chase Nielsen, Hallmark's navigator, was told he would be executed. He was blindfolded and led outside by two guards. They dragged him along a gravel path, and when they stopped, he heard a squad of soldiers march up and stop close by. He stood still, his back to the firing squad, waiting for the shot. Sweat poured down his face as he heard a shouted command. He thought of trying to run but knew that it was useless. He could not see through the blindfold and his legs were still weak from the knee-spreading torture.

The interpreter began to laugh. He explained that as Knights of the Bushido of the Order of the Rising Sun, they never executed people at sundown, only at sunrise. But unless Nielsen decided to cooperate, the interpreter added, he would die when the sun came up.

He was taken back to his cell and given sandwiches and coffee. An hour later, guards hauled him up by the chain on his handcuffs, which bound his hands behind his back, and looped it over a peg on the wall. He hung there, with his toes barely touching the floor, all night. Pain coursed through his wrists, arms, shoulders, and chest. Mercifully, he passed out and remained unconscious most of the night.

In the morning, he, Meder, and Hallmark were brought together in a room. Each was stunned by how awful the others looked. They were not allowed to speak, but just seeing each other provided some small measure of comfort. They were given sandwiches and coffee, blindfolded, and taken aboard a plane, where they were tied to their seats. They would be flown to Tokyo. It was April 25.

★ ★ ★ ★

Neither Hallmark's nor Farrow's crew was aware that the other was in the same Tokyo prison, undergoing the same treatment. By then, the men were in such poor shape that they were aware of little beyond their individual circles of agony. The torture had not diminished. If anything, the presence of additional prisoners caused the interrogators to increase their efforts to learn about the raid.

For eighteen days the questioning continued, twenty-four hours a day. The prisoners were not permitted to sleep, wash, shave, or eat above the level of semi-starvation. New interrogators were brought, all of whom had lived in the United States and knew something about the culture, the people, and the slang. They asked many questions about America, but mostly probed for details of the raid. The

Japanese still would not accept that the army bombers had flown off a carrier. They showed the men pictures of carriers and told them to describe the *Hornet*. When the men answered, they invented some colorful descriptions.

One day they were shown a set of maps and charts taken from one of the downed B-25s. When the prisoners saw them, they realized they had endured the weeks of torture for nothing. The Japanese had found the maps shortly after the raid and thus had known most of the answers to their questions all along.

That did not put an end to the interrogations, but it did slow their pace. The fliers were allowed to sleep through the night and were questioned only during the day. The severity of their treatment during those sessions did not lessen, however, and by then they were weakened by dysentery. The Japanese offered no medical assistance. Their rooms contained only a hole in the floor for a toilet, and the odor, heightened by the heat and humidity of the closed cells, was overpowering. Sometimes it was almost a relief to be taken out for interrogation.

On May 22 the men were led individually to an interrogation room, as on so many other occasions, but this time no questions were asked. Instead, they were seated at a table with a pen and a pile of papers written in Japanese, and ordered to sign their names. When they asked what the papers were, they were told they contained their confessions to war crimes against the Japanese people.

If they did not sign, they were told, they would be executed. Weak, hungry, and beyond caring, each man signed a set of fabricated questions and answers he could not read, which implicated them in crimes against civilians. Bobby Hite's statement asked if he had done any strafing. The answer the Japanese gave was, of course, yes.

"Heretofore," the false confession read, "I haven't revealed any information on this point, but the truth is that about five to six minutes after leaving the city we saw in the distance what looked like an elementary school with many children at play. The pilot steadily dropped altitude and ordered the gunmen to their stations. When the plane was at an oblique angle, the skipper gave firing orders, and bursts of machine-gun fire sprayed the ground. Of course, since all this took place in a moment's time, I have no idea as to the extent of the damage inflicted."

Bill Farrow's phony confession dealt with the indiscriminate bombing of civilians as well as with the strafing of the school-children.

"I don't know what excuse to make for [the bombing of civilians] other than to state the fact that we were a temporary crew with inadequate training. I cannot make any assertion that we bombed our targets and nothing else. Moreover, at the time the Japanese antiaircraft guns were especially active, and since our only thought was to drop our bombs quickly and make a hurried dash for safety, I believe it is natural that some damage was inflicted on residences, and some civilians may have been killed. On this score, as commander of the plane, I am fully cognizant of my responsibilities."

The statement went on, "There is truly no excuse for [strafing the elementary school]. I have made no mention of this incident before, but after leaving Nagoya, I do not quite remember the place, there was a place which looked like a school, with many people there. As parting shot, with a feeling of 'damn those Japs,' I made a power dive and carried out some strafing. There was absolutely no defensive fire from below."

For Dean Hallmark, the Japanese had written, "In all probability there was a considerable amount of indiscriminate bombing.

"Since it was our intention to bomb Tokyo and escape to China quickly, we also dropped bombs over objectives other than those targets specified, and made a hasty escape. Therefore, we also bombed residential homes, killing and wounding many people."

Harold Spatz, the engineer-gunner in Farrow's crew, also allegedly confessed to strafing the school. "It was an extremely inexcusable deed. Shortly after leaving Nagoya, while flying southward along the coast, the pilot immediately upon perceiving a school steadily reduced altitude and ordered us to our stations. I aimed at the children in the schoolyard and fired only one burst before we headed out to sea. My feelings at the time were 'damn those Japs,' and I wanted to give them a burst of fire. Now I clearly see that this was truly unpardonable and in all decency should not have been committed."

Jack DeShazer, the bombardier, was reported to have said, "Since in this type of bombing it is inevitable that the bombs will scatter to the residential areas, from the beginning I expected such an eventuality and acted accordingly. As far as we were concerned, the quicker we discharged our bombs and caused a lot of casualties and escaped, the better it was for us. Colonel Doolittle and the other ranking officers, as well as our pilot, did not especially call our attention to these things. Of course, since the primary objective was the petroleum tanks, the surrounding residences were clearly discernible."

And so it went, page after page, describing crews too frightened and too eager to escape to stick to only military targets. The statements showed a lack of concern at the time of the raid about the killing of civilians. They discussed Doolittle's guilt for not having forbidden such attacks and expressed the prisoners' remorse for having committed them. At the same time, the confessions were worded to show a cold acceptance of such acts as a reality of the kind of war America was waging against Japan.

"Personally, I am extremely sorry," the statement in Bob Meder's name read, "but in modern warfare such things cannot be helped. Inasmuch as demoralizing the spirit of the people is one of the objectives, there is no alternative other than to ignore our feelings."

Once the men had signed their confessions, the interrogations ceased. Two weeks later, with their wrists and ankles bound by metal cuffs, they were led to the prison courtyard, where a photographer took their picture. They were bundled into four American automobiles, two prisoners to each car, and driven to a railroad station. They had not washed, shaved, or changed clothes in two months and were still suffering from dysentery. They were offensive objects of curiosity to the passersby.

The men spent two days on a train to Nagasaki. It was hot and crowded, and they remained shackled, but at least they were given their first decent food. Once in Nagasaki, they spent the night in a hot, fetid cell, the first time they had been together and allowed to talk freely since their capture. They eagerly recounted their experiences to one another.

The next morning they were put aboard a ship and for two days were well treated and well fed. The ship docked at Shanghai on June 19, and the prisoners were taken to the Bridge House jail, an apartment building the Japanese had converted to a prison. They were crowded into a cell with fifteen Chinese prisoners. Even with the decent food they had received the past few days, they were in a weakened, sickly condition. Hallmark could not stand by himself. The others had to, because there was not enough room for everyone to lie down to sleep at the same time. Some of the Chinese prisoners were comatose and near death.

It was a hellhole of filth, stench, death, disease, and overpowering heat. Although the previous weeks had been "a nightmare," wrote Jake DeShazer's biographer, the weeks to come were ones of "stark horror."

★ ★ ★ ★

The Chinese people who had aided the Doolittle Raiders, and thousands of others who did not even know of their existence, were also undergoing days of horror at the hands of the Japanese. Emperor Hirohito and other Japanese leaders were incensed that American planes had violated their homeland, but they harbored a greater wrath toward the Chinese people who had helped the Doolittle fliers when they landed in eastern China. The Japanese were determined to make the Chinese pay for that help and to deter them from assisting Americans in the future.

On April 20, two days after the bombs fell on Japan, Hirohito instructed his senior army commander in China, Gen. Yasuji Okamura, to prepare a punitive expedition against the people of Chekiang province, where Doolittle's men had found refuge. A few days later the emperor approved orders for an offensive sweep through the adjoining provinces, to "destroy the air bases from which the enemy might conduct aerial raids on the Japanese homeland.

"The captured areas will be occupied for a period estimated at approximately one month. Airfields, military installations, and important lines of communication will be totally destroyed. . . .

"The commander-in-chief of the China Expeditionary Army will begin the operation as soon as possible. He will concentrate on the annihilation of the enemy and destruction of key enemy air bases in the Chekiang area."

The orders unleashed a bloodbath. It began on May 15, when 100,000 Japanese troops broke the informal and uneasy truce that had been in force in eastern China. Facing little opposition, they ravaged an area the size of Pennsylvania. It went on for the next three months.

"When they finally withdrew in mid-August 1942," wrote historian David Bergamini, "they had killed 250,000 Chinese, most of them civilians. The villages at which the American fliers had been entertained were reduced to cinder heaps, every man, woman, and babe in them put to the sword. In the whole of Japan's brutal eight-year war with China, the vengeance on Chekiang would go down unrivaled except by the ferocious march on Nanking in 1937."

The Western world recoiled when the Nazis sacked the village of Lidice in Czechoslovakia, massacred 172 men and boys, and sent 195 women to the Ravensbruck concentration camp. That atrocity received, as it deserved, front-page newspaper coverage. The destruction of Lidice occurred on June 9, 1942, three weeks after the Japanese campaign of terror began, which killed a quarter of a million people in eastern China. The mass slaughter in China, however, received little attention from the press, despite reports from American witnesses to the brutality. U.S. newspapers did not publicize the extent of the devastation until a year later, relegating it to an inside page.

*The New York Times* of May 26, 1943, reported on page three the experiences of two American Catholic priests. When the Japanese withdrew from the countryside in mid-August, Father George Yager, Bishop Charles Quinn, and other priests moved back into their former missions and found nothing but destruction and desolation confronting them. Towns were completely laid waste. The whole countryside reeked of death in every form. Poor country people who had stayed on, hoping to be allowed to continue to work their fields, had been savagely tortured and put to death.

"From some of the villagers who had managed to escape death we heard stories far too brutal and savage to relate. Just one charge was not heard—cannibalism. But outside of that, take your choice and you can't miss the savage nature of the Japanese army."

In May 1944, *Reader's Digest* reported on a story by an American Protestant missionary, Charles L. Meeus, who visited an area sacked by the Japanese a few months after the destruction occurred. At Ihwang, where the residents had helped Doc Watson and his crew, Meeus met an eighty-year-old schoolteacher who told him how proud the village's inhabitants had been to feed the Americans and guide them to safety so they would be able to make more bombing raids on Japan.

But then the Japanese came to Ihwang. "They killed my three sons," the schoolteacher said, "they killed my wife, Ansing; they set fire to my school; they burned my books; they drowned my grandchildren in the well." *

The man in whose house Watson had been given shelter was wrapped in a blanket by the Japanese. They soaked the blanket with kerosene and forced the man's wife to set it afire. Hundreds of other townspeople were drowned in wells, shot, bayoneted, or beheaded.

The Chinese fishermen who had helped Hallmark, Nielsen, and Meder when they washed up on the shore were lined up and mowed down by machine-gun fire. The Japanese rampaged through the village, killing and wounding everyone within sight.

The heavily outnumbered Chinese army troops throughout the area fell back to Chuchow, which they planned to defend. Some forces withdrew inside the city's walls, hoping to lure the Japanese into attacking them. The main body of Chinese troops deployed in the range of hills north and south of Chuchow, ready to hit the

---

* The old man had survived by hiding in the same well all night. He took Reverend Meeus to the wreckage of Watson's plane, *Whirling Dervish*, and Meeus took a small piece of the cowling from the right engine nacelle, which eventually was turned over to the Doolittle Raiders Association, after the war.

enemy on its flanks, once the Japanese had committed themselves to an attack. Japanese planes spotted the troops in the hills, however, and with the element of surprise lost, the Chinese withdrew, ending any hope of defending the city.

With the opposition vanquished, the Japanese destroyed the Chuchow airfield so effectively it could never be used again. They forced four thousand Chinese peasants to work for three months, digging trenches three feet deep and eight feet wide, spaced at 120-foot intervals at right angles across the runway. The Japanese also demolished the airfields at Chü-hsien, Yushan, and Lishui. Claire Chennault wrote that those airfields "were so thoroughly destroyed that it was easier to build new fields than to restore the damage."

Although the Japanese succeeded in punishing those who had given aid to the American fliers, they failed in their larger goal of preventing the Chinese from helping other fliers in the future. Before the war was over, hundreds of pilots and crews downed in China would be led to safety by the Chinese people, whose will to defy their conquerors had not been broken by those three terrible months in the summer of 1942.

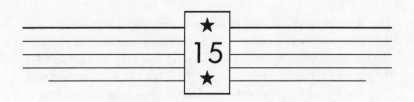

15

# I've Been Away

Memorandum for General Arnold
May 12, 1942

Have one of your people draft what you think should be the citation for a Medal of Honor for Doolittle. It should be ready at the time of his return, having had prior approval by the president. It will be necessary to keep this citation secret for a long time. However, the fact of the award of the Medal of Honor should be made public the day it becomes known that Doolittle is in town. I wish to arrange the affair so that he is kept under cover until received by the president and decorated.

We should have prepared in advance a press release of the matter and that can best be done in your office. We also should have prepared a proposed statement by Doolittle, which may take the place of a press release—except as to the Medal of Honor and reception by the president. It is quite probable that Doolittle would wish to modify the statement, but as speed will be necessary we should have a rough draft prepared in advance.

G. C. Marshall
Chief of Staff

★ ★ ★ ★

The War Department had not issued any official statement about the raid on Tokyo. Neither Doolittle's name nor that of the USS *Hornet* had been released, and Marshall and Hap Arnold still felt the need to remain secretive about the affair. It was not that they were concerned that the raid was a failure because of the loss of men and planes. They knew by then that the majority of the fliers were safe. But they believed secrecy was necessary to protect those men in Japanese hands, as well as Lawson, McClure, Clever, and White, who had not yet reached safety in unoccupied China. Also, they did not want the American people, or the Japanese, to know that all sixteen planes had been lost.

In addition, the pressure on the War Department to release information about the raid had lessened. The purpose of the raid—to provide a much-needed boost to American morale—had been achieved, spectacularly so. But a month had passed, and other actions, notably the fall of Corregidor on May 6, had taken over the headlines in the daily papers. The bombing raid on Japan was yesterday's news.

★ ★ ★ ★

At five o'clock on the morning of May 18, Mrs. Doolittle received a telephone call at her mother's home in Los Angeles, where she had been staying for a month. It was General Arnold. He asked her to come to Washington. He told her to stay close to the phone, and that when he had made her travel arrangements, he would call back. He did not tell her why she was to come to Washington, and she did not ask. If Hap Arnold wanted her there, that was good enough. She was sure it had something to do with Jimmy, and she was fairly sure Jimmy had led the raid on Japan the month before. She also felt certain that her husband was all right. Arnold had sounded too cheerful to be preparing her for bad news.

Arnold telephoned again a few hours later. She had a seat on an airliner departing Los Angeles at 4:15 that afternoon, to arrive in Washington the following morning. While she was preparing to leave, Doolittle was already on his way to Washington.

It had been two weeks since he had left China, and he'd spent most of that time in airplanes of various kinds. He was outfitted in a pith helmet, bush jacket, shorts, and knee socks he had purchased in Calcutta. He thought it was a silly way for a new brigadier general to dress, but he could hardly travel around the world in the uniform in which he had landed in a Chinese rice paddy fertilized with night soil. This was the best he could do as a replacement.

He went from Chungking to Kunming, to Myitkyina in Burma and on to Calcutta, making the last leg of the trip in a DC-3 that managed to take off with seventy-two people aboard, probably a record for an airplane designed to carry twenty-one. The plane belonged to China National Airways Corporation. Doolittle spoke to the pilot before takeoff.

"I hope to hell you know what you're doing," Doolittle said.

The pilot looked at the disheveled, middle-aged man in the motley clothing that bore no insignia of rank or service, and said, "There is a war going on over here."

From India, Doolittle journeyed west to Iran and Egypt, south to Khartoum and Dakar, across the Atlantic to South America, and north to Puerto Rico and Washington. When he arrived, Arnold told him to stay out of sight in his apartment and to tell no one he was there, not even Joe. Doolittle took advantage of the forced isolation and began writing his report of the mission.

Joe Doolittle, on the flight from Los Angeles, was the only woman passenger aboard. Every time she wanted to use the plane's single lavatory, she found it occupied. She was relieved to hear there would be a one-hour stopover in Pittsburgh in the morning so she could wash up from the overnight flight and fix her hair to look presentable when she reached Washington.

She stepped off the plane in Pittsburgh and headed for the terminal. An army officer took her by the arm and hustled her toward a small air corps plane waiting to fly her to the capital immediately. The officer insisted there was no time for her to stop in the terminal, and when she boarded the plane, she found, to her dismay, that it had no lavatory. When she landed at Washington's nearby airport, she was determined to find a rest room before she went anywhere else.

As soon as she stepped off the plane, she was met by another army officer, who seemed nervous and impatient.

"We have a car waiting for you, Mrs. Doolittle," he said, "but we've really got to hurry."

"I've got to hurry, too," Joe said. "No matter where you want me to go, it can't be as important as the place I want to go."

The officer was momentarily flustered.

"But, Mrs. Doolittle," he said, "we're due at the White House in ten minutes."

"The White House?"

★ ★ ★ ★

Doolittle received a phone call in his Washington apartment that morning. It was Hap Arnold, telling him that a car would pick him up in one hour. At the appointed time, Doolittle recalled, "I was picked up, and in the car with me were General Arnold and General Marshall. We started out in complete silence, and finally I said, 'Well now, I'm not too sharp. If you were to tell me what this is all about, I'm sure I could comport myself better.'"

Marshall and Arnold exchanged glances.

"We are going to the White House," Marshall said, "where the president will give you the Medal of Honor."

Doolittle was too stunned to speak.

"Well," Marshall said, "you don't seem very pleased."

"I don't think I earned the Medal of Honor," Doolittle said. "The Medal of Honor, to me, [is] something that [is] given where one chap lost his life saving somebody else's life. So I don't think I earned it."

Hap Arnold stopped smiling. So did George Marshall, who made it clear to Doolittle that he did not recommend someone for the nation's highest award lightly, without proper consideration. Doolittle disregarded the rising anger in Marshall's voice and the stern expressions of both superior officers. He had never been one to remain quiet when he felt he had something important to say.

"I still don't like it," he said. "General, I lost sixteen planes and eleven men. The big medal means a great deal to me, and I honestly don't think I deserve it."

"You did a really great job, Doolittle," Marshall said. "You deserve it all right."

But Doolittle persisted.

"Not," he said, "any more than some of the men who have gotten it outside of combat these past few years. Sure, they did good jobs, but you know well how everyone felt about their getting the medal."

Doolittle mentioned the example of Charles Lindbergh, who was awarded the Medal of Honor for his nonstop flight across the Atlantic, and he said he thought that was wrong. It was equally wrong to give him the medal now, just for flying a combat mission, particularly one in which he had lost all his planes.

Marshall listened patiently but with obvious annoyance. He had not expected to have to defend his recommendation for the medal, certainly not to the person he had selected to receive it.

"I know all that," Marshall said. "I recommended that you be given the Congressional Medal of Honor in order to raise the medal back to the level where it belongs."

"Well," Doolittle said, "if that's how you feel about it, all right. I feel that I don't deserve it, but I can tell you I'll spend the rest of my life trying to earn it."

When they reached the White House, Doolittle had a few minutes for a reunion with his wife, who looked, as she put it, "like a carpetbagger." He inquired after their children and asked if she had received his letter. When she said no, he said that was because he had never had a chance to write one!

Hap Arnold was grinning again by the time they were ushered into the president's Oval Office, and Marshall appeared to have reverted to his usual calm demeanor.

President Roosevelt was in a happy mood. He was delighted with the public response to the Tokyo raid, which he considered to be his own idea, and pleased to be presenting the Medal of Honor to the man who had led it.*

Despite General Marshall's concern for secrecy, Roosevelt invited

---

* Roosevelt had been told nothing about the plan to bomb Japan until after the planes had taken off from the *Hornet*. Admiral King had then briefed the president in person.

the White House reporters into the office to witness the ceremony. He joked with them and pointed out that no newspaper reporter, not even a syndicated columnist, had guessed that the great Jimmy Doolittle had led the raid on Japan. He said that Doolittle had returned that day from the secret base at Shangri-La.

Doolittle told the reporters that none of his planes had been shot down, which was true. He also said that "none was damaged to an extent that precluded its proceeding to its destination"—also true. The planes had, indeed, reached their destination, China. That none had been able to land there as planned, and that consequently all had been lost, was not mentioned, nor would it be for another year.

When Roosevelt finished bantering with the reporters, he announced that Doolittle would hold a press conference that afternoon at the War Department. Then the president turned to Marshall, who read the Medal of Honor citation aloud.

"Brigadier General James H. Doolittle, United States Army, for conspicuous leadership above and beyond the call of duty, involving personal valor and intrepidity at an extreme hazard to life. With the apparent certainty of being forced to land in enemy territory or to perish at sea, General Doolittle personally led a squadron of army bombers manned by volunteer crews in a highly destructive raid on the Japanese mainland."

Marshall handed the citation to Mrs. Doolittle, who rolled and twisted the paper so nervously in her hands that Marshall wanted to take it back, to keep her from tearing it.

Doolittle leaned down for Roosevelt to pin the medal on his chest. The second of Sergeant Leonard's predictions, made on that cold hillside in China a month before, had come true.

★ ★ ★ ★

Doolittle remained concerned over the situation of those Raiders whose fate was still unknown. Messages arrived from General Bissell in Chungking almost daily, reporting the latest developments. On May 19, Bissell told Arnold that Trav Hoover and his crew were safe and on their way to Chungking. It was definite that Hallmark, Nielsen, and Meder had been captured by the Japanese, but Bissell had no word on Hallmark's other crew members, Dieter and Fitzmaurice.

The following day, Bissell reported that Lawson, McClure, Clever, and White were on their way to Chuchow, and that Chinese army units were trying to protect them from Japanese advances in the area. There was no guarantee that the fliers would be able to evade the enemy. The outcome was still much in doubt. So far as Bissell knew, Bill Farrow's crew remained in the hands of the Chinese puppet forces in Japanese-occupied territory. Three weeks later he reported that the Chinese government was trying to ransom them, but there was little hope of success.

While he waited for additional information, Doolittle did his best to comfort the families of his men. On the day after the Medal of Honor ceremony, when newspapers throughout the country announced that he had led the raid on Tokyo, he began to write letters to the next of kin of the seventy-nine men who had been on the mission with him. Most of the letters were easy to write because the men were known to be safe.

To the mother of his copilot, Dick Cole, in Dayton, Ohio, Doolittle wrote:

I am pleased to report that Dick is well and happy, although a bit homesick. I left him in Chungking, in China, a couple of weeks ago. He had recently completed a very hazardous, extremely important and most interesting flight—the air raid on Japan. He comported himself with conspicuous bravery and distinction. He was awarded the Distinguished Flying Cross for gallantry in action, and also was decorated by the Chinese government.

Transportation and communication facilities are extremely bad in the Far East and so it may be some time before you hear again from Dick directly. I assure you, however, that everything is going smoothly with him and although plans for the future are uncertain, he will probably be returning home sometime in the not too distant future.

I am proud to have served with Dick, who was my copilot on the flight, and hope that I may have an opportunity to serve with him again.

Other letters were more difficult. To Ted Lawson's mother, in Los Angeles, Doolittle wrote:

> I am sorry to be obliged to advise that your son was wounded in action. We have been unable to ascertain the exact extent of the wounds. . . . We were advised yesterday by cable from China that [Lawson and his crew] are on their way out en route to Chungking. From Chungking they will proceed to India and then on home.

As with every letter, he told Mrs. Lawson how proud he was to have served with her son and how brave Ted had been, and also about the medals he had received.

To Dean Hallmark's mother, in Dallas, Doolittle wrote how sorry he was to have to bring bad news.

> However, it is not as bad as it might be. Your son, according to the most reliable information that we are able to obtain, landed in Japanese-occupied territory in China and has been taken prisoner. Every effort was and still is being made to extricate him from Japanese hands but to date we have not been successful. You may depend on everything possible being done in this direction.

He added a postscript to his letter to Mrs. Hallmark, the same one he added to the letters of all those whose loved ones remained in jeopardy: "As the above information is of military significance, it is requested that it be kept in the strictest confidence."

There was another obligation Doolittle attended to during that time, and that was to the man who had packed the parachute he used when he bailed out over China. It was a long-standing air corps tradition to send a box of cigars to the packer of a chute that opened successfully (the packer's name was on the inspection card).

After he'd taken care of that, he went to the neighborhood drugstore to buy a tube of toothpaste. He did not know about the new wartime measure that required turning in the old used tube before purchasing a new one. He was also startled by the high war tax on many items, and commented on it to the druggist.

"Don't take it out on me," the man said. "Don't you know there's a war on?"

"Sorry," Doolittle said. "I've been away."

★ ★ ★ ★

Lt. Hank Miller, the navy flier who had taught the Doolittle pilots how to take off from a carrier deck, was back where he had started, teaching cadets at Pensacola how to fly. His continuing attempts to get a combat assignment had been thwarted. In early June he received a telephone call from an officer in Washington who was involved with personnel assignments.

"Are you the Henry Miller of Shangri-La?"

"Yes, sir."

"Can you get up to Washington on Wednesday?"

"I sure will."

Miller was certain the call could mean only one thing, a special assignment like the one that had taken him out to the Pacific.

"Oh boy," he recalled saying to himself, "this is just great, another deal like the Doolittle raid. I was glad to get out of the instructing business at Pensacola and go to war again."

He got on an airliner, and when he changed planes at Jacksonville, he recognized Fred Braemer, who had been the bombardier on Doolittle's plane. Braemer was on the final leg of his journey halfway around the world from Chungking to Washington.

As soon as the plane had landed, Miller went to the navy department to see the officer who had phoned him.

"Commander," he said, "I am here, ready to go again."

"Did you bring your white uniform up?"

"Yes, sir," Miller said, more than a bit puzzled. A combat assignment did not normally call for a white uniform.

"Didn't anybody tell you what you were supposed to come up here for?"

"No."

"You're going to a dinner party. You and Jimmy Doolittle are supposed to tell the secretary of the army and the secretary of the navy about the Doolittle raid from the army and the navy standpoint."

Miller was disappointed, but orders were orders. He reported for duty to a private dining room at the Mayflower Hotel, on Connecticut Avenue, where, over drinks and dinner, he and Doolittle told their stories.*

★ ★ ★ ★

By the end of June, enough of the Doolittle Raiders had returned to the States to warrant holding a ceremony to present the Distinguished Flying Cross. Although the fliers had been notified of the award in Chungking, the medals had not been presented there because Stilwell's headquarters did not have any. Doolittle sent out orders dated June 15, 1942, to "all officers and men with me at Shangri-La," requesting them to report to Room 4414 of the Munitions Building in Washington. Security about the details of the mission was still a priority, something he made clear in paragraph two of the orders.

"You will grant no interviews with the press nor pose for photos and in your communications to your homes [you] will advise them simply that you are back in the United States. Use the utmost caution until such time as you have been given a directive . . . on what you can say and do, so as not to jeopardize the security of others going into the field. In other words, be most cautious with everyone except authorized intelligence officers of the United States Army."

On June 27, at Washington's Bolling Field, twenty-three of the Raiders lined up against a backdrop of obsolete B-18 bombers. The air force band and color guard stood at attention, along with several platoons of soldiers. The Washington, D.C., *Sunday Star* referred to the men of Doolittle's command as "members of the United States military mission to Shangri-La," and praised Doolittle for his "achievement in leading the men on the raid without losing a plane." Several of the wives attended the ceremony, watching proudly as their men were decorated by Hap Arnold. It was a glori-

---

* Hank Miller returned to Pensacola, but in November he was transferred to fighters. He commanded air groups aboard the carriers *Princeton* and *Hancock* in the Pacific. In February 1965, as commander of Task Force 77, he launched the first of a series of carrier strikes on North Vietnam from the carriers *Ranger*, *Coral Sea*, and *Hancock*. He retired from active service in 1971 at the rank of rear admiral.

ous moment and well-deserved recognition for what they had accomplished.

A smaller ceremony was held a week later at Walter Reed Army
Hospital to honor Ted Lawson, Mac McClure, and Doc Watson.
Lawson and McClure's trip home had taken two weeks. Accom-
panied by Dr. White and Bob Clever, their first stop was Dinjan,
India, where they met Bob Gray and Dick Joyce, who had been
reassigned to flying transports.

At New Delhi, the fliers stayed at the luxurious Hotel Imperial.
Lawson hobbled around the city on his crutches, looking for gifts to
take home to his family. He and McClure searched for apple pie à la
mode, something they had dreamed about for weeks. They found
lots of ice cream, but no apple pie.

The next stop was Karachi, where they were joined by Ross
Greening, Jack Hilger, Charles Ozuk, and several other Raiders
also on their way home. The group flew to Cairo, where Clever and
Ozuk were stricken with appendicitis. Both men tried to reboard the
plane, wanting to get home no matter how sick they were, but White
wisely sent them to a hospital.

At the next stop, a U.S. military base somewhere along the Nile,
they saw a copy of the June 1 issue of *Life* magazine, which contained an article about the raid. Lawson studied his picture in the
magazine, looked in the mirror, and concluded they were two different people. Then it was on to Nigeria, where they found Jack Sims,
Ses Sessler, and Griff Williams.

On the way across the Atlantic, while the others slept, Lawson
made his way to the cockpit. The pilot motioned him to take the
copilot's seat. Lawson very much wanted to know what it felt like to
fly a plane again, but was reluctant to ask. The pilot sensed it from
the look on Lawson's face and graciously turned over the controls.
Lawson flew the big transport for an hour, and it made him feel a
little better.

From Brazil they flew to Trinidad, which boasted welcome trap-
pings of American civilization—ice-cold Coca-Cola and slot ma-
chines. Once they reached Palm Beach, Florida, Lawson and Hilger
took advantage of being stateside by consuming an outrageous

breakfast of two quarts of milk, two chocolate milkshakes, bacon and eggs, and several hamburgers.

They landed at Bolling Field on June 16 and an army ambulance drove Lawson and McClure to the hospital. They were taken to Doc Watson's room. Watson had arrived the week before and had been operated on for his arm and shoulder injuries. They had dinner on trays—McClure and Lawson asked for seconds—and while they were eating, in walked Jimmy Doolittle, apologizing for not having met their plane at Bolling.

Doolittle returned to Walter Reed Army Hospital on July 6, accompanied by Maj. Gen. M. F. Harmon, chief of the air staff of the Army Air Force, Secretary of the Treasury Morgenthau, McClure's mother, Watson's wife and parents, and Lawson's wife. The three fliers sat up in wheelchairs for the ceremony. When General Harmon pinned the Distinguished Flying Cross to their pajamas, Doolittle looked on with a big proud smile on his face.*

★ ★ ★ ★

Doolittle was growing restless, eager for a new command. Hap Arnold kept him busy for a while with a round of visits to defense plants to give morale-building talks to workers, as well as radio speeches and personal appearances to boost the war effort. Doolittle quickly became tired of these activities, wanting a more active role in the war.

Arnold was not sure what to do with him. He knew that some career officers resented Doolittle's rapid two-step promotion and his high visibility for leading a combat mission, something many of them had done without fanfare. Other officers resented the fact that Doolittle had, in their view, deserted the service for ten years to compete in air races and make big money while they had endured low budgets and slow promotions. Arnold was having difficulty finding

---

* Lawson remained in the hospital until May 1943 and served as liaison officer at the American air mission in Santiago, Chile. He was retired for physical disability in February 1945. McClure stayed in Walter Reed until June 1943 and served as air navigation instructor until he was hospitalized again for five months and retired on disability. Watson was hospitalized until July 1944. He remained in the air force after the war, and retired at the rank of lieutenant colonel in 1961.

a suitable post for Doolittle. The first commander to whom he recommended Doolittle—Douglas MacArthur—turned him down flat. There was room for only one celebrity in MacArthur's command.

Arnold set his sights on the European theater and sent Doolittle to London in early August, with the idea that he would serve under Eisenhower to organize and command Ike's new Twelfth Air Force. The only problem was that Eisenhower took an immediate dislike to Doolittle.

Eisenhower knew of Doolittle long before the Tokyo raid and respected him as a pilot, but he was doubtful of Doolittle's ability to administer a large military unit because of his absence from the armed forces at that time in his career when he might have been chosen to attend Command and General Staff School to study organizational and leadership skills. Ike simply didn't think Doolittle had had enough experience. Also, when the two men met for the first time in Eisenhower's London headquarters, Doolittle expressed openly, as was his way, his disagreement with Eisenhower on the uses of air power.

After the meeting, Eisenhower cabled Arnold to say he did not want Doolittle in his command. He asked for Tooey Spaatz or Ira Eaker instead. Arnold said Ike could have anyone he wanted, but he still recommended Doolittle. Reluctantly, Ike acceded to Arnold's wishes, but the antagonism between the two men was apparent. Doolittle wrote that "it made [Ike] dislike me even more because he thought I was being forced down his throat. . . . I could see his dislike while making my presentations. It was difficult not to be upset by it."

Doolittle organized the Twelfth Air Force and proved his worth to Eisenhower, although it took a long time. The Twelfth was heavily involved in the invasion of North Africa and the subsequent land campaign, and Doolittle did his job so well that Eisenhower recommended him for promotion to major general by November 1942, but not before there was another confrontation.

Doolittle was testing a new model Supermarine Spitfire at his base at Oran, Algeria, when Ike called from his headquarters on Gibraltar. When informed what Doolittle was doing, an angry Eisenhower said that Doolittle was to report to him as soon as possible.

Doolittle flew to Gibraltar to meet with his boss. Eisenhower said that he understood Doolittle had been "up in a Spitfire looking for Germans." This was not precisely the case, but Doolittle did not argue. (He said later he enjoyed being characterized that way.)

"Yes, sir," Doolittle said. "A new airplane—a Spit IX—just came down and I wanted to try it out."

"Listen, Doolittle," Ike said, "you can either be a major general in charge of my air or you can be a second lieutenant and you can go fly Spitfires looking for Germans. I can fix that tomorrow. Which do you want?"

"I'd rather be a major general handling your air."

"All right," Ike snapped. "Stay at it."

After the war, Eisenhower liked telling the story about Jimmy Doolittle going up in a Spitfire looking for Germans, but it took a year for him to be convinced that Doolittle was more than a daredevil, irresponsible, hotshot pilot. Yet even during that year, Eisenhower promoted him, decorated him, and gave him command of the Fifteenth Air Force in the Mediterranean. In mid-July 1943, the man who had led sixteen planes on America's first air raid on Tokyo personally led five hundred planes on the first raid on another Axis capital, Rome. And on January 6, 1944, Lieutenant General Doolittle replaced Ira Eaker as commander of the Eighth Air Force in England. He had finally proved himself to Eisenhower.

★ ★ ★ ★

Ski York and his crew—Bob Emmens, Nolan Herndon, Ted LaBan, and Dave Pohl—still under house arrest at Okhuna, were told by their keeper, Mike, of an article in the daily paper. It described the ceremony at Bolling Field in Washington at which twenty-three of the Doolittle Raiders had been decorated. The men were shocked. The news suggested that only twenty-three of the remaining seventy-five had survived. Worse, they had not heard anything from the American embassy officials in over two months, despite their promise to stay in touch.

They had spent the past two months sitting on the porch, watching people walk past the house, playing chess, and trying to learn Russian. Mike brought them a volleyball and a net, but Emmens twisted his ankle in a game against their Russian wardens and had to wear a cast for several weeks. Mike rounded up a piano and a small pool table to amuse them, but what they really wanted was word from the embassy, some sign they had not been forgotten. They kept asking Mike to contact the embassy but never knew if he did.

By the middle of July, supplies were getting scarce. Cigarettes went first. All the Americans smoked, and they then took to rolling their own out of newspaper and coarse Russian tobacco. Food was running low, and for a time they were out of vodka, which had always been as plentiful as water. A month later, Mike gave them sets of rough white muslin underclothing. It was the first time they had been given any clothes, and it could mean only one thing. They were going to remain interned in Russia for a long time.

Several days later, Mike announced that they would be leaving in a few hours, but he refused to say where they were going. They were taken aboard a train and put in a compartment with a small supply of food. They knew then that the journey would not be a long one. The train headed north, toward Moscow, which gave them a glimmer of hope, but then it turned northeast. The hope of getting to the embassy quickly faded.

After two days on the train and two more on a boat, they disembarked at the village of Okhansk, in the foothills of the Ural Mountains on the western edge of Siberia. Mike explained that they had been brought here to protect them from the German advance. He didn't say if the U.S. Embassy had been informed about their move, but he promised to let officials there know. The men doubted that they could believe him.

On September 1, 1942, they settled in a primitive, unpainted wooden house. The toilet was a hole in the floor, and the bathhouse was a log hut out back. They would be there for seven months. Shortly after their arrival, Mike announced that someone was coming from Moscow to see them. Their hopes rose again. It had been four months since they had seen another American. They busied themselves writing letters to their families for the embassy people to mail, polishing their brass, and pacing in front of the house. A large quantity of food and vodka was delivered, but nobody came. The men sat up until two o'clock in the morning, too keyed up to sleep.

When they had nearly given up, a yacht came upriver at one o'clock the next afternoon, bringing several Russian military officers and four Americans: Page and Michela; Maj. Gen. Follett Bradley of the Army Air Force, who was in Russia to arrange delivery of lend-lease supplies; and U.S. Ambassador William Standley. They brought gifts for the fliers—toothpaste, cigarettes, American magazines, and an English-Russian grammar book. The last seemed a bad sign. The visitors had little to report on the Doolittle raid. All they knew was that no planes had been shot down over Japan and that one or maybe two crews had been captured.

York spoke privately to the American visitors about how bored and desperate they were, and he asked if the embassy officials could help them escape by supplying them with maps and compasses. Ambassador Standley said they could do nothing along those lines, but they were trying to get them released through diplomatic means. He did not believe it would be soon, however. They left after only two hours, itself a disappointment, but promised to send the embassy physician to examine them.

The weather turned damp and cold. By the end of September the village streets had turned to mud, and a few days later a foot of snow covered the ground. Now the men could not even go outdoors. The American doctor had not yet arrived, and they knew that if he did not come soon, he would not be able to reach them until the spring thaw.

"Our morale was becoming lower day by day," Emmens wrote. "It was becoming necessary to be extremely careful of the things we said and the manner in which we said them to one another. Any serious rift among ourselves would be bad."

They started playing hearts every night for two hours, keeping score on a weekly basis. Each Friday night the winner was announced, and punishment was meted out to the losers, who were swatted on the rear by the others. It helped to relieve the tension and give vent to any anger or animosity that had developed during the week.

The Russian guards thought the fliers were crazy, but they, too, looked forward to the Friday-night sessions. Mike decided to join them in the card game, but was the biggest loser that week. To the Americans, it was the best Friday night of all, but Mike decided not to play again.

On October 15 the embassy doctor arrived in a horse-drawn sleigh, bringing cigarettes, whiskey, and American books and magazines. He gave them a supply of aspirin and quinine and stayed two days. It was a treat to talk to someone who brought news of the rest of the world. They did not know he was the last American they would see for the rest of their time in Russia.

# I Request that the Penalty Be Death

On April 28, ten days after the Doolittle raid, Japanese Prime Minister Hideki Tojo called a conference of his bureau chiefs. The purpose of the meeting was to decide the fate of the eight captured American airmen. Should they be executed or given lengthy prison sentences? Should they be treated as prisoners of war or as war criminals? A sharp difference of opinion soon became apparent between Tojo and Gen. Hajime Sugiyama, chief of the Imperial General Staff.

Sugiyama, expressing the wishes of Emperor Hirohito, argued that an example must be made of the captured fliers by executing them. If they were not executed, he said—if they were merely imprisoned—that would be no deterrent against future attacks on the Japanese homeland. The Americans had to be made to understand that their fliers would pay the supreme penalty for bombing Japan. This was why the Japanese military had opposed the Geneva Prisoner-of-War Convention in 1929. And now that Japan herself had been attacked, Sugiyama insisted, it was even more imperative to take a hard line with the captured fliers. Otherwise, Japan could expect to be attacked many more times during the war.

Tojo argued against executing the fliers on the grounds that it would be viewed as a barbaric act by the rest of the world and might endanger a few thousand Japanese citizens interned in the United States—diplomats, journalists, and businessmen whose repatriation had yet to be arranged. Tojo also believed that there was no legal basis for executing the American prisoners.

He did think, however, that the captured fliers should be punished, and he called the raid "contrary to international law. It was not against troops but against noncombatants, primary school students, and so forth. . . . since this was not permitted by international law, it was homicide." He agreed with Sugiyama that some punishment was necessary to deter future air raids, but disagreed on the form that punishment should take.

The debate continued for weeks, but by midsummer it was clear that Sugiyama's desire for execution would prevail. Bowing to the inevitable, Tojo wanted to ensure that the executions would be legal. Accordingly, "regulations for punishment of enemy air crews" were approved on August 13, 1942.* By the terms of this act, which was applied retroactively to include the Doolittle fliers, the bombing and strafing of civilian targets was punishable by death or a prison term of ten years to life, depending on the severity of the crime.

With the legal justification for execution in place, it remained only to conduct a trial of the prisoners, a show trial in which verdict and punishment had already been decided.

★ ★ ★ ★

The eight American prisoners had been housed in the same cell in Shanghai's Bridge House jail since mid-June. Their physical condition and morale deteriorated daily, even after the Chinese prisoners were removed so they had the cell to themselves. There was barely enough food to sustain life—weak tea and miserly portions of rice containing worms and maggots. At first they could not force themselves to eat it, no matter how hungry they were, but Chase Nielsen persuaded them that they had to if they intended to survive. He was

* See Appendix 2.

determined to stay alive so that one day, he could tell the world what the Japanese had done to them.

Dean Hallmark became so ill with dysentery that he fainted. The men had to carry him to the toilet "about every fifteen minutes," Jake DeShazer said. Eventually, their own exhaustion forced them to stop.

They had not bathed, shaved, or changed clothes since their last day on the *Hornet*. Their bodies were covered with bites from lice, bedbugs, and rats. They were required to sit cross-legged all day on the floor, without leaning against the walls, a painfully confining position for Westerners who were not used to it, as Japanese were. If the guards saw them shift position, they would poke a pole through the cell bars and smack them on the head.

A guard who caught Bobby Hite and Bill Farrow leaning against the wall charged into the cell and hit Hite with his sheathed sword. Hite grabbed the scabbard and pulled it out of the guard's hands. The guard maintained his hold on the sword and pointed it at Hite. Farrow stepped beside Hite and they both dropped into a crouch, menacing the guard with their wrestler's stance. The guard backed out of the cell, and all of their jailers seemed less hostile after that. A few even grew cautiously friendly.

A few weeks later, some British members of the Shanghai police force, allowed by the Japanese to continue to perform their duties, took up a collection for the English and American prisoners in Bridge House. They were able to provide decent food once a day— corn, eggs, meat, real coffee, and tea. It lasted only two weeks. The Americans were then able to bribe an amenable Japanese guard with the money they had been permitted to keep. He brought them clean clothes, but what boosted their morale even more was arranging to have a bath and have their beards clipped and heads shaved. Then they had a feast—steak, vegetables, jam, and French bread— the last such meal they would have for three years. Within hours, Hallmark collapsed, and three days later he looked like a skeleton. He was unconscious much of the time and too weak to get up, even when the others could rouse him. And the others were not in much better condition themselves.

On August 28 they were taken from their cell and put on a truck. Hite and Farrow had to carry Hallmark on a stretcher. He was delirious. They were driven across Shanghai to the Ward Road jail, where they were led into a small courtroom. Five Japanese officers sat behind a long table. The Americans stood in a row facing them. Hallmark lay on the floor on his stretcher, unaware of what was going on. Flies landed on his body, but he was too weak to brush them away. Suddenly, George Barr passed out. When he came to, he was given a chair from which to watch as their trial began.

The judge, Maj. Gen. Shoji Ito, the chief justice officer of the Thirteenth Army Military Court in Shanghai, spoke in Japanese. This would be the only portion of the proceedings to be translated into English for the American fliers. Ito asked each of the prisoners to tell the court briefly the story of his life, starting from the time he was in high school. The seven men—Hallmark could not respond— told something of their past, distorting their experiences in the air corps as much as possible. Their words were translated for the Japanese officers, but they seemed bored, not at all interested in the Americans' answers. None of them took notes.

There was no reason for anyone to take notes because the outcome of the trial had already been dictated by the chief of the general staff, General Sugiyama. He sent an emissary, Colonel Arisue, to Shanghai with orders that were revealed in the war crimes trials after the war: "To carry out the trial in a very strict manner, and that punishment must be very strict. As a matter of fact," Arisue said, "the chief of the general staff was expecting the death sentence."

The prosecutor, Maj. Itsura Hata, read the charges against each man and presented the evidence, including their confessions. "It is evident," Hata said, "that they are guilty in a view of military law; therefore I request that the penalty be death sentence." The case was presented in Japanese but not translated into English. The judge read a lengthy prepared statement, which the interpreter said was the verdict of the court and the sentences. When the prisoners asked what the sentences were, he said the judge had ordered him not to tell them. The trial was over.

Japanese soldiers picked up Hallmark's stretcher and took him back to Bridge House. He was dumped in a cell with twenty prisoners of several nationalities, and for six weeks he lay on the floor, too weak to move. No medical care was provided.

The other seven Americans were placed in individual cells in a building next to the courthouse. They were kept in solitary confinement for twenty days before being allowed out for a brief period of exercise each day. The food was as sparse as it had been at Bridge House, but at least there they had had the comfort of one another's presence. Now they faced the days and nights alone, each with the nagging worry that the court's sentence, which might be carried out at any time, was death.

★ ★ ★ ★

They had, indeed, been sentenced to death, but the decision to carry it out had yet to be made. The fliers were caught in the middle of the battle between the army and the cabinet, between Sugiyama and Tojo. At eleven-thirty on the morning of October 3, 1942, Prime Minister Tojo appeared at the Imperial Palace to speak with Koichi Kido, the lord privy seal and the emperor's closest adviser. Tojo reported on the trial and the death sentences that had been handed down, and argued for leniency. At the most, he suggested, only some of the fliers should be executed, not all of them. That afternoon, Kido spent ten minutes with Emperor Hirohito, explaining Tojo's position.

General Sugiyama had tried to get an appointment with Kido first, but was unsuccessful. When he arrived that afternoon, Kido had already presented Tojo's request for leniency to the emperor. Sugiyama stated his position, arguing for the execution of all the fliers immediately, but he was too late. Hirohito agreed with Tojo that only those found guilty of killing schoolchildren should be executed. The others would be sentenced to life imprisonment.

On October 10, Sugiyama cabled the decision to Gen. Shunroku Hata, supreme commander of Japanese forces in China.

The verdict issued by the military tribunal concerning the punish-

ment of the American airmen who raided the Japanese homeland is
considered to be fair and just.

However, upon review, we believe that with the exception of both
pilots, and gunner Spatz, the death sentence should be commuted.

The five whose death sentences were commuted shall be sentenced
to life imprisonment. As war criminals, their treatment shall not be
that accorded ordinary prisoners of war.

Even in the event of an exchange of war prisoners, they may not be
repatriated to the United States forces.

Dean Hallmark, Bill Farrow, and Harold Spatz would die. Their
executions were set for October 15. The day before, Hallmark was
brought back from Bridge House and placed in a cell in the same
building as the others. They were not aware of it because they were
still in solitary confinement.

One at a time, the three condemned men were taken into a room
and told they would be executed the following day. Sgt. Sotojiro
Tatsuta, the prison warden, told the men through an interpreter
that they could write brief letters to their families.

"Don't let this get you down," twenty-three-year-old Bill Farrow,
from Darlington, South Carolina, wrote to his mother. "Remember
God will make everything right and that I will see you all again in the
hereafter."

Harold Spatz, twenty-one years old, of Lebo, Kansas, wrote to his
father. "I want you to know I died fighting for my country like a
soldier."

"I hardly know what to say," wrote twenty-eight-year-old Dean
Hallmark, from Robert Lee, Texas, who had become lucid enough
to be aware of the situation. "They have just told me I am liable to
execution. I can hardly believe it." He urged his mother to "try to
stand up under this and pray."

The men waited in their cells until four o'clock the next afternoon, when they were driven by truck to a public cemetery near the
prison. Three small wooden crosses stood in a row on freshly cut
grass. A squad of soldiers marched over the lawn. Three troopers
were detailed to the perimeter to serve as guards, while the other six

were formed into two lines, one behind the other, some twenty feet in front of the Americans.

Maj. Itsura Hata, the prosecutor in their trial, arrived, along with Sergeant Tatsuta, the prison warden, and Chosei Fujuta, the court clerk. Also present as official witnesses were the prosecutor for the military district, three medical officers, members of the Shanghai military police, and an interpreter. A small altar was set up on a table behind the firing squad, and an incense burner was lit. Even executions had a ritual, and the Japanese took pains to follow it.

Major Hata read the official death decree, which was translated into English, then spoke to the Americans informally. He did so, he said at his own trial after the war, to make them feel calmer about their death. He bowed to the three weak, gaunt fliers and stepped back so that the warden could have his say.

"I do not know what relation I had with you in the previous life," warden Tatsuta said, according to his testimony during his war crimes trial in 1946, "but we have been living together under the same roof and on this day you are going to be executed, but I feel sorry for you. Your lives were very short but your names will remain everlastingly."

He recalled that one of the prisoners—he was not sure which—had thanked him for his consideration during the imprisonment. It was a statement that sounded more than a little self-serving, but then Tatsuta was on trial for his life.

The prisoners were made to kneel on the ground in front of the wooden crosses, and their arms were tied to the ends of the horizontal crossbars. They were blindfolded, and a large splotch of black ink was daubed squarely in the center of each man's forehead. The spots were the targets. When the command to fire was given, all three were hit with precision. No second shots were required, and Hallmark, Farrow, and Spatz died instantly.

In 1946, four men were tried in Shanghai's Ward Road jail for their part in the brutal treatment of the captured Doolittle fliers and for the executions. On trial were Lt. Gen. Shigeru Sawada, commander of the Japanese Thirteenth Army in China; Capt. Ryuhei

Okada, a member of the court that had convicted the Doolittle fliers; Lt. Yusei Wako, a prosecutor; and Capt. (formerly Sgt.) Sotojiro Tatsuta, the warden of the Ward Road jail. Others thought responsible had already died or could not be located.

Wako received a nine-year sentence; the others were given five-year jail terms. The maximum penalty that could have been imposed was death, and the families and friends of the executed fliers, as well as many other Americans, were outraged at the lenient sentences.

The U.S. Military Commission found that "the offenses of each of the accused resulted largely from obedience to laws and instructions of their government and their military superiors. They exercised no initiative to any marked degree. These circumstances . . . do not entirely absolve the accused from guilt. However, they do compel unusually strong mitigating considerations."

Chase Nielsen had vowed to his buddies to stay alive—even if he had to eat rice with worms and maggots—to tell the world about their treatment at the hands of the Japanese. He fulfilled his vow when he appeared as a witness in the trial at the Ward Road jail. Nielsen wrote to Doolittle that the guards "really cringed when I walked in." He added, "I sit here with tears in my eyes when I think what has happened to the ones who were in the Jap prison camps and feel that I want to do what little I can to help those who came back and to help prosecute those who were responsible for the executing of the others."

Prime Minister Tojo survived a suicide attempt after Japan surrendered. He was tried as a war criminal by the International Military Tribunal, Far East, and hanged in 1948. General Sugiyama was successful in his suicide and so evaded other punishment for war crimes.

★ ★ ★ ★

The morning after the executions, the other American prisoners— Nielsen, Meder, Hite, Barr, and DeShazer—were allowed to take baths, after which they were led from their cells by soldiers in dress uniforms carrying rifles and sabers. Each man thought he was being taken to his place of execution. Instead, they were led back into the courtroom to face fifteen solemn Japanese officers. They wondered why Hallmark, Farrow, and Spatz were missing. They had not seen Hallmark for nearly two months, since their last appearance in court, but so far as they knew, the others had been in their cells the day before.

They had little time to ponder their absence. The chief judge began to read a statement in Japanese. The words were translated into English, and the men were stunned by what they heard. They were, the judge said, guilty of indiscriminately bombing schools and hospitals and machine-gunning innocent civilians. They had been sentenced to death, but owing to the mercy of the emperor, their sentences had been commuted to life imprisonment.

Immediately after the sentence was pronounced, guards surrounded the prisoners and marched them back to their individual cells. "I had expected to be executed," Jake DeShazer said. "It was really a relief to know that they were now planning to let us remain alive. I could not help feeling a strange sense of joy. . . . At the same time, it seemed almost hopeless to think of ever being free again, since the most probable thing would be that we would be executed when America did win the war."

Two days later it appeared that the judge had changed his mind. The fliers were brought together in the prison courtyard where the warden, Tatsuta, speaking through an interpreter, told them they had been found guilty of war crimes for killing civilians, and had been sentenced to death.

The men stared at him, unbelieving, and Tatsuta asked the translator exactly what he had told them. The two men spoke for a few minutes, and the translator smiled and said he had made a mistake. The Americans were sentenced to prison for life, not to death.

Tatsuta took them into the courtroom, where their possessions had been stacked in eight neat piles. They were allowed to sort through them and take whatever they wanted back to their cells.

The men looked at the three untouched piles. Each was sure that Hallmark, Farrow, and Spatz had been killed, but no one wanted to say so aloud. As they gathered their belongings, they whispered the conjecture that the three had been taken someplace else.

They resumed their daily routine in their separate nine-by-five-foot cells. They were allowed out for a half hour every morning to brush their teeth and wash their faces, and later for a brief period of exercise. They were able to exchange a few quick words during those times, when the guards were not looking. Otherwise, there was nothing to do—no books, newspapers, radio, or companionship, no letters from home or Red Cross packages. As war criminals, they were entitled to nothing.

They could shout to one another from their cells, but that brought punishment from the guards. Their only link became a prisoner-trusty who served as their interpreter. His name was Caesar Luis dos Remedios; his father was Portuguese and his mother Japanese. He slipped them notes with their food, messages of encouragement from one another, and news on the progress of the war. He told them about a big sea battle at a place called Midway, which he thought the Japanese had lost.

He managed to get them out of solitary during the dreadfully cold winter. The cells were unheated, and the two blankets issued to each man were inadequate protection for sleeping on the bare floor. The men were sure they would never survive, and said as much to the trusty. He went to see Tatsuta on their behalf and persuaded the warden to help.

The men were given three blankets apiece and brought together in a larger cell, ending the awful isolation. The companionship improved their morale, but their physical condition reached a new low. They had begun to show symptoms of beriberi, a disorder brought on by a deficiency of vitamin $B_1$. Their muscles and joints ached and they became irritable, unable to concentrate or control their temper. As weak as they were, they almost came to blows. The condition could easily have been relieved by a proper diet, but the Japanese did nothing to help.

Bobby Hite was the most affected, and one morning in late January he passed out while doing push-ups. When he revived, he experienced double vision and paralysis. A Japanese doctor examined him and administered an injection that knocked him out for forty-eight hours. When he woke up, he found only Bob Meder in the cell with him. The others had been moved elsewhere. For ten days

Meder fed him, kept him wrapped in blankets, and talked about anything that came to his mind, in an effort to bolster Hite's spirits.

Together again in a single cell, the men passed the winter. Their trusty continued to bring them war news, plus a Valentine's Day greeting in February, birthday good wishes to Barr in April, and a few precious books.*

On April 17, 1943, almost one year to the day after the B-25 bombing raid on Japan, their stay in Shanghai ended. They were taken to the prison courtyard, blindfolded, handcuffed, and tied to a guard. Then they were driven to the airport, placed on a plane, and handcuffed to their seats. Their destination was a prison an hour west of Nanking. Five American prisoners arrived in Nanking that day. Only four would leave.

★ ★ ★ ★

It was bitterly cold in Russia that winter of 1942–43. By the end of November, the temperature was fixed below zero. There had been no further contact with the U.S. Embassy since the doctor's visit in mid-October. Mike spent less and less time with them. He was away most days and many nights. Emmens and York had learned enough Russian by then to get along without him. They could speak to the women who cooked and took care of the house, and could understand most of the news on the radio.

In December they ran low on food. Mike was no help, but the woman in charge of the kitchen found out that their food was stored at the district headquarters, and that no one would bring it out because of the weather. Despite a temperature of minus forty degrees, she walked to the depot, borrowed a truck, and brought back six cartons of food, some of it lend-lease from the United States. The food was rationed carefully, for they were not sure when they would be able to get more.

The men celebrated Christmas by chopping down a tree in the woods and decorating it with bits of cotton. They serenaded one another with Christmas carols after dinner. A few days later they

---

*After the war, Caesar Luis dos Remedios was instrumental in gathering evidence against Japanese accused in the war crimes trial held at the Ward Road jail.

were invited to the village school to be guests at a children's party. They gladly accepted the invitation.

The children looked hollow-eyed and hungry. Their heads had been shaved, probably because of lice. They put on a play in which a Russian army unit recaptured a town from the Germans. One of the Russian soldiers left his post to see if his wife and mother had survived the German occupation. Because of this act of desertion, he was shot as a traitor. The moral was that a person's obligation to the state is greater than any obligation to family or anyone else.

After the play, the children crowded around the Americans, fingering their uniforms and their shiny watches and rings. One boy asked Emmens if there were any other wristwatches like his in America, and if anyone could own a watch. The men found the experience depressing, and they declined invitations to other children's parties.

By January of 1943, their morale was sinking. The weather kept them indoors, and they remained bored and listless. The poor diet was causing bleeding gums and raw, flaky skin. If only they had some way to keep busy, to help in the war effort—Russia was, after all, an American ally—then they could better tolerate the climate, scarce food, and confinement.

York decided to write to Joseph Stalin, asking that the men be released to go back to what they had been trained for, fighting the Japanese and the Germans. Failing that, he asked Stalin to move them to a warmer climate and give them work.

Mike was horrified at the idea of writing to the Russian dictator. Suppose Stalin became angry at the impertinence of the Americans and decided to ship them deep into Siberia? Mike might have to go with them. Still, he helped correct their Russian grammar and said he would mail the letter for them, but, as usual, they did not know if they could trust him to do it. Then, one evening late in January, Mike failed to show up for dinner. They never saw him again.

Near the end of February the temperature rose to zero, and occasionally as high as ten degrees above. The fliers began to talk about making plans to escape after the spring thaw. A month later, two Russian army officers—a major and a captain—knocked on the door and asked to speak to them. The senior officer pulled a letter from his briefcase.

"This letter was received in Moscow a short time ago," he said. "Did you write it?"

When York admitted he had written the letter, the major smiled and said that they could not be allowed to leave the country, but it had been decided to move them to a warmer climate and give them jobs. When he asked how soon they could be ready to leave, York said in one hour.

The Russian women who had been caring for them for seven months broke into tears at the news. Although the five Americans had lost weight on the poor diet, the women had gained, for they were getting better rations than they would have otherwise. Emmens assured them that the war would soon be over and things would get better for the Russian people. They didn't seem to believe him.

The Russian major, unfailingly polite and courteous, led them off in a four-car caravan on a twelve-hour drive to the city of Molotov, where they were housed in a decent hotel, fed well, and measured for Russian uniforms. The next day they were given olive-drab pants, pullover blouses, black boots, wide leather belts, and caps with the red star insignia.

That night they were taken to see a performance of *Swan Lake* by the Leningrad Kirov Ballet, and allowed the freedom of walking back to their hotel by themselves, with no guards. The following night the major took them to see an American film, *One Hundred Men and a Girl.* It was the fifth time they had seen it.

The next day they flew south to Chkalov, where they stayed in a hotel and were taken to the opera to see *Eugene Onegin,* based on the Pushkin poem. The movie the following evening was *The Great Waltz.* The major told them that the rest of their journey would be by train, and when they boarded, they were surprised to find themselves in a car with other people. It was the first time they had not been isolated while traveling.

Emmens, Herndon, LaBan, and Pohl shared two compartments, but York was shown to a compartment with a Russian civilian, whose possessions, prominently displayed, proved a surprise. He had an English-language novel, a can of Maxwell House coffee, a can of Spam, and an overcoat bearing the label of a well-known London tailor.

The man's name was Kolya. He spoke English, seemed to know about the Tokyo raid—though he had no information on survivors—and became friendly with the Americans during the eight-day trip south. The train passed through Tashkent and Samarkand, and the major said their destination was Ashkhabad, which, by coincidence, was where Kolya lived. York spoke to him at length about their desire to get out of Russia, and he began to wonder if Kolya might help them. Kolya had promised to take them to the opera in Ashkhabad, and to see that they got sufficient food. It looked as though they had found a useful friend.

When they arrived in Ashkhabad, they saw a range of mountains less than one hundred miles to the south. On the other side of the mountains lay Iran, and freedom. The major took them to the house assigned to them, but when he saw it, he gaped in disbelief. It was little more than a hovel built of dried mud, containing two dingy rooms. The kitchen was in a tiny hut in back. The water supply was an open faucet in the yard, beyond which stood an outhouse with no roof, merely a board placed over an open pit.

"Home sweet home," Emmens said.

"These bastards," York said. "These dirty goddamned bastards!"

It was April 9, 1943, almost a year since they had landed in Russia.

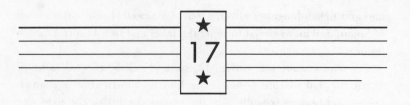

# You Can Go
# Home Now

President Roosevelt kept the news of the executions of the three Doolittle fliers secret until April 1943, one year after the raid. As early as October 19, 1942, only four days after the executions, the Japanese published newspaper articles for both foreign and domestic consumption about "the cruel, inhuman and beastlike American pilots who . . . dropped incendiaries and bombs on non-military hospitals, schools and private houses and even dive-strafed playing schoolchildren [and] were captured and court-martialed and severely punished according to military law."

On October 21, Japan's Domei news agency, in an English-language broadcast, said the captured fliers had confessed to their war crimes.

"William J. Farrow, U.S. Army Air Corps, typifies the spirit in which U.S. airmen attacked Tokyo. When questioned, he told the Japanese authorities: 'I saw school kids playing around a building which looked like a grammar school. I felt I might as well give the Jap kids a taste of bullets while I was at it. So I dived down toward them and machine-gunned them. I felt sorry for them, but hell, ain't they enemy kids?'"

The broadcast also quoted an alleged confession from Hallmark, and mentioned Spatz and DeShazer. "Meanwhile, it is recalled that punishment has already been meted out to some captured U.S. airmen." None of the radio or newspaper reports specifically mentioned execution. The punishment was always referred to as "severe," however, and American government officials suspected that meant the death penalty.

Working with the Swiss ambassador in Tokyo, the U.S. Department of State attempted to find out if their suspicions were correct. By the middle of February 1943, there was no longer any doubt. In response to a formal inquiry from the Swiss government about the captured fliers, the Japanese replied on February 17:

Primo: Imperial Government had intention to bring before court-martial and severely punish as enemies of humanity those members crews enemy planes who after having raided Japanese territory, [Manchuria], or zones of Japanese military operations fall in hands Japanese and who after inquiry reveal themselves guilty cruel or inhuman acts.

Secundo: Members of crews American planes who fell into Japanese hands after raid April 18 last on Japan have intentionally bombed and set fire to non-military installations such as hospitals, schools and crowds situated far from military installations. What may be more stigmatized is the fact they wounded and killed little innocent schoolchildren who played in the grounds of their school by machine-gunning, deliberately mowing them down although recognizing them as such. . . . The American government will understand that such persons are unpardonable as enemies of humanity. The Imperial government cannot (repeat not) treat such guilty as prisoners of war.

Tertio: The guilt of such persons having been established by court inquiry, the death penalty was pronounced according to martial law. However, following commutation punishment granted as special measures to larger part condemned, sentence of death was applied only to certain of accused.

The Japanese refused to reveal the names of the executed fliers, the sentences imposed on the others, or where they were being held, nor would they allow the Swiss ambassador to visit them.

Roosevelt wrote to Secretary of State Cordell Hull that he was "deeply stirred and horrified" to learn of the executions. He proposed taking a strong stand against Japan in retaliation, including the threat of retribution against Japanese prisoners of war in American hands. He wanted to warn Japan that if they continued to violate the international rules of warfare, America would "visit upon the officers of the Japanese government responsible for such uncivilized and unhuman acts the punishment they deserve."

The president delayed replying to the Japanese for two months, from February to April, because of his fear—shared by many senior members of the government—that it would jeopardize the safety of the seventeen thousand Americans taken prisoner by Japan through their conquests in the Pacific. The Japanese might treat them even more brutally if the United States protested too strongly the execution of the Doolittle fliers. That consideration had to be balanced, however, against Japan's threat to punish severely any fliers who attacked Japan in the future, or who engaged in what the Japanese would claim to be war crimes. That threat had to be challenged. America expected to launch more raids against Japan in the future, and couldn't let her fliers believe they would be executed if shot down.

In the end, Roosevelt decided that "the note to the Japanese government [should be] so strong that it will not further hurt the persons of Americans now in their custody—civilians and members of the armed forces—if I give out the full facts." He also decided to tell the American people about the execution of the prisoners of war, to give them "the full facts" as well.

There was only one problem. The American people had never been told that any of the Doolittle Raiders had been captured. So far as they knew, all the fliers had survived the mission. Admitting the capture of the fliers now might give the appearance of a year-long coverup. Also, the fact that all sixteen airplanes had been lost had never been published. It was decided that all this information should be forthcoming, especially since it might eventually be revealed by other sources anyway, particularly by the Chinese. The details of the raid were scheduled to be released on April 20, 1943, and the news of the executions two days later.

The day before, a story appeared in *The New York Times* relating how Doolittle and his fliers had taken off from an aircraft carrier and not from a secret land base the president referred to as Shangri-La. A United Press reporter, Donald Coe, had talked with Doolittle and ten of the Raiders who were serving with him in North Africa, for a story commemorating the first anniversary of the raid. Somehow his article was approved by army censors, revealing that the planes had been launched from a carrier, although the name of the ship was not disclosed.

Coe's story described how the Raiders had wanted to arrange a reunion to mark the anniversary, but could not do so because the men were scattered at bases all over the world. "Hell," Bill Bower said, "we haven't any whiskey for a celebration anyway." When asked if he would like to bomb Tokyo again, Bower said, "I'd like to leave right now. I wonder if we will try it again—maybe even tomorrow on the anniversary. I'll bet those Japs are sweating a little tonight." *

Bower may have been right. Shortly before April 18, Japanese radio warned the people that they might be bombed again. "It cannot be doubted," the broadcaster said, "that the enemy is intending

---

* Since the end of the war, the Doolittle Raiders have held annual reunions. One of the most memorable of these took place on April 18, 1947, at the Deauville Hotel in Miami, Florida. On the morning after, the night watchman, Tom Willemstyn, sent a memo to the hotel manager. "The Doolittle boys added some gray hairs to my head. This has been the worst night since I worked here. They were completely out of control. I let them make a lot of noise in 211 but when about fifteen of them with girls went in the pool at 1:00 A.M. (including Doolittle) I told them (no swimming allowed at night). Doolittle told me that he did not wanted to make trouble and that they were going to make one more dive and would leave. But they were in the pool until 2:30 A.M. I went up twice more without results. They were running around in the halls in their bathing suits and were noisy up until 5:00 A.M." The hotel manager asked the Raiders to sign the memo as a souvenir. The paper, with nearly thirty signatures, is among the Doolittle Papers in the Manuscript Division of the Library of Congress. The Doolittle Raiders Association in later years has supported civic and air force activities, and awards an annual scholarship to an outstanding aerospace science and engineering student.

to throw the country into confusion by indiscriminate bombing attacks." He added that America "has recently feverishly been trying to attempt a second air raid." The first attack had revealed the "beastly character" of the United States for all the world to see. Since the Americans were losing everywhere in the Pacific, the Japanese people were told, the only thing left for them to do was to bomb the Japanese mainland again.

The War Department's official communiqué on the Doolittle raid was released at nine-thirty on the evening of April 20. It stated for the first time that Shangri-La, in reality, was the USS *Hornet*, which subsequently had been sunk on October 26, 1942, in the Battle of Santa Cruz.* The plan of the mission was described at length, including the intended landings in eastern China.

"Because of a combination of circumstances," the War Department communiqué reported, "the planes were unable to reach their assigned landing fields. One came down in Soviet Russian territory. The others made forced or crash-landings in China—some in Japanese-occupied territory—or in water off the Chinese coast. All their planes were wrecked."

Seven men were injured in the crashes, the public was told, and one, Leland Faktor, was killed. Bill Dieter and Don Fitzmaurice (whose death in the crash of Hallmark's plane was still not known) were listed as missing in action. Although the press release offered as much information as was available about the aftermath of the Doolittle raid, the government was, not unexpectedly, criticized for having issued misleading statements the year before. War Department spokesmen explained the delay in releasing the information in terms of not wanting to endanger the missing fliers, the crew of the *Hornet*, or the Chinese who had helped the Americans to escape. Also, the government said, "If the secret could always have been kept from the Japanese—which in the end was impossible—it would naturally have added to the tension with which Japan awaits the attacks that still lie ahead."

---

*Capt. Charles Perry Mason and most of the *Hornet*'s crew were rescued by other American ships; 129 men were lost.

Editorial writers across the nation applauded those reasons for keeping the plan of the raid secret, but they chastised the War Department for having deceived the American people by saying that none of the planes "was damaged to an extent that precluded its proceeding to its destination," when, in fact, none of the planes reaching China landed safely.

"It is," wrote *The New York Times*, "to this use of the misleading statement and not at all to the policy of secrecy justified by military expediency, that the American public has a right to object, and to object strongly. . . . The harm comes when the facts leak out—as they leaked out about [the extent of the damage at] Pearl Harbor, and as they have been leaking out for many months about the raid on Tokyo—and the public, feeling itself to have been misled, begins to suspect the accuracy and completeness of the communiqués of our armed forces. Suspicion of this kind is a hard and damaging blow to morale in a democracy."

For a brief time, journalists, congressmen, and other influential persons began to question whether the Doolittle raid had been as successful as the earlier reports had claimed. But all such doubts were forgotten two days later, when word of the executions was announced.

A wave of revulsion and rage swept the country in reaction to this news. The response was almost as strong as the anger that had followed the sneak attack on Pearl Harbor. People were outraged. President Roosevelt issued the news "with a feeling of deepest horror," and he used such words as "barbarous," "depravity," "savages," and "killing in cold blood," to describe both the event and the Japanese. Secretary of State Hull declared, for the first time, that the United States would settle for nothing less than the "unconditional surrender" of Japan. There would be no negotiated peace with a country that executed prisoners of war.

Gen. Hap Arnold issued a message to all members of the Army Air Force:

"In violation of every rule of military procedure and of every concept of human decency, the Japanese have executed several of your brave comrades who took part in the *first* Tokyo raid. These men died as heroes. We must not rest—we must redouble our efforts—until the inhuman warlords who committed this crime have been utterly destroyed.

"Remember those comrades when you get a Zero in your sights—have their sacrifice before you when you line up your bombsights on a Japanese base."

In North Africa, Jimmy Doolittle issued a statement calling for the United States to bomb Japan until she crumbled and begged for mercy. He said that he and his Raiders stood ready to repeat their mission, only this time on a larger, more devastating scale.

Admiral Halsey was irate when he learned of the executions. A friend with him at the time recalled the moment for Halsey's biographer. The friend said it was the first time he noticed the birthmark on Halsey's neck. "I saw it because it turned purple. [Halsey] stuck out that ram-bow jaw and he ground his teeth. Those eyebrows of his began to flail up and down. . . . All he could shout was, 'We'll make the bastards pay! We'll make 'em pay!'"

New York City's mayor, Fiorello La Guardia, told a cheering crowd at a war bond rally on Wall Street that America would not take revenge on the Japanese prisoners in her hands. "That is not our way. But by the living God, we will take it out on the dirty, contemptible, brutal and bestial gentlemen of Japan at the proper time."

From coast to coast, in every city and town, American citizens did the only thing they could to express their resolve to beat the Japanese: they bought war bonds in record numbers. In the twenty-four hours following the announcement of the executions, more than $11 billion worth of bonds were sold, the largest one-day sale in the war.

Japan reacted quickly to American anger in a Domei news agency English-language radio broadcast, charging that the American people had been disappointed by the insignificant results of the Doolittle raid and that the government was now trying to deflect their attention by the hysterical announcement that the executions had been illegal and inhuman. Nothing could hide the fact that the raid had been a failure, Domei said.

"General Doolittle has assumed the false colors of a hero in a conspiracy with President Roosevelt. Doolittle, commander of the raid on Japan one year ago, failed to do anything, so we have the pleasure of offering him the title of 'Did-little.'"

The broadcast concluded that Japan would leave nothing undone to prevent future air raids. A warning was issued: "Don't forget, America—make sure that every flier that comes here has a special pass to hell, and rest assured it's strictly a one-way ticket."

★ ★ ★ ★

York and his crew read about the executions in a Russian newspaper a few days after Roosevelt made the announcement. "It made us feel ashamed of complaining about our lot," Emmens said. Their lot involved working in a factory, overhauling training planes. They took a bus to and from their job each day, and every evening a Russian officer came to the house to bring food and tobacco. The only other contact they had was their friend from the train, Kolya, who entertained them in his home, taking care first to close the shutters.

By the end of their third week in Ashkhabad, after they had asked him many times, Kolya agreed to help them escape to Iran. He cautioned that it would take time to arrange, and he warned that if they tried to escape on their own and were caught, they would be sent to Siberia. Five weeks later, Kolya told York about an Iranian named Abdul Arram, who could have them smuggled out of the country. York would have to deal with Arram himself. Kolya could not risk being seen in the man's company.

After much haggling, Arram agreed to take the men to Mashhad, the first town across the border, for $250. Kolya came to the house with five bottles of vodka, a loaf of black bread, and a small tin of caviar for their journey. The Americans gave him gifts—U.S. dollars, clothes, and a small alarm clock he had admired.

"Kolya was speechless," Emmens wrote. "He started with Ski and passed to each of us with a gripping handshake followed by a hug and a kiss on each cheek. It was all quite dramatically touching. And yet there was something pitiful in seeing this grown man become so upset over receiving such trifles."

Kolya gave his belt to York and a penknife to Emmens and apologized for having nothing to give to the others. He was so proud, he said, to know Americans. He waited with them until midnight, when Arram arrived with his truck and driver.

They said good-bye to Kolya and climbed in the back of the truck. They drove south for an hour before pulling off the highway onto a dirt road. The driver stopped. At once, Emmens was worried that they had been duped, that Arram was planning to kill them there for their money. No one would ever know what had become of them. But Arram and the driver had only stopped to switch license plates. They proceeded south for another hour, and Arram turned them over to a guide and drove away. The Americans followed the guide uphill, in single file, at a rapid pace.

They walked, they crawled on hands and knees, they ran in a crouch past boulders ten feet high, until the guide stopped and threw out his arms to indicate they had crossed the frontier. It was 4:20 on the morning of May 27, 1943. They were out of Russia, but they were not yet free. Russian troops controlled the roads from the border to a point south of Mashhad to protect convoys of lend-lease supplies from Kurdish bandits. There was still the chance that the Americans would be captured and returned to the Soviet Union.

The guide led them to a road where they found Arram waiting in his truck. They climbed aboard, headed south, and drove until daylight, when they approached a Russian checkpoint. The Americans, from under the cover of a tarpaulin, heard Arram talking with the Russian guards. Boots crunched on the gravel near the rear of the truck. Emmens felt the tarpaulin being raised and found himself staring into a face barely a foot from his. He could see the stubble of a beard on the man's cheeks. He closed his eyes and when he opened them again, the man was gone. Some of their $250 had apparently gone for bribes.

They drove on in a light rain, passing Russian sentries every three or four miles, but none of them stopped the truck. By noon the sun was shining, and Arram stopped and motioned them out. He pointed to a town about four miles away and said it was Mashhad. This was as far as he was going—there were too many Russian guards ahead, he said. York argued with him, reminding him he had promised to get them into town, but Arram was adamant. He would go no farther. He wheeled the truck around and drove off.

The fliers scrambled into one of the many bomb craters that pitted the barren countryside, and consumed the food and vodka Kolya had given them. "Well, here we are," York said, "a couple of miles out of Mashhad, Persia, sitting in a bomb crater eating black caviar, black bread, and drinking vodka. I wonder how many other Americans have done this?"

One barrier remained between them and freedom, a Russian sentry post on a bridge just north of the town. They talked it over and decided there was no point in all of them risking capture. York and Emmens would try to get past the guards and from there to the British consulate; there was no U.S. consulate in Mashhad. If they were successful, they would have the British send a car for the other three. If no help came in two hours, Herndon, LaBan, and Pohl would be on their own. York and Emmens marked the rim of the crater with the five empty vodka bottles, so that they could identify the spot for the British, pulled their caps low over their eyes, and started off.

As they approached the bridge, they noticed that the guard was inspecting every cart and truck, but not stopping people crossing on foot. They timed their arrival at the guard post to coincide with the approach of a truck. The guard, busy checking the contents of the truck, did not even look at them. York and Emmens walked into Mashhad, elated to be free, and saw two armed Russian soldiers heading toward them. They turned and pretended to be looking in a shop window, and the soldiers strolled by without noticing them.

Kolya had drawn them a crude map showing the location of the British consulate, which they found without any problem. York walked up to the Iranian guard at the entrance and said he wanted to see the British consul.

"British consul no here," the guard said.

It was an awful moment. Had they come all that way only to be stranded, with no identification, no knowledge of the language, and no way to reach safety?

But the guard was speaking again.

"Vice-consul here!" he said.

★ ★ ★ ★

The Japanese had transferred the five American prisoners to Nanking on April 17, 1943. They were housed in a recently constructed military prison. Bobby Hite said it was like moving from the worst slum imaginable to a picture-book home out of *House and Garden* magazine. Because the facility was new, there were no lice or bedbugs or rats. Even the blankets were reasonably new, and four of them per man. The food was the same—dirty rice and tea—though there was a bit more of it.

That was the good news they found on their arrival. The bad news was that they remained in solitary confinement, with only fifteen minutes a day out of their cells for exercise, and a few minutes for washing. With luck, they could whisper a few furtive words to one another during those moments.

The prison guards talked to them occasionally, usually about the progress of the war and how the Americans were losing it. They told the prisoners the United States could not possibly win, so, of course, there was no hope for their release. They would die in a Japanese prison. Sometimes a guard would admit that Japan might be defeated, but if that happened, he said, the prisoners would be beheaded. There was no hope for them either way.

With nothing to occupy them during that spring and summer, and in the absence of any belief they might be released, their mental and emotional states deteriorated to the point where they began to hallucinate, often imagining they saw huge piles of food. They lost themselves in daydreams, reveries in which they relived happy times from the past. It became increasingly difficult to return to reality, to cope with the rigors of daily existence, when the mental world they could create was so pleasant and peaceful.

To maintain their sanity, the men forced themselves to engage in elaborate mental games. If the physical world was bleak, the mental world could, for a time, be lively and rich. Chase Nielsen built a house in his mind, nail by nail, brick by brick, with attention to such details as the choice of doorknobs and the landscaping. George

Barr constructed a complex neon sign, Bobby Hite cleared the land tree by tree for a fully working farm. Jake DeShazer wrote poetry on a mental blackboard, and Bob Meder reviewed books he had read, making outlines of them, and sometimes reciting poetry he had memorized in school.

Fall came early to Nanking and, with it, concern about surviving another winter. The cells were unheated, and the men grew more frail with every passing month. Meder was particularly feeble. Late in September he developed dysentery and lost so much weight he could no longer take exercise during their time outdoors. Soon he was too wasted to speak.

Two months later he developed beriberi. One day, during the exercise period, he reminded Nielsen of a promise they had all made to one another, to visit the families of those who died. He asked Nielsen to pray for him. A Japanese guard shouted at them to stop their conversation. Nielsen ignored the guard and continued to talk to Meder, hoping to raise his spirits. The guard kept yelling and Nielsen went on talking.

When the exercise period ended, Nielsen helped Meder to his feet and led him inside. The guard followed and struck Nielsen in the face. Nielsen calmly relaxed his hold on Meder and slapped the guard across the face. The other guards looked on in disbelief. The first guard raised his scabbard to beat Nielsen with it, but the corridor was too narrow to permit a full swing. Nielsen dodged the blows easily. After a few minutes the guard gave up, and the prisoners were led back to their cells. Nielsen waited for the beating he thought was inevitable as punishment for slapping a guard, but nothing happened. He was not singled out for retaliation, and a few guards seemed to admire his courage.

Bob Meder, twenty-six years old, from Cleveland, Ohio, died on December 1, 1943. The Japanese conducted a funeral service for the man whose life they could have saved with a little decent medical treatment. The four American survivors heard the sounds of hammering, and the next day they were taken into Meder's cell, one at a time. Not even in mourning would they be brought together. The body lay in a wooden coffin with a wreath of flowers and a Bible on the lid. Meder was cremated, and the small black box of ashes was placed in an empty cell, along with his few possessions.

His death was a blow to the others. They brooded over the loss, grieving alone, asking themselves why death had claimed this man whose humor and good will had helped sustain them through the last horrible nineteen months. Each of them, in his own way, began to look to religion for answers and solace.

Meder's death changed their lives in another way. Japanese prison officials began to fear the consequences of their neglect of the prisoners. They became concerned that they would be held responsible for this death if Japan lost the war. And by the beginning of 1944, losing the war was a real possibility. The warden tried to make amends, asking the Americans what they would like to have. It was an astonishing question for those sickly, undernourished men to hear from a Japanese officer. They gave him a list of all kinds of American food, which they knew would be impossible to obtain, and also asked for some books.

The warden added a daily supply of bread to their rations and increased the number of meals from two to three. He brought them five religious books, including the Bible. The men devoured the books, passing them back and forth and almost memorizing them. This intensive, exclusive immersion in spiritual readings provided an anchor and gave them something to sustain them through the days ahead.

Jake DeShazer seemed especially moved, and he worked deliberately to change his life in accordance with biblical teachings. He soon had the opportunity to put his beliefs into practice. While he was being returned to his cell from an exercise period, a guard hit him viciously in the back, shouting at him to hurry up. He slammed the cell door on DeShazer's bare foot and kicked the foot with his boots.

DeShazer's immediate reaction was hatred, but an inner voice reminded him of Jesus's command to love one's enemies. For the next several mornings, DeShazer was friendly toward the guard. At first the man was suspicious and regarded him with distrust. But after a few mornings of smiles and pleasant greetings from De-Shazer, the guard began to talk to him and never brutalized him again. He occasionally brought DeShazer a little extra food, a generous and courageous act. DeShazer concluded that his kindly behavior had worked and that he was reaping the reward.

The summer of 1944 was the hottest on record for Nanking. The cells were like ovens. The doors were solid wood and the small windows were so high that no fresh air could circulate. Hite ran a high fever and seemed on the point of death. Prison officials were alarmed at the prospect of a second death among the Doolittle fliers, now that the war was going so badly for them. They replaced Hite's cell door with a screen and gave him medical attention. With care and the onset of cooler weather, he improved.

The winter of 1944–45 proved to be the coldest on record. The ground remained covered with snow from December to March, and the men shivered in their unheated cells. The Japanese issued heavier clothing, and when that proved insufficient, they gave them back their American uniforms to wear over their prison clothes. Even with the additional layers, they felt chilly all the time.

On Christmas Day of 1944, they heard the sound of airplane engines and saw fighters—probably P-51s—zoom overhead and attack a nearby refinery and some oil storage tanks. They cheered when they heard the explosions and the chatter of machine-gun fire. If the Americans were close enough to send fighter planes to Nanking, surely the war would soon be over. They waited eagerly every day for more planes, but none came, and their expectation of a quick victory and freedom soon faded.

The cold weather continued, the boredom and monotony continued, and from time to time the Japanese renewed their savagery toward the prisoners. George Barr was the target one freezing day. Because he was the tallest of the prisoners, and had bright red hair and beard, he was frequently singled out for extra kicks and punches. This time the guards almost killed him. It started because Barr refused to wash his feet in the snow as ordered, before returning to his cell after the exercise period. They usually washed their feet at a hydrant inside the building, but this time the guards demanded that Barr use a snowbank.

After Barr refused, one of the guards beat him on the legs with his sword. Barr wheeled around and punched the guard in the face. Other guards overpowered him and kept him outside while Hite, DeShazer, and Nielsen were taken back to their cells. Barr was thrown to the ground and forced into a straitjacket with his arms behind his back. The laces were pulled so tight he could barely breathe.

The pain and the panic when he gasped for air were like nothing he had ever felt. There was a tremendous pressure in his skull as he struggled, like an animal, to breathe. He was certain he was going to die, sure that his head would burst.

The other prisoners heard his screams and were sure he was being beaten to death. The guards grinned as they watched Barr writhe in the snow. After nearly a half hour of this torment, Barr's frantic movements had loosened the laces enough so that he could take a few gasps of air.

One guard looked at his watch, and when a half hour had elapsed, he nodded to the others. They knelt down next to Barr, and he was sure they were going to untie him. Instead, they drew the laces tighter and made him endure another thirty minutes of agony. When they led him back to his cell, one of the guards gave him a cigarette, the first he had smoked in three years. He said he appreciated the gesture, but the hour he had spent in the straitjacket was the most gruesome treatment he had received in three years of horrors. Not even the beatings and tortures inflicted by the Kempei Tai just after his capture compared to that.

In the middle of June 1945, the prisoners left Nanking, after more than two years, for another prison, another unknown place with new guards, new routines, and new dangers. One morning they were taken from their cells, handcuffed, and draped in large green raincoats. Hoods were fitted over their faces. They were tied to guards and placed on a train.

As usual when they were moved from one prison to another, they were comparatively well fed in transit and not physically abused. They stayed on the train for three days. Just before they pulled into a station, their guards told them they were arriving in Peking, almost six hundred miles north of Nanking. They were driven to a large military prison that housed more than one thousand Japanese soldiers, serving sentences for various crimes. It was to be their last prison, and in many ways it was worse than Nanking.

In solitary confinement once more, without even daily exercise periods to break the tedium, they had little chance to see one another. Now they were allowed out of their cells only once a week, for a bath. At first they were required to sit cross-legged on the floor throughout the day, but after several weeks they persuaded the guards to find them something to sit on. Each man was given a tiny stool whose seat was a two-by-four board about eight inches long. It was not much of an improvement, but it did get them off the floor and allow them to straighten their legs. They were made to sit quietly all day, facing the rear of the cell. At night they had straw mats to sleep on. The meals were worse than the stuff they had been given at Nanking.

The poor food, lack of exercise, and almost total isolation, combined with their growing despair, led to a rapid decline in strength and health. DeShazer, ill from dysentery, counted seventy-five painful boils on his body. He became delirious and kept repeating verses he had memorized from the Bible.

He was so weak he could not sit upright on the stool, yet he knew he would be punished for lying down during the day. He got on his knees, faced the cell door, and started to pray, to let the guards know about the wonderful religious spirit he felt was with him. A guard banged on the door and warned him to get back on his stool, but DeShazer continued to pray. Several guards entered the cell, seeming awed by his behavior, and they laid him gently on the straw mat. A Japanese doctor gave him some injections, and he was brought milk, eggs, good bread, and nourishing soup.

One morning toward the end of that summer, DeShazer heard an inner voice commanding him to pray, without stopping, for peace.

He did so, from seven o'clock that morning until two in the afternoon. Then the voice told him he did not have to pray any longer because the victory had been won. The war was over.*

The date was August 9, 1945, the day on which the atomic bomb was dropped on Nagasaki. A few hours after the attack, Emperor Hirohito expressed the wish to his military leaders that the war should end. The next day, Japan informed the Allied forces she would surrender, but the American prisoners would not learn about it for another ten days.

On August 13 there was an abrupt and mysterious change in the monotonous pattern of the prisoners' lives. That morning there was no bugle call, no signal for them to fold neatly their grass mats and flea-ridden blankets, to mop the floors, and to stand at attention for the familiar cell inspection, the way every other day had begun. Chase Nielsen noticed that fewer guards were patrolling the cell block and that they were quieter than usual. A few hours later, Nielsen spotted tall plumes of smoke carrying light-colored ashes drifting skyward. It looked as though the Japanese were burning their official papers.

Any change in the routine that marked the days was troubling, particularly one that suggested to the Americans that their captors might be preparing to leave. Nielsen wondered where the fliers would be taken next. He hoped it was south, to someplace warmer. He doubted that he could survive another winter like the last one. But he couldn't banish the nagging fear that if the Japanese were, indeed, leaving, they might not be taking their prisoners with them. They might execute them and bury them here instead.

The relaxed security continued for a week. "I had to live with my thoughts and hopes and prayers," Nielsen said. Then, on August 20, he heard several guards talking loudly as they approached his cell. He tensed as they stopped outside the door. They opened it and helped him out. They also brought out Barr, Hite, and DeShazer.

The guards stopped talking. The Americans looked at one an-

---

*DeShazer's inner voice also told him he had been called to spread the word of God among the Japanese people. After the war, he returned to Japan as a missionary.

other and smiled but said nothing. They were hustled into the prison office and ordered to stand at attention while a prison official addressed them. The man spoke slowly, waiting while an interpreter translated his words into English.

The war was over, he said. The emperor had seen fit to end it. He hoped they could all be friends now.

"He didn't say who won the war," Nielsen remembered, "but we knew. He didn't have to tell us."

The official looked at the prisoners and repeated his announcement.

"The war is over. You are now free to go home."

Recalling his experiences forty years later, Chase Nielsen described his feelings.

"I had always thought that when the war ended or whenever I was released, I'd shout and dance and talk to everyone who would listen . . . but all I could do was shrug my shoulders and weep."

The Japanese guards presented the fliers with the uniforms they had been wearing when they were captured, the clothing they had worn when they took off from the *Hornet*, their only physical link with that time so long ago. The last of the Doolittle Raiders were going home.

# APPENDIX 1

# Tokyo Raiders,
# Order of Takeoff,
# April 18, 1942

Takeoff No. 1 (bail out over China)

    P       Lt. Col. James H. Doolittle

    CP    Lt. Richard E. Cole

    N      Lt. Henry A. Potter

    B      Sgt. Fred A. Braemer

    E-G   Sgt. Paul J. Leonard (killed in bomb attack, North Africa, January 18, 1943)

Takeoff No. 2 (crash-landing, China)

    P       Lt. Travis Hoover

    CP    Lt. William N. Fitzhugh

    N      Lt. Carl R. Wildner

    B      Lt. Richard E. Miller (killed in action, North Africa, January 22, 1943)

    E-G   Sgt. Douglas V. Radney

Takeoff No. 3 (bail out over China)

    P       Lt. Robert M. Gray (killed in crash en route to China from India, October 18, 1942)

    CP    Lt. Jacob E. Manch

    N      Lt. Charles J. Ozuk

    B      Sgt. Aden E. Jones

E-G   Cpl. Leland D. Faktor (killed bailing out over China, April 18, 1942)

Takeoff No. 4 (bail out over China)
P    Lt. Everett W. Holstrom
CP   Lt. Lucian N. Youngblood
N    Lt. Harry C. McCool
B    Sgt. Robert J. Stephens
E-G   Cpl. Bert M. Jordan

Takeoff No. 5 (bail out over China)
P    Capt.David M. Jones (POW in Germany, 2½ years)
CP   Lt. Ross R. Wilder
N    Lt. Eugene F. McGurl (killed in crash, Burma, June 3, 1942)
B    Lt. Denver V. Truelove (killed in action, Sicily, July 9, 1943)
E-G   Sgt. Joseph W. Manske

Takeoff No. 6 (crash-landing, China)
P    Lt. Dean E. Hallmark (executed by Japanese, October 15, 1942)
CP   Lt. Robert J. Meder (died in Japanese prison, December 1, 1943)
N    Lt. Chase J. Nielsen (POW of Japanese, 3½ years)
B    S/Sgt. William J. Dieter (killed in crash, April 18, 1942)
E-G   Sgt. Donald E. Fitzmaurice (killed in crash, April 18, 1942)

Takeoff No. 7 (crash-landing, China)
P    Lt. Ted W. Lawson
CP   Lt. Dean Davenport
N    Lt. Charles L. McClure
B    Lt. Robert S. Clever (killed in crash, U.S., November 20, 1942)
E-G   Sgt. David J. Thatcher

**Takeoff No. 8 (landing in Russia, crew interned)**

| | |
|---|---|
| P | Capt. Edward J. York |
| CP | Lt. Robert G. Emmens |
| N-B | Lt. Nolan A. Herndon |
| E | S/Sgt. Theodore H. LaBan |
| G | Sgt. David W. Pohl |

**Takeoff No. 9 (bail out over China)**

| | |
|---|---|
| P | Lt. Harold F. Watson |
| CP | Lt. James N. Parker |
| N | Lt. Thomas C. Griffin (POW in Germany, 2 years) |
| B | Sgt. Wayne M. Bissell |
| E-G | S/Sgt. Eldred V. Scott |

**Takeoff No. 10 (bail out over China)**

| | |
|---|---|
| P | Lt. Richard O. Joyce |
| CP | Lt. J. Royden Stork |
| N | Lt. Horace E. Crouch |
| B | Sgt. George E. Larkin, Jr. (killed in crash en route to China from India, October 18, 1942) |
| E-G | S/Sgt. Edwin W. Horton, Jr. |

**Takeoff No. 11 (bail out over China)**

| | |
|---|---|
| P | Capt. C. Ross Greening (POW in Germany, 2 years) |
| CP | Lt. Kenneth E. Reddy (killed in crash, U.S., September 3, 1942) |
| N | Lt. Frank A. Kappeler |
| B | S/Sgt. William L. Birch |
| E-G | Sgt. Melvin J. Gardner (killed in crash, Burma, June 3, 1942) |

**Takeoff No. 12 (bail out over China)**

| | |
|---|---|
| P | Lt. William M. Bower |
| CP | Lt. Thadd H. Blanton |
| N | Lt. William R. Pound, Jr. |

B  Sgt. Waldo J. Bither

E-G Sgt. Omer A. Duquette (killed in crash, Burma, June 3, 1942)

Takeoff No. 13 (bail out over China)

P  Lt. Edgar E. McElroy

CP  Lt. Richard A. Knobloch

N  Lt. Clayton J. Campbell

B  Sgt. Robert C. Bourgeois

E-G Sgt. Adam R. Williams

Takeoff No. 14 (bail out over China)

P  Maj. John A. Hilger

CP  Lt. Jack A. Sims

N-B Lt. James H. Macia

E  S/Sgt. Jacob Eierman

G  Sgt. Edwin V. Bain (killed in action, Rome, July 20, 1943)

Takeoff No. 15 (crash-landing, China)

P  Lt. Donald G. Smith (killed in crash, British Isles, November 12, 1942)

CP  Lt. Griffith P. Williams (POW in Germany, 2 years)

N-B Lt. Howard A. Sessler

E  Sgt. Edward J. Saylor

G  Lt. Thomas R. White, Medical Corps

Takeoff No. 16 (bail out over China)

P  Lt. William G. Farrow (executed by Japanese, October 15, 1942)

CP  Lt. Robert L. Hite (POW of Japanese, 3½ years)

N  Lt. George Barr (POW of Japanese, 3½ years)

B  Cpl. Jacob D. DeShazer (POW of Japanese, 3½ years)

E-G Sgt. Harold A. Spatz (executed by Japanese, October 15, 1942)

# APPENDIX 2

# Japanese Regulations for Punishment of Enemy Air Crews (August 13, 1942)

Article 1.  These military regulations shall be applicable to enemy flyers who have raided Japanese territories, Manchukuo [Manchuria], or our operational areas and have come within the jurisdiction of the Japanese Expeditionary Forces in China.

Article 2.  Those who have committed the following acts shall be liable to military punishment:
  (1) Bombing, strafing, and other attacks with the object of threatening or killing and injuring ordinary people.
  (2) Bombing, strafing, and other attacks with the object of destroying or damaging private property of a non-military nature.
  (3) Bombing, strafing, and other attacks against objects other than military objectives, except those carried out under unavoidable circumstances.
  (4) Violations of wartime international law. The same shall be applicable to those who, with the object of carrying out the acts enumerated in the preceding paragraph, have come to raid Japanese territories, Manchukuo, or our operational areas and have come within the jurisdiction of the Japanese Expeditionary Forces in China before accomplishing this object.

Article 3.  Death shall be the military punishment. However, life imprisonment or more than ten years confinement may be submitted for it according to extenuating circumstances.

Article 4.  Death shall be by shooting. Confinement shall be effected in a detention place and prescribed labor imposed.

Article 5.  Under special circumstances the execution of military punishment shall be remitted.

Article 6.  In respect to confinement, the provisions of the criminal law concerning penal servitude shall be correspondingly applicable, in addition to the provisions of these military regulations.

Supplementary Regulations. These military regulations shall be enforced from 13 August 1942. These military regulations shall be applicable also to the acts committed previous to their enforcement.

> Military Ordinance No. 4
> of the Japanese Expeditionary
> Forces in China
> 13 August 1942
> Shunroku Hata, Supreme Commander
> of the Japanese Forces in China

# ACKNOWLEDGMENTS AND SOURCES

The major repositories of information on the Doolittle raid are the U.S. Office of Air Force History, Bolling Air Force Base, and the U.S. Air Force Historical Research Center, Maxwell Air Force Base. From the holdings at Bolling, military historian Bernard C. Nalty supplied a number of reports and interviews, including the Ross Greening monograph, *The First Joint Action* (submitted to the faculty of the Armed Forces Staff College, Norfolk, Virginia, Fourth Class, 21 December 1948). Mr. Nalty also offered valuable suggestions for research, and his assistance and interest are much appreciated. Lynn O. Gamma of the reference division at Maxwell provided extensive research assistance and supplied documentation including the interviews with General Doolittle and Colonel Bower, and the microfilm records "Report on Doolittle raid on Tokyo, 18 April 1942, with collection of interviews, messages, and maps" (Assistant Chief of Air Staff, Intelligence, roll A1250), "Tokyo raid material, 1942" (Historical Division, roll A1289), and "Reports on B-25 aircraft" (roll A8259).

The National Archives has the *Proceedings of the International Military Tribunal, Far East*, which contains material relating to the treatment of Japanese prisoners of war and to the trial, sentencing, and execution of several of the Doolittle fliers. I am grateful to John Taylor of the Military Reference Branch for his guidance through these tens of thousands of pages and for his additional leads. I also wish to thank Wilbert Mahoney of the Military Reference Branch, who located several files on the Doolittle raid, including Doolittle's own plans and subsequent report.

The Operational Archives Branch of the Naval Historical Center at the Washington Navy Yard provided material from the war diaries of the USS *Hornet* and USS *Enterprise*, plus additional material on the Tokyo raid. Hannah M. Zeidlik, Chief of the Historical Resources Branch of the Army Center of Military History in Washington provided documents on the raid prepared by S. L. A. Marshall for the Historical Division of the War Department's Special Staff.

It was a pleasure to work with Paul Stillwell, Director of Oral History for the United States Naval Institute, Annapolis, Maryland, and Susan Sweeney of the Oral History Department, who searched their extensive files and provided transcripts of interviews with General Doolittle, Rear Admiral Henry Miller, Captain Stephen Jurika, and others. The interviews are excellent and carefully annotated. The prompt response and helpful comments from Mr. Stillwell and Ms. Sweeney deserve my greatest thanks. Admiral Donald Duncan's oral history, conducted by the Columbia University oral history program, is available in abbreviated form in *The Pacific War Remembered: An Oral History Collection*, edited by John T. Mason, Jr., and published by the Naval Institute Press (1986).

The Manuscript Division of the Library of Congress made available the papers of Doolittle, Henry H. Arnold, and Cordell Hull. The Doolittle Papers include the report of the flight surgeon, T.R. "Doc" White ("Report to the Air Surgeon of activities covering the period from March 1, 1942 to June 16, 1942"). The National Air and Space Museum houses the huge collection of air force photographs, and I thank Larry Wilson for guiding me to the appropriate pictures for this book. Additional photos were supplied by Elizabeth Ferguson, Archivist of the San Diego Aero-Space Museum. Mrs. Ferguson, the niece of Admiral Marc Mitscher, also offered helpful personal comments.

John N. Jacob, Archivist-Librarian at the George C. Marshall Foundation, Lexington, Virginia, conducted a search of the Marshall archives and sent documents relevant to the raid. Raymond Teichman, Supervisory Archivist for the Franklin D. Roosevelt Library, Hyde Park, New York, provided similar assistance, as did Nanci A. Young, Archivist, Yale University Library, New Haven, Connecticut, for the Henry L. Stimson papers.

Richard A. Knobloch, chairman of the Doolittle Raiders Association, provided a current roster of members, and a number of the fliers and their widows responded fully and graciously to my request for assistance. General Doolittle himself replied most kindly; his views on the raid are, of course, well documented, most recently in the 1983 United States Naval Institute interview. I especially wish to acknowledge the help of Richard Cole, Jacob DeShazer, Thomas Griffin, Charles "Mac" McClure, Joseph Manske, and Chase Nielsen. Marie Zimmermann (Mrs. Earl Zimmermann), the widow of pilot Don Smith, sent a stack of informative newspaper clippings with her letter. L'Gean Youngblood, the widow of pilot Lucian Youngblood, provided a copy of Major Youngblood's own account of the raid as well as other useful material. I thank all these people for taking the time to share their recollections with me.

I am pleased to acknowledge the assistance of several members of the crew of the USS *Hornet*, including Stephen Jurika, Edgar G. "Ozzie" Osborn, Donald Kirkpatrick, and Oscar Dodson. Admiral Dodson also provided copies of his magazine articles about the *Hornet*.

Anyone writing about the Doolittle raid owes a debt of gratitude to two historians whose books on the raid appeared in the same year— 1964. They are C.V. Glines and James M. Merrill. Glines was able to interview a number of the Raiders who have since died, and Merrill compiled much interview data from Japanese observers of the raid. Thus, both writers were able to record valuable eyewitness statements that would otherwise be unavailable. Since these books were published, a number of additional interviews have been conducted, most notably by the United States Naval Institute, the U.S. Office of Air Force History, and the Columbia University oral history program.

My special thanks go to Captain Thomas B. Payne, USN (Ret.), whom I first met some years ago, when I interviewed him for my book on the USS *Houston*. Tommy's assistance and encouragement throughout the Doolittle project have been invaluable. He has supplied me with lists of books and addresses, put me in touch with retired navy pilots and veterans' groups, and offered wonderful comments about shipboard life.

I am always grateful for the assistance of Col. John R. Vance, USA (Ret.), an astute military historian, and a prisoner of war following the fall of Corregidor. Thanks also to Comdr. Ronald Sperry, USN (Ret.), who provided a thorough critique of the manuscript and offered insightful comments about the mission and its historical background.

It is with both pleasure and gratitude that I acknowledge the substantial contributions to this book of my wife, Sydney Ellen. Her skill and training as researcher, in leading an impatient author through the mazes of archives and libraries; as editor, in pointing to ambiguities, inconsistencies, and, occasionally, just plain bad prose; and as indexer, in locating every relevant concept for the reader to find influenced the project through every stage from idea to finished book. Her deeply felt care and commitment to the book—and to its author—are evident on every page.

# CHAPTER NOTES

## 1. A Shiver over Japan

Doolittle quotations in Merrill, *Target Tokyo*, p. 135. Fuchida quotation in Larrabee, *Commander in Chief*, p. 366. Comment on Yamamoto in Potter, *Yamamoto*, p. 179. Ugaki quotation in Toland, *The Rising Sun*, p. 386. Kuroshima quotation in Prange, *Miracle at Midway*, p. 25.

## 2. That Might Be a Good Idea

Roosevelt quotations in Reynolds, *The Amazing Mr. Doolittle*, p. 175, and Coffey, *Hap*, p. 269. *Saratoga* task force bound for Wake Island discussed in Schultz, *Wake Island*, pp. 190–92, and Prange, *Miracle at Midway*, p. 6. The Marine Corps general quoted is Maj. Gen. Omar T. Pfeiffer, Fleet Marine Officer and Assistant War Plans Officer, CinCPAC; the admiral is Joseph M. Reeves, former Commander in Chief of the United States Fleet. Ugaki quotation in Prange, *Miracle at Midway*, p. 24. Comments on Admiral King in Spector, *Eagle Against the Sun*, p. 126. King quotation in Glines, *Doolittle's Tokyo Raiders*, p. 18. Low conversations in Reynolds, *The Amazing Mr. Doolittle*, pp. 171–72. Duncan quotations in Duncan oral history; additional comments in Merrill, *Target Tokyo*, p. 21. Portal quotation in Copp, *Forged in Fire*, p. 209. Arnold quotations in Copp, *Forged in Fire*, p. 209, and Arnold, *Global Mission*, p. 277.

### 3. I Have Never Felt Fear

Doolittle quotations in interviews with U.S. Office of Air Force History, September 26, 1971; U.S. Naval Institute, February 15, 1983; and CBS-TV program "Top Flight," October 27, 1987. Additional quotations in Glines, *Jimmy Doolittle*, pp. 13, 93; Thomas and Jablonski, *Doolittle*, p. 40; and Coffey, *Hap*, p. 248. Eaker quotation in Coffey, *Hap*, p. 100. Life at Eagle Pass, Texas, described in Thomas and Jablonski, *Doolittle*, p. 56. The Pulitzer air race described in Thomas and Jablonski, *Doolittle*, p. 74. Arnold quotation in Arnold, *Global Mission*, p. 299. Arnold-Doolittle meeting, January 17, 1942, described in Glines, *Jimmy Doolittle*, p. 126.

### 4. The B-25B Special Project

Doolittle's report on the B-25B special project is in the National Archives (384.7 AAG). Doolittle quotations in Glines, *Doolittle's Tokyo Raiders*, pp. 25–26, and Reynolds, *The Amazing Mr. Doolittle*, p. 180. Arnold quotations in Arnold, *Global Mission*, p. 289. Modifications to the B-25B described in the Greening monograph, "The First Joint Action." Events on the USS *Hornet* described in Griffin, *A Ship to Remember*, pp. 19, 45, 48, and Taylor, *The Magnificent Mitscher*, pp. 104, 112, 113; additional information in Dodson, "The Doolittle Raid." Fitzgerald quotation in Glines, *Jimmy Doolittle*, p. 131. Duncan quotations in Duncan oral history. Lawson quotations in Lawson, *Thirty Seconds over Tokyo*, pp. 7, 14. Bower quotations in interview with U.S. Office of Air Force History, October 27, 1971. Hilger quotation in Reynolds, *The Amazing Mr. Doolittle*, p. 179.

### 5. Tell Jimmy to Get on His Horse

Quotations from Cole, Griffin, McClure, and Manske in letters to the author. Bower quotations in interview with U.S. Office of Air Force History, October 27, 1971. Lawson quotations in Lawson, *Thirty Seconds over Tokyo*, pp. 22, 29, and interview with *New York Times*, April 23, 1943, p. 4. Doolittle quotations in interviews with U.S. Office of Air Force History, September 26, 1971, and U.S.

Naval Institute, February 15, 1983; additional information in the Greening monograph, "The First Joint Action," and in Glines, *Doolittle's Tokyo Raiders*, p. 46. Miller experiences in Miller oral history. White quotation in White, "Report to the Air Surgeon." The crew of the *Hornet* discussed in Griffin, *A Ship to Remember*, p. 51. Duncan experiences in Duncan oral history. Nimitz-Halsey conversation in Potter, *Bull Halsey*, p. 56.

## 6. I'll Be Seeing You

Doolittle quotations in interview with U.S. Naval Institute, February 15, 1983; additional quotations in Glines, *Doolittle's Tokyo Raiders*, pp. 66, 75; Lawson, *Thirty Seconds over Tokyo*, p. 31; and the Greening monograph, "The First Joint Action." Miller-Doolittle conversations in Miller interview with U.S. Naval Institute, March 24, 1971 (abbreviated version in Miller oral history). Lawson quotations in Lawson, *Thirty Seconds over Tokyo*, p. 33. Bower quotations in interview with U.S. Office of Air Force History, October 27, 1971. Mitscher-Duncan conversation in Taylor, *The Magnificent Mitscher*, p. 116. Duncan quotation in Duncan oral history. Arnold cables to Stilwell from U.S. Air Force Historical Research Center (microfilm roll A1250, frames 472, 473, 488). York quotation from U.S. Air Force Historical Research Center (microfilm roll A1289, frame 0839). White quotation in White, "Report to the Air Surgeon." Potter on Halsey's version of the Halsey-Doolittle meeting in Potter, *Bull Halsey*, p. 395. Halsey quotations in Halsey and Bryan, *Admiral Halsey's Story*, pp. 101, 103. Griffin and McClure recollections in letters to the author.

## 7. This Is a Breeze

Doolittle quotations in Reynolds, *The Amazing Mr. Doolittle*, pp. 194, 198–99. Miller conversations with Doolittle and with Mitscher in Miller interview with U.S. Naval Institute, March 24, 1971. Jurika quotations in interview with U.S. Naval Institute, March 17, 1976; and in a letter to the author. Bower quotations in interview with U.S. Office of Air Force History, October 27, 1971. Greening quotations in monograph, "The First Joint Action." Lawson quotations in Lawson, *Thirty Seconds over Tokyo*, p. 35. McClure quotations in a letter to the author. Events aboard the *Hornet* in Griffin, *A Ship to Remember*, p. 52, and Taylor, *The Magnificent Mitscher*, p. 117. Mitscher after-action report (USS *Hornet*, CV-8, Report of Action, April 18, 1942) from U.S. Air Force Historical Research Center; additional information from report of Maj. Harvey Johnson, Jr., Adjutant, B-25B special project, National Archives (384.7 AAG). DeShazer quotation in Watson, *DeShazer*, p. 32. "How to Make Friends" in Morison, *The Rising Sun in the Pacific*, p. 391. Akers quotation in Glines, *Doolittle's Tokyo Raiders*, p. 85. Griffin and Manske quotations in letters to the author. Story of Mitscher and the young poker player in Karig and Kelley, *Battle Report*, p. 297. Tokyo broadcast in *New York Times*, April 18, 1942, p. 3. Stilwell quotation in *The Stilwell Papers*, p. 81. Harp quotation in *This Is It!* p. 13.

## 8. This Force Is Bound for Tokyo

*Enterprise* sailors quoted in Potter, *Bull Halsey*, pp. 58–59. Halsey quotations in Halsey and Bryan, *Admiral Halsey's Story*, p. 102; Merrill, *A Sailor's Admiral*, p. 35; and Potter, *Bull Halsey*, p. 61. Halsey after-action report (USS *Enterprise*, Report of Action, April 18, 1942) from U.S. Air Force Historical Research Center. Letters requesting Japanese medals be returned to original owners in National Archives (384.7 AAG); additional information in the Greening monograph, "The First Joint Action," and Griffin, *A Ship to Remember*, p. 66. Tokyo radio broadcast in Potter, *Bull Halsey*, p. 59. Doolittle quotations in Greening monograph, "The First Joint Action." Information on attempts to prepare the east China airfields from draft report submitted to Col. S. L. A. Marshall on the Tokyo raid, July 18, 1943 (U.S. Office of Air Force History); and U.S. Air Force Historical Research Center (microfilm rolls A1250, frame 491; A1289, frames 940-942). Smith-Hutton quotation in interview with U.S. Naval Institute, July 25, 1974. Radio intercept from *Nitto Maru* reported in Glines, *Doolittle's Tokyo Raiders*, p. 123. De-

Shazer quotation in Watson, *DeShazer*, p. 38. Jurika quotation in interview with U.S. Naval Institute, March 17, 1976. Miller quotation in interview with U.S. Naval Institute, March 24, 1971. Mitscher quotation in Taylor, *The Magnificent Mitscher*, p. 121.

## 9. Army Pilots, Man Your Planes

Doolittle quotations in interview with U.S. Naval Institute, February 15, 1983, and "Personal Report," Chungking, China, May 4, 1942 (Doolittle Papers, Library of Congress). Mitscher conversation with Doolittle reported in Reynolds, *The Amazing Mr. Doolittle*, pp. 201–2. Mitscher after-action report (USS *Hornet*, CV-8, Report of Action, April 18, 1942) from U.S. Air Force Historical Research Center. Bower quotation in interview with U.S. Office of Air Force History, October 27, 1971. DeShazer, Kirkpatrick, and Osborn quotations in letters to the author. Additional DeShazer quotation in Watson, *DeShazer*, p. 39. Comments of standby crews reported in Merrill, *Target Tokyo*, p. 67. Hilger quotation in Merrill, *Target Tokyo*, p. 69. Lawson experiences in Lawson, *Thirty Seconds over Tokyo*, pp. 51, 57–58. Information on B-25 takeoff routine in *Pilot's Manual for B-25 Mitchell* (Army Air Forces, Air Service Command, Patterson Field, Ohio). Miller quotations in interview with U.S. Naval Institute, March 24, 1971; additional quotation in Lawson, *Thirty Seconds over Tokyo*, p. 54. Jurika quotations in interview with U.S. Naval Institute, March 17, 1965. Emmens quotation in Emmens, *Guests of the Kremlin*, pp. 1–3. *Enterprise* log quoted in Halsey and Bryan, *Admiral Halsey's Story*, p. 103. "Haul ass with Halsey" in Potter, *Bull Halsey*, p. 61. Story of picket boat skipper in Glines, *Doolittle's Tokyo Raiders*, p. 115. Ring poem in Griffin, *A Ship to Remember*, p. 71. Description of air-raid drill in Tokyo, April 18, 1942, from "Report and Analysis on Tokyo Raid," U.S. Air Force Historical Research Center (microfilm roll A1289, frames 0904-0906).

## 10. They Were Shooting at *Us*

Information on the raid and quotations from pilots and crews from U.S. Air Force Historical Research Center, especially "Assessment of Damage, Tokyo Raid" (microfilm roll A1289, frames 0812-0826), "Memorandum for the Commanding General, Army Ground Forces, Report on Tokyo Raid, 2 October 1943" (microfilm roll A1289, frames 0827-0842), and "Report and Analysis on Tokyo Raid" (microfilm roll A1289, frames 0904-0965). Doolittle quotations in interview with U.S. Naval Institute, February 15, 1983. Reports of conversations between Doolittle and crew (Braemer, Leonard, Potter) in Reynolds, *The Amazing Mr. Doolittle*, pp. 204, 206. Lawson and Davenport quotations in Lawson, *Thirty Seconds over Tokyo*, pp. 59, 100. Experiences of York and his crew reported in Emmens, *Guests of the Kremlin*, pp. 5–6, 9, 11, 12. Quotations from Potter, Jones, and Scott in *New York Times*, June 28, 1942, p. 18. Griffin quotation in a letter to the author. Information on misidentifying Nakajima Type-97 as Zero from U.S. Air Force Historical Research Center (microfilm roll A1289, frame 0928).

## 11. If My Wife Could See Me Now

Information on the raid and quotations from pilots and crews from U.S. Air Force Historical Research Center, especially "Interviews with Pilots and Air Crews Conducted After the Raid" (microfilm roll A1250, frames 0196-0247), "Report and Analysis on Tokyo Raid" (microfilm roll A1289, frames 0904–0965), and "Assessment of Damage, Tokyo Raid" (microfilm roll A1289, frames 0812–0826, which includes quotations from Japanese newspapers and radio broadcasts). Toland quotation in Toland, *The Rising Sun*, p. 385. Grew quotation in Grew, *Ten Years in Japan*, p. 453. Smith-Hutton quotations in Smith-Hutton interview with U.S. Naval Institute, July 25, 1974, and Jurika interview with U.S. Naval Institute, April 1, 1976. Jurika quotation in interview with U.S. Naval Institute, March 17, 1965. Quotations from Greening, Hilger, and Saylor in *New York Times*, June 28, 1942, p. 18. Lavalle quotation in *New York Times*, April 25, 1943, p. 26. Additional accounts of Japanese reactions to bombing in Merrill, *Target Tokyo*, pp. 80, 92–96, 105–6; summary of damage from raid on p. 105. Bower quotation in interview with U.S. Office of Air Force History, October 27, 1971. DeShazer quotations in Watson, *DeShazer*, p. 45. Sakai quotations in Sakai, *Samurai*, pp. 148, 149.

## 12. Thanks for a Swell Ride

Information on the raid and its aftermath, and quotations from pilots and crews, from U.S. Air Force Historical Research Center, especially "Interviews with Pilots and Air Crews Conducted After the Raid" (microfilm roll A1250, frames 0196–0247), and "Report and Analysis on Tokyo Raid" (microfilm roll A1289, frames 0904–0965, which includes S. L. A. Marshall report). Experiences of York and crew reported in Emmens, *Guests of the Kremlin*, pp. 17, 31, 33. Experiences of Lawson and crew reported in Lawson, *Thirty Seconds over Tokyo*, p. 78. Experiences of Nielsen, Griffin, Mc-Clure, and Manske in letters to the author. Manch and Stork quotations in *New York Times*, April 25, 1943, p. 27. Experiences of Doolittle and crew reported in Reynolds, *The Amazing Mr. Doolittle*, pp. 208–9, 211. Farrow, Hite, and Nielsen experiences in Glines, *Four Came Home*, pp. 50, 65, 68. Bower quotations in interview with U.S. Office of Air Force History, October 27, 1971. DeShazer quotation in Watson, *DeShazer*, pp. 50–51.

## 13. We Lost Some of the Boys

Quotations from Japanese newspapers and radio broadcasts in *New York Times*, April 18, 1942, pp. 1, 3; April 19, 1942, pp. 1, 38. Landis quotation in *New York Times*, April 20, 1942, p. 3. Air force documentation on the raid, and messages from Bissell, from draft report submitted to Col. S. L. A. Marshall on the Tokyo raid, July 18, 1943 (U.S. Office of Air Force History). Message from Doolittle through Soong to Arnold from U.S. Air Force Historical Research Center (microfilm roll A1250, frame 0527); information on Doolittle's original version of this message in "Personal Report," Chungking, China, May 4, 1942 (Doolittle Papers, Library of Congress). Memoranda, Arnold to Roosevelt, from U.S. Air Force Historical

Research Center (microfilm roll A1250, frames 0538, 0539). Stimson quotations in Prange, *Miracle at Midway*, p. 27. Shangri-La story in Rosenman, *Working with Roosevelt*. Message from Ambassador Standley, War Department, Incoming Message, April 22, 1942, from U.S. Air Force Historical Research Center (microfilm roll A1250, frame 0544). Message from Marshall to Doolittle, War Department, Outgoing Message No. 527 (c/o Stilwell), April 22, 1942, from George C. Marshall Foundation (box 65, folder 11). Leonard and Doolittle quotations in Reynolds, *The Amazing Mr. Doolittle*, p. 213. Doolittle's reaction to Leonard's request reported by Associated Press, December 14, 1986, in an interview marking Doolittle's ninetieth birthday. Doolittle's evaluation of the results of the raid in interview with U.S. Air Force Office of Information, June 23, 1965, "Historical Documentation of Lt. Gen. James H. Doolittle." Donkey story reported in Greening monograph, "The First Joint Action." Lawson experiences in Lawson, *Thirty Seconds over Tokyo*, pp. 106, 112–14, 120–21, 141, 156. Halsey letter to Doolittle in Merrill, *A Sailor's Admiral*, p. 35. Bower quotation in interview with U.S. Office of Air Force History, October 27, 1971. Experiences of Griffin and McClure in letters to the author. Letter from Madame Chiang courtesy of Mrs. Lucian Youngblood.

## 14. Days of Stark Horror

Experiences of York and crew in Emmens, *Guests of the Kremlin*, pp. 47, 64, 90. Experiences of fliers captured by the Japanese in George Barr's report ("Rough draft of a story by Capt. George Barr, pertinent to the trials in Shanghai of those Japanese officials held responsible for the execution of three Doolittle fliers who participated in the raid on Tokyo," March 30, 1946), in the Doolittle Papers, Library of Congress; and in "Report on the Matter Concerning the Investigation of the American Airmen who Raided the Japanese Homeland, Military Police Report No. 352, May 26, 1942, in the National Archives (RG 331); Nielsen's torture described in Glines, *Four Came Home*, pp. 80–81; DeShazer's experiences in Watson, *DeShazer*, p. 64. Bergamini on retaliatory raids against the Chinese in Bergamini, *Japan's Imperial Conspiracy*, pp. 1173–74. Meuss re-

310 THE DOOLITTLE RAID

port in *Reader's Digest*, May 1944; additional reports in *New York Times*, May 26, 1943, p. 3. Chennault quotation in Chennault, *Way of a Fighter*, p. 169.

## 15. I've Been Away

Memorandum from Marshall to Arnold about Medal of Honor from George C. Marshall Foundation (box 65, folder 11). Mrs. Doolittle's experiences in Reynolds, *The Amazing Mr. Doolittle*, pp. 220–23. Doolittle remark to CNAC pilot in *New York Times*, April 26, 1943, p. 6. Doolittle conversation with Marshall and Arnold about Medal of Honor in Doolittle interview with U.S. Naval Institute, February 15, 1983. Additional Doolittle remarks, and Medal of Honor citation, in *New York Times*, May 20, 1942, p. 4. Doolittle letters to fliers' families in Doolittle Papers, Library of Congress. Doolittle conversation with druggist reported in Thomas and Jablonski, *Doolittle*, p. 204. Miller experiences in interview with U.S. Naval Institute, March 24, 1971. Doolittle orders to Raiders, June 15, 1942, regarding DFC ceremony, in Doolittle Papers, Library of Congress. *Sunday Star* report on ceremony, June 28, 1942, p. A5. Lawson experiences in Lawson, *Thirty Seconds over Tokyo*, pp. 173, 177. Experiences of York and crew in Emmens, *Guests of the Kremlin*, pp. 109, 158. Doolittle-Eisenhower relationship described in Thomas and Jablonski, *Doolittle*, pp. 207–8, 218–19.

## 16. I Request that the Penalty Be Death

Information on the trial, sentences, and execution of the Doolittle fliers from the *International Military Tribunal, Far East*, pp. 14600, 27904–6, 28873, 38621–22; "Regulations for Punishment of Enemy Air Crews" (reprinted as Appendix 2), pp. 14662–64 (National Archives, RG 331). Additional information and last letters from Farrow, Hallmark, and Spatz in Glines, *Four Came Home*, pp. 116–19; and in Watson, *DeShazer*, pp. 72–73. Nielsen quotation from letter to Doolittle in Doolittle Papers, Library of Congress. Quotation from U.S. Military Commission in Piccigallo, *The Japanese on Trial*, p. 72. Experiences of York and crew in Emmens, *Guests of the Kremlin*, pp. 178, 220–22, 242.

## 17. You Can Go Home Now

Japanese newspaper articles from U.S. Air Force Historical Research Center (microfilm roll A1250, frame 0513), Office of the Military Attaché, Chungking, No. 318. Domei broadcasts from War Department, Bureau of Public Relations, Analysis Branch, Foreign Broadcast Digest No. 270-FRD (Doolittle Papers, Library of Congress). Other Japanese radio broadcasts quoted in *New York Times*, April 19, 1943, p. 8; April 23, 1943, pp. 1, 4. Japanese government response to Swiss government inquiry from U.S. Air Force Historical Research Center (microfilm roll A1250, frames 0323–0325), Message, Bern (Switzerland) to Secretary of State, Washington, February 23, 1943. Roosevelt comments to Hull in Roosevelt, *FDR: His Personal Letters*, p. 1420. Coe article on first anniversary of raid in *New York Times*, April 19, 1943, p. 8. Newspaper coverage of War Department communiqué, editorial response, and announcement of executions, in *New York Times*, April 22, 1943, pp. 1, 3, 22. Arnold memorandum to air force personnel, April 21, 1943, in Arnold Papers, Library of Congress. Halsey reaction to executions in Merrill, *A Sailor's Admiral*, p. 36. La Guardia reaction in *New York Times*, April 23, 1943, p. 8. Experiences of York and crew in Emmens, *Guests of the Kremlin*, pp. 248, 269, 278, 282, 289. Barr torture reported in Glines, *Four Came Home*, pp. 145–46. DeShazer experiences in Watson, *DeShazer*, pp. 117, 120, 124. Nielsen quotations in letters to the author.

# BIBLIOGRAPHY

Adams, H. H. *1942: The Year that Doomed the Axis.* New York: David McKay, 1967.

Adams, H. H. *Harry Hopkins.* New York: G. P. Putnam's Sons, 1977.

Arnold, H. H. *Global Mission.* New York: Harper and Row, 1949.

Bergamini, D. *Japan's Imperial Conspiracy.* New York: William Morrow, 1971.

Chennault, C. L. *Way of a Fighter.* New York: G. P. Putnam's Sons, 1949.

Coffey, T. M. *Hap: The Story of the U.S. Air Force and the Man Who Built It, General Henry H. "Hap" Arnold.* New York: Viking, 1982.

Copp, DeWitt S. *Forged in Fire: Strategy and Decisions in the Air War over Europe, 1940–1945.* Garden City, New York: Doubleday, 1982.

Craven, W. F., and J. L. Cate (eds.). *The Army Air Forces in World War II.* Vol. 1, *Plans and Early Operations, January 1939 to August 1942.* Chicago: University of Chicago Press, 1948.

Dorwart, J. M. *Conflict of Duty: The U.S. Navy's Intelligence Dilemma, 1919–1945.* Annapolis: Naval Institute Press, 1983.

Dull, P. S., and M. T. Umemura. *The Tokyo Trials: A Functional Index to the Proceedings of the International Military Tribunal, Far East.* Ann Arbor: University of Michigan Press, 1957.

Duncan, D. B. "Secret Planning for the Tokyo Raid." In *The Pacific War Remembered: An Oral History Collection*, edited by J. T. Mason, Jr. Annapolis: Naval Institute Press, 1986.

Emmens, R. G. *Guests of the Kremlin*. New York: Macmillan, 1949.

Fahey, J. C. *U.S. Army Aircraft, 1908–1946*. Falls Church, Virginia: Ships and Aircraft, 1946.

Fuchida, M., and M. Okumiya. *Midway: The Battle that Doomed Japan*. Annapolis: Naval Institute Press, 1955.

Glines, C. V. *Doolittle's Tokyo Raiders*. Princeton: D. Van Nostrand, 1964.

Glines, C. V. *Four Came Home*. Princeton: D. Van Nostrand, 1966.

Glines, C. V. *Jimmy Doolittle: Daredevil Aviator and Scientist*. New York: Macmillan, 1972.

Grew, J. C. *Ten Years in Japan*. London: Hammond, Hammond, 1944.

Griffin, A. T. *A Ship to Remember: The Saga of the* Hornet. New York: Howell, Soskin, 1943.

Halsey, W. F., and J. Bryan. *Admiral Halsey's Story*. New York: Curtis, 1947.

Harp, E. B. "God Stood Beside Us." In *This Is it!*, edited by H. Davis. New York: Vanguard Press, 1944.

Hayes, G. P. *The Joint Chiefs of Staff and the War Against Japan*. Annapolis: Naval Institute Press, 1982.

Hull, C. *Memoirs of Cordell Hull*. New York: Macmillan, 1948.

Karig, W., and W. Kelley. *Battle Report: Pearl Harbor to Coral Sea*. New York: Rinehart, 1944.

King, E. J., and W. Whitehill. *Fleet Admiral King: A Naval Record*. New York: W. W. Norton, 1952.

Larrabee, E. *Commander in Chief: Franklin Delano Roosevelt, His Lieutenants, and Their War*. New York: Harper and Row, 1987.

Lawson, T. W. *Thirty Seconds over Tokyo*. New York: Random House, 1943.

Lewin, R. *The American Magic: Codes, Ciphers and the Defeat of Japan*. New York: Farrar Straus & Giroux, 1982.

Lundstrom, J. B. *The First South Pacific Campaign: Pacific Fleet Strategy December 1941–June 1942*. Annapolis: Naval Institute Press, 1976.

Merrill, J. M. *A Sailor's Admiral: A Biography of William F. Halsey.* New York: Thomas Y. Crowell, 1976.

Merrill, J. M. *Target Tokyo: The Halsey-Doolittle Raid.* Chicago: Rand McNally, 1964.

Miller, H. L. "Training the Doolittle Fliers." In *The Pacific War Remembered: An Oral History Collection,* edited by J. T. Mason, Jr. Annapolis: Naval Institute Press, 1986.

Morgenthau, H. *From the Morgenthau Diaries,* edited by J. M. Blum. Boston: Houghton Mifflin, 1959–67.

Morison, S. E. *The Rising Sun in the Pacific, 1931–April 1942.* Boston: Little, Brown, 1948.

Piccigallo, P. R. *The Japanese on Trial: Allied War Crimes Operations in the East, 1945–1951.* Austin: University of Texas Press, 1979.

*Pilot's Manual for B-25 Mitchell.* Fairfield, Ohio: Army Air Forces, Air Service Command, Patterson Field, 1942.

Pogue, F. *George C. Marshall: Ordeal and Hope, 1939–1942.* New York: Viking, 1966.

Potter, E. B. *Bull Halsey.* Annapolis: Naval Institute Press, 1985.

Potter, J. D. *Yamamoto: The Man Who Menaced America.* New York: Viking, 1965.

Prange, G. W. *Miracle at Midway.* New York: McGraw-Hill, 1982.

Reynolds, Q. *The Amazing Mr. Doolittle: A Biography of Lieutenant General James H. Doolittle.* New York: Appleton-Century-Crofts, 1953.

Roosevelt, F. D. *FDR: His Personal Letters, 1928–1945.* vol. 2. Edited by E. Roosevelt. New York: Duell, Sloan and Pearce, 1950.

Rosenman, S. I. *Working with Roosevelt.* New York: Harper and Row, 1952.

Russell, E. F. L. *The Knights of Bushido: The Shocking History of Japanese War Atrocities.* New York: E. P. Dutton, 1958.

Sakai, S. *Samurai.* New York: E. P. Dutton, 1957.

Schultz, D. *Wake Island: The Heroic Gallant Fight.* New York: St. Martin's, 1978.

Sherwood, R. E. *Roosevelt and Hopkins: An Intimate History.* New York: Harper and Row, 1948.

Spector, R. H. *Eagle Against the Sun: The American War with Japan.* New York: Free Press, 1985.

Stilwell, J. W. *The Stilwell Papers*. Edited by T. H. White. New York: William Sloane, 1948.

Taylor, T. *The Magnificent Mitscher*. New York: W. W. Norton, 1954.

Thomas, L., and E. Jablonski. *Doolittle: A Biography*. Garden City, New York: Doubleday, 1976.

Toland, J. *The Rising Sun: The Decline and Fall of the Japanese Empire, 1936–1945*. New York: Random House, 1970.

Tolischus, O. D. *Tokyo Record*. New York: Harcourt, Brace and World, 1943.

*U.S. Strategic Bombing Survey: Effects of Strategic Bombing on Japanese Morale*. Washington, D.C.: U.S. Government Printing Office, 1947.

*U.S. Strategic Bombing Survey: Interrogations of Japanese Officials*. Washington, D.C.: U.S. Government Printing Office, 1946.

Watson, C. H. *DeShazer: The Doolittle Raider Who Turned Missionary*. Winona Lake, Indiana: Light and Life Press, 1950.

Willmott, H. P. *Empires in the Balance: Japanese and Allied Pacific Strategies to April 1942*. Annapolis: Naval Institute Press, 1982.

# INDEX

A-20 bombers, 7
Air races, 30–31, 35, 37–40
Aircraft insignia, 153
Akers, Frank, 48–49, 51, 100, 102
Alameda Naval Air Station, 85–88
Aleutian Islands, 48, 89, 113, 180,
    205
Alexander, E. H., 117
American embassy, Tokyo, 118,
    136–137, 162–163
AMMISCA (American military
    mission to China), 78, 79
Antiaircraft defenses (Tokyo), 10,
    109, 147–150, 152–154, 156–
    158, 161, 162, 164, 167
Aoki, Mrs. Ryu, 160
Arisue, Colonel, 263
Army Air Corps-Navy relations,
    94–96, 98, 100–101, 104–105
Arnold, Henry H. "Hap," 7, 25,
    40, 82, 204, 209, 210, 244,
    246–248, 252, 254–255, 279
    and Chinese landing fields, 55,
    78–81, 106–107, 115–116
    and plans for raid, 16–18, 42–
    44, 47–48, 56, 67, 71–73

and reports to Roosevelt, 206–
    207, 211–212
Arram, Abdul, 281–283
Ashkhabad, Russia, 273, 281
Avenger torpedo planes, 71


B-17 bombers, 16, 17, 209
B-18 bombers, 14, 17, 56, 252
B-23 bombers, 14, 43, 56
B-25 Mitchell bombers:
    bomb load, 45, 63, 101, 125
    carburetors, 65, 81–83, 87, 143
    compasses, 104, 147
    displayed in Tokyo, 216
    fuel consumption, 64–65, 69, 70,
        77, 139, 141–143, 145, 152,
        154
    fuel tanks, 44–45, 58, 67, 82
    gun turrets, 46, 56–57, 67, 82,
        140, 141, 145, 151, 154
    modifications and maintenance,
        14, 43–48, 54, 67, 68, 81–83,
        87, 97, 103–104, 114–115
    preparations for carrier takeoff,
        124–128

propeller blades, 69, 82
radio equipment, 46–47, 78
selected for raid, 14–15, 43, 56–57
test launching, 50–52
wingspan, 14, 43, 50
B-26 bombers, 14, 42, 43
Backus, Edward N., 117
Bain, Edwin V., 169, 295
Barr, George, 132, 170–171, 201, 295
prisoner of Japanese, 232, 233, 263, 267, 270, 285–291
*Bat Out of Hell* (B-25), 70, 132–133, 144, 201–202, 216
Battle of Java Sea, 59
Battle of Midway, 4, 71, 86, 209, 269
Battle stations drill, 93–94
Bendix Corporation, 65
Bendix trophy race, 38
Bergamini, David, 240
Bettis, Cyrus, 30
Birch, John, 215, 221
Birch, William L., 166, 294
Bissell, Clayton L., 81, 115–117, 204, 205, 209, 212, 217, 248–249
Bissell, Wayne M., 198, 294
Bither, Waldo J., 167, 196, 295
Bitter, Bruno, 164
Blanton, Thadd H., 295
Bogart, Larry, 96, 112
Bolling Field, 252, 254
Bombsights, 66
Bourgeois, Robert C., 167–168, 295
Bower, William M., 57, 60, 65, 67, 70, 77, 82, 88, 90, 94, 105, 124, 166–167, 196, 216, 218, 277, 294
Bradley, Follett, 258

Braemer, Fred A., 147, 148, 182, 251, 292
Brereton, Lewis H., 107, 117
Brewster Buffalo fighters, 9
Bridge House jail (Shanghai), 239, 261–262, 264, 265
British consulate (Mashhad, Iran), 283–284
British embassy (Tokyo), 118, 136–137
Browning, Miles, 74, 84–86

Camp Dick, Texas, 24
Camp Dix, New Jersey, 24
Campbell, Clayton J., 167, 295
Carrier takeoffs (B-25s), 127–133
training for, 13, 14, 43, 49–52, 61–64, 67, 86
Casualties, American, 187, 189–190, 266, 285
Japanese, 173
Chen, Doctor, 220
Chennault, Claire L., 6, 15, 55–56, 80, 211, 215, 217–218, 242
Chiang Kai-shek, 6, 55, 79–81, 107, 115–116, 204, 218–219
Chiang Kai-shek, Madame, 218–219
Chinese airfields, as possible staging bases, 6–7, 15, 16, 48
as refueling bases for B-25s, 15, 54–56, 78–81, 96, 101, 102, 106–108, 111, 115–118, 178–179
Chinese civilians, aid fliers, 213–214, 220–225, 230
Japanese retaliation against, 239–242
Chinese government, and secrecy, 55, 78–79, 107
Chinese Order of the Clouds (medal), 218–219

Chuchow, China, 54, 55, 116, 117, 182, 193, 196, 205, 216, 217, 241–242

Chü-hsien, China, 195, 221, 224, 242

Chungking, China, 55, 79–81, 96, 111, 116–118, 172–173, 197–199, 213, 214, 218, 221, 222, 224

Churchill, Winston, 12

Clever, Robert S., 142, 191–192, 220–225, 244, 249, 253, 294

Coe, Donald, 277

Cole, Richard E., 60, 127, 139, 182, 183, 249, 292

Confessions of American fliers (Japanese propaganda), 236–238, 274–275

Creehan, Pat, 126

Crouch, Horace E. "Sally," 193, 294

Cunningham, Winfield Scott, 9

Curtiss Hawk fighters, 30, 31, 33, 117

Curtiss-Wright Aircraft Company, 31, 32, 36

DB-7 bombers, 7

DC-3s, 117, 181, 225, 245

Daniels, Josephine "Joe." see Doolittle, Mrs. James H.

Daniels, Josephus, 27

Date line error, 111, 116

Dauntless dive bombers, 119, 134

Davenport, Dean, 88, 141, 190–192, 220–225, 293

Demolition bomb load, 45, 101, 125

DeShazer, Jacob D., 98–99, 120, 126, 130, 132–133, 144, 170–171, 295

prisoner of Japanese, 201–202,

231, 238, 239, 262, 267–268, 275, 285–291

Devastator torpedo planes, 71, 134

Dieter, William J., 188–190, 230, 249, 278, 293

Distinguished Flying Cross (DFC), 212, 252–254

Dodson, Oscar, 50

Doolittle, James H. "Jimmy," 1–4, 18–48, 53–56, 58, 60–78, 81–93, 95–97, 101–104, 107, 111–115, 122, 124, 143, 179, 204–206, 212–217, 219, 244–252, 254–256, 277, 280, 292

bombing raid on Tokyo, 126–130, 139–140, 147–149, 181–185

early life, 19–42

and Eisenhower, 255–256

and Halsey, 83–85

letters to Raiders' families, 249–250

Medal of Honor, 243, 246–248

promotion to brigadier general, 212, 217

Doolittle, Mrs. James H. "Joe," 22, 23, 25, 27, 29, 32, 36–39, 90, 244–248

Doolittle Raiders:

Association, 241, 277

awarded DFC, 212

casualties, 187, 189–190, 266, 285

interned in Russia, 143–144, 155–156, 179–181, 210, 226–229, 256–259, 270–273, 281–284

order of takeoff, 292–295

prisoners of Japanese, 202, 210, 216, 219, 229–239, 248–249, 260–270, 274–276, 284–291

staff officers, 67

training, 13–15, 43, 44, 49–52, 54, 56, 58–71, 77, 86, 89, 90, 95, 96, 99–100, 102
volunteers for mission, 58–61
dos Remedios, Caesar Luis, 269–270
Douglas DB-7 bombers, 7
Duncan, Donald, 13–16, 18, 42, 43, 47, 49–53, 67, 71–75, 78
Duquette, Omer A., 196, 295

Eagle Pass, Texas, 26–27
Eaker, Ira C., 25, 255, 256
Early, Stephen, 206, 211
Easter services, USS *Hornet*, 105–106
Eglin Field, 44, 59–70, 76–77
Eierman, Jacob, 295
Eighth Air Force, 209, 256
Eisenhower, Dwight D. "Ike," 208–209, 255–256
Emmens, Robert G., 131, 142–144, 155, 294
   interned in Russia, 179–180, 256–259, 270, 272, 273, 281–283
*Enterprise* aircraft carrier, 9, 74, 85, 106, 133–136. *See also* Task Force 16
Executions of American fliers, 265–266
   public reaction, 274–281

F4F Wildcat fighters, 134
Faktor, Leland D., 187, 215, 221, 278, 293
Farrow, William J., 114, 132–133, 170–171, 216, 295
   prisoner of Japanese, 201–202, 231–235, 237, 249, 262–263, 274
   execution, 265–266

Ferry Command, 80
Fifteenth Air Force, 256
First-aid supplies, 68–69, 83, 98, 102
Fitzgerald, John, 49, 51
Fitzhugh, William N. "Foggy," 186, 292
Fitzmaurice, Donald E., 188–190, 230, 249, 278, 293
Fletcher, Frank Jack, 9
Flying Tigers, 7–8, 55, 211, 225
Forman, Harrison, 173
Fourteenth Air Force, 215
Fourth Interceptor Command, 208
Fuchida, Mitsuo, 3
Fuel consumption on bombing raid, 139, 141–143, 145, 152, 154
Fujuta, Chosei, 266

Gardner, Melvin J., 165, 192, 294
Gee Bee racer, 39
Geneva Prisoner-of-War Convention, 260
Gerstner Field, 24
Gray, Robert M., 144, 150–151, 186, 216, 253, 292
*Green Hornet* (B-25), 70, 152–153, 188
Greening, C. Ross, 58, 62, 65–67, 95, 98, 114, 165–167, 194–195, 215, 216, 253, 294
Grew, Joseph, 162–163
Griffin, Thomas C., 60, 68, 90, 100, 156, 197–198, 219, 294
Grumman F4F Wildcat, 134
Gunnery practice, 65–67, 102

Hallmark, Dean E., 152–153, 188–190, 293
   prisoner of Japanese, 216, 229–

(Hallmark, Dean E. *cont.*)
231, 234–235, 237, 239, 241,
248, 250, 262–266, 268, 274
execution, 265–266
Halsey, William F., 71, 74–75, 84–
86, 106, 109–114, 118–123,
133, 216–217, 280
decision to launch B-25s, 122–
123
*Hari Carrier* (B-25), 194
Harmon, Millard F. "Miff," 72–73,
254
Harp, Edward, 105–106
Hata, Itsura, 263, 266
Hata, Shunroku, 264, 297
Henderson, George, 96
Hengyang, China, 222, 225
Herndon, Nolan A., 143, 155, 294
interned in Russia, 256–259,
272, 283
High-octane aviation fuel, 40, 55
Hilger, John A., 58, 60, 66, 67, 82,
85, 87, 102, 126, 144, 146,
168–171, 199, 216, 253, 295
Hirohito (Emperor), 205, 239, 260,
264, 290
Hite, Robert L., 144, 295
prisoner of Japanese, 201–202,
231, 236, 262–263, 267, 269–
270, 284–291
Holstrom, Everett W. "Brick,"
140–141, 151, 195, 221, 293
Honjo, Seikichi, 160
Hoover, Travis, 67, 130, 139, 149,
150, 184–186, 221, 248, 292
*Hornet* aircraft carrier, 5, 13, 15,
48–53, 70–72, 78, 83–86, 88–
106, 124–136, 171–172, 231,
232, 236, 278
B-25s taken aboard, 85, 88–
90

B-25s launched, 124–133
*Hornet* crew, relations with
Doolittle fliers, 94–96, 98,
104–105
*Hornet* officers, remarks on
Doolittle fliers, 94–95, 100–
101
Horton, Edwin W., 145, 158, 193–
194, 294
Howze, Harry, 55
Hull, Cordell, 276, 279

Ihwang, China, 198, 241
Iida, Minoru, 160
Imperial Palace, Tokyo, 101, 115,
147, 157
Incendiary bomb load, 45, 101, 125
International Date Line, 111, 116
International Military Tribunal,
Far East (war crimes trials),
267
Inubo Saki lighthouse, Japan, 120,
149, 150, 157, 167
Iran (Persia), 273, 281–284
Ito, Shoji, 263

Japanese army bombers and fighters, 109, 110, 151, 153–154,
158
Japanese civilian reaction to raid,
159–162, 174–175
Japanese medals returned, 112
Japanese navy, intercepts U.S.
radio messages, 109–110, 113,
120–122
patrol planes, 133–134, 146
picket boats, 11, 12, 110, 113,
118–123, 133
Japanese news media reports on
raid, 146, 155, 172–175, 203–
205, 216

Japanese regulations for punishment of enemy air crews, 261, 296–297

Johnson, Harvey, 67, 102

Jones, Aden E., 150–151, 187–188, 293

Jones, David M., 58, 62, 67, 125, 151–154, 195–196, 221, 225, 293

Jordan, Bert M., 140–141, 293

Joyce, Richard O., 145–146, 157–158, 193–194, 253, 294

Jurika, Stephen, 93, 94, 99–100, 103, 105, 108, 112, 120, 129, 133, 136, 155, 163, 171–172, 183, 184, 198

Kappeler, Frank A., 165, 195, 294

Kawai, Iwao, 161

Kawasaki Ki. 61 (Japanese fighter plane), 165

Kelly Field, 27

Kempei Tai, 232–234

Khabarovsk, Russia, 181, 226, 227

Kian, China, 117, 225

Kido, Koichi, 264

King, Ernest J., 5, 7, 8, 11–13, 15–18, 47, 71, 74, 247

Kirkpatrick, Don, 126

Knobloch, Richard A., 167–168, 198, 295

Knox, Frank, 9, 112

Kobe, air raid on, 15, 48, 102, 168–170

Kolya, 273, 281–283

Kondo, Nobutake, 121

Kuibshyev, Russia, 228

Kunming, China, 117, 225

Kuroshima, Kameto, 4

Kweilin, China, 80, 117, 118, 225

LaBan, Theodore H., 143, 294 interned in Russia, 256–259, 272, 283

La Guardia, Fiorello, 280

Landis, James, 208

Langley Field, 27, 49, 56

Larkin, George E., 158, 294

Lavalle, Ramon Muniz, 163–164

Lawson, Ted W., 57, 60, 64, 70, 88, 95, 98, 112, 126, 130–131, 141–142, 153–154, 190–193, 200, 220–225, 244, 249, 250, 253, 254, 293

Lend-lease supplies, 46, 54, 79, 282

Leonard, Paul J., 1, 3, 148, 182, 183, 185, 212–213, 217, 248, 292

Lindbergh, Charles A., 19, 33, 247

Ling, Captain, 230–231

Linhai, China, 220–223

Lishui, China, 117, 224, 242

Lockheed Hudson bombers, 7

Low, Francis S., 5, 7, 9, 11–13, 16, 18, 42, 47, 75

Low-level flying, 64, 70, 77

MacArthur, Douglas, 8, 59, 255

Macia, James H. "Herb," 168–169, 295

Magruder, John, 79

Manch, Jacob E. "Shorty," 144–145, 150, 187–188, 293

Manske, Joseph W., 60, 68, 104, 195, 293

March Field, 57, 77

Marshall, George C., 7, 8, 47, 56, 79, 91, 116, 204, 206, 207, 209, 211, 212, 243, 244, 246–248

Marshall, S. L. A., 177

Mashhad, Iran, 281–284

McCarthy, James, 49, 51, 52
McChord Field, 56
McClellan Field, 76–78, 81–83,
    86–87
McClure, Charles L. "Mac," 60,
    64, 88, 90, 95, 97, 153, 191–
    192, 220–225, 244, 249, 253,
    254, 293
McCook Field, 24, 29–31. See also
    Wright Field
McCool, Harry C., 140, 293
McElroy, Edgar E. "Mac," 167–
    168, 198, 225, 295
McGurl, Eugene F., 293
Meder, Robert J., 188–190, 293
    prisoner of Japanese, 229–231,
    234–235, 238, 241, 248, 267,
    269–270
    death, 285–286
Medical supplies, 68–69, 83, 98,
    102
Meeus, Charles L., 241
Merrill, James M., 174
Michela, Joseph, 229, 258
Mid-Continent Airlines, 44, 47
Midway, 4, 71, 86, 209, 269
Mike (Mikhail Schmaring), 226–
    229, 256–259, 270–271
Miller, Henry L., 61–64, 69, 76–
    77, 86–89, 92–93, 97, 103,
    122, 126, 129, 130, 135, 251–
    252
Miller, Richard E., 149, 292
Mills, William C., 58, 60
Mitchel Field, 30, 34, 36
Mitchell, Billy, 27, 28
Mitscher, Marc A. "Pete," 49–53,
    70, 78, 86, 88, 89, 92–93, 95,
    97, 98, 105, 112, 119, 123,
    124, 126, 128, 129, 171
    criticizes B-25 takeoffs, 135
Morgenthau, Henry, 254

Nagasaki, 238, 290
Nagoya, air raid on, 15, 48, 102,
    144, 168–170
Naguma, Chuichi, 121
Nakajima Type-97 (Japanese fighter
    plane), 158
Nandian Island, 200, 220
Nanking, China, 270, 284–288
Nashville (cruiser), 120–121, 123,
    134, 135
New York Times, The, 31, 203,
    240, 277, 279
Nielsen, Chase J., 188–190, 293
    prisoner of Japanese, 229–231,
    234–235, 241, 248, 261, 267,
    284–291
Nimitz, Chester, 71, 74, 98, 106,
    112, 122
Nishiura, Susumu, 159
Nitto Maru (Japanese picket boat),
    120–121, 123, 133
North American Aircraft Company,
    64, 216

O Shima (O Island), 161, 167
Okada, Ryuhei, 266–267
Okamura, Yasuji, 239
Okhansk, Russia, 257
Okhuna, Russia, 228, 256
Operational plans for raid, 13–16,
    18, 47–48, 53–56, 72, 74,
    101–102, 106, 114–115
Osaka, air raid on, 15, 102, 169
Osborn, Edgar "Ozzie", 127–132
Ozuk, Charles J., 151, 186–188,
    221, 253, 293

P-36 fighters, 65
P-38 fighters, 41, 57
P-39 fighters, 41, 57
P-40 fighters, 7, 41, 65
Pacific Fleet, 6, 84, 122, 207

Page (U.S. embassy official, Moscow), 229, 258

Parachute jumps over China, 182, 187, 194–199, 201, 250

Parker, James N., 197–198, 294

Parker, Mr. and Mrs., 220, 223

Pearl Harbor attack, 3, 5–7, 11, 17, 57, 59, 84, 161, 207, 279

Picket boats (Japanese patrol boats), 11, 12, 110, 113, 118–123, 133

sunk by *Nashville*, 120–121

Pohl, David W., 142, 144, 294

interned in Russia, 256–259, 272, 283

Portal, Charles, 16–18

Potter, E. B., 84

Potter, Henry A., 139–140, 148, 182, 184, 185, 292

Pound, William R., 166–167, 295

Prisoners of war, 202, 210, 216, 219, 229–239, 248–249, 260–270, 274–276, 284–291

alleged confessions, 236–238, 274–275

interrogations, 202, 231–235

torture, 103, 230–235, 287–288

Pulitzer trophy race, 30

Quigley, Daniel, 112

Quinn, Charles, 240

Radio homing signals, 106–107, 116, 117

Radio JOAK (Japanese propaganda station), 155, 172

Radney, Douglas V., 149, 292

Ream Field, 25

Reddy, Kenneth E., 195, 294

Retaliation, expected by Japan for Pearl Harbor attack, 10–11, 54

expected by U.S. for Doolittle raid, 207–209

Reuters on alleged bombing raid, 112–113

Reynolds, Quentin, 6

Ring, Stanhope C., 135

Rockwell Field, 24–26

Roosevelt, Franklin D., 6–9, 16, 17, 27, 47–48, 207, 210–211, 234, 247–248, 274, 276, 281

Rosenman, Samuel I., 210

Royce, George, 96

*Ruptured Duck* (B-25), 70, 104, 141, 153–154, 190

Russia, assistance requested for raid, 7–8, 16, 46, 54, 79, 115, 144

fliers interned in, 179–181, 210, 226–229, 256–259, 270–273, 281–284

SBD Dauntless dive bombers, 119, 134

Sacramento Air Depot, 68, 72, 82. *See also* McClellan Field

Sakai, Saburo, 175

*Saratoga* aircraft carrier, 8–9

Sato, P. E., 162

Sawada, Shigeru, 266

Saylor, Edward J., 169, 295

Schmaring, Mikhail "Mike," 226–229, 256–259, 270–271

Schneider seaplane trophy race, 30–31

Scott, Eldred V., 145, 156–157, 197–198, 294

Sessler, Howard A. "Ses," 170, 200, 253, 295

Seventeenth Bombardment Group, 44, 56–58, 60

Shanghai, 202, 231, 234, 270

Bridge House jail, 239, 261–262, 264, 265

Ward Road jail, 263, 266–267, 270

Shangri-La, 210–211, 248, 251, 252, 277, 278

Shell Oil Company, 35–40, 55

Sims, Jack A., 253, 295

Smith, Donald G., 132, 144, 146, 169–171, 199–200, 220, 221, 295

Smith-Hutton, Henri, 118, 162–163

Smith-Hutton, Jane, 163

Soong, T. V., 206

Soucek, Apollo, 99

Soviet Union. *see* Russia

Spaatz, Carl A. "Tooey," 48, 255

Spatz, Harold A., 295
  prisoner of Japanese, 237, 268, 275
  execution, 265–266

Spitfire (British fighter plane), 255–256

Spurrier, Lieutenant, 116–117

Stalin, Joseph, 7–8, 16, 271

Standard Oil Company, 80

Standley, William H., 210, 258

Stephens, Robert J., 151, 293

Stilwell, Joseph W. "Vinegar Joe," 79–81, 106–107, 115–116, 204, 209, 211

Stimson, Henry L., 8, 47, 209

Stork, J. Royden "Roy," 194, 294

Sugiyama, Hajime, 260–261, 263, 264, 267

Suzuki, Kikujiro, 160

Swiss ambassador to Japan, 162–163, 275

Swiss government information on raid, 206, 275–276

TBD-1 Devastator torpedo planes, 71, 134

TBF Avenger torpedo planes, 71

Task Force 16 (Mike), 14–15, 53, 71, 84–86, 106, 109–115, 118–123, 133–136. *See also Hornet*

Tatsuta, Sotojiro, 265–269

Tenth Air Force, 107

Thatcher, David J., 141, 154, 191–193, 220–222, 224, 294

Thompson trophy race, 39

Tojo, Hideki, 159, 260–261, 264, 267

Tokyo, air-raid drill, 118, 136–137, 162, 163
  air raid on, 15, 48, 101, 139–158
  antiaircraft defenses, 10, 109, 147–150, 152–154, 156–158, 161, 162, 164, 167
  damage, 173–174
  false report of bombing, 112–113

Tokyo Bay, 149–153, 157, 166–169

Tokyo Rose, 9

Toland, John, 159

Tolischus, Otto, 164

Torture of prisoners-of-war, 103, 230–235, 287–288

Truelove, Denver V., 152, 293

Turner, Roscoe, 48

Twelfth Air Force, 255

UC-67 transport plane, 14

Udet, Ernst, 37

Ugaki, Matome, 3, 10, 121

U.S. Embassy, Tokyo, 118, 136–137, 162–163

U.S. government reaction to raid, 204–206, 244, 252, 278–279

U.S. Military Commission (war crimes trials), 267

U.S. military reports on raid, 177–178, 204–210

U.S. news media reports on raid, 203–206, 208, 210

Vladivostok, 8, 16, 46, 54, 79, 115, 144, 179–181, 210

Vormstein, H., 112

Wake Island, 6, 8–9, 16, 207

Wako, Yusei, 267

Wall, Robert, 132

Walter Reed Army Hospital, 32, 225, 253, 254

War bonds sales, 280

War crimes trials, 266–267, 270

War Department, on raid, 278–279 on secrecy, 244, 252

Ward Road jail (Shanghai), 263, 266–267, 270

Watson, Harold F. "Doc," 126, 145, 156–157, 197–198, 241, 253, 254, 294

Wells, Florence, 164

Wenchow, China, 230, 231, 234

Western Defense Command, 208

*Whirling Dervish* (B-25), 145, 157–158, 241

*Whiskey Pete* (B-25), 70, 144, 150, 186

White, Dr. Thomas Robert "Doc,"
66, 68–69, 83, 98, 102, 169, 200, 220–225, 244, 249, 253, 295

Wilder, Ross R., 196, 293

Wildner, Carl R., 149, 185, 292

Williams, Adam R., 295

Williams, Griffith P., 221, 253, 295

Wiseman, O. B., 119

Wong, Mister, 230–231

Wright Field, 31, 44–46. *See also* McCook Field

Yager, George, 240

Yamamoto, Isoroku, 3–4, 10–11

Yokohama, air raid on, 15, 48, 102, 147–158, 165–168

Yokosuka, air raid on, 150, 157, 158, 167, 168

York, Edward J. "Ski," 58, 62, 65, 67, 83, 88, 95, 131, 142–144, 155–156, 294 interned in Russia, 179–181, 226–229, 256–259, 270–273, 281–283

Youngblood, Lucian N., 140, 151, 293

Yushan, China, 117, 196, 242

Zeroes (Japanese fighter planes), 133, 134, 158